The

Autograph

Tree

William Henry

MERCIER PRESS

For

My Daughter Lisa

Youthful Days in Coole

MERCIER PRESS

Cork

www.mercierpress.ie

© William Henry, 2020

ISBN: 978 1 78117 639 9

A CIP record for this title is available from the British Library.

Printed and bound in the EU.

CONTENTS

Acknowledgements   5

'Coole Park' by W. N. Sheerin   7

Introduction   9

    Augusta Persse, 'Lady Gregory'   15

    Robert Gregory   27

    William Butler Yeats   37

    Jack Butler Yeats   48

    John Millington Synge   58

    Sara Allgood   70

    Frank Fay   77

    William George Fay   84

    George William Russell   94

    John Quinn   106

    Augustus John   113

    James Dickson Innes   124

    George Bernard Shaw   131

    Lennox Robinson   142

    Sean O'Casey   149

    George Moore   161

    Douglas Hyde   171

    Violet Florence Martin, 'Martin Ross'   182

    Lady Margaret Sackville   193

Countess of Cromartie   200
John Masefield   204
Robert Ross   213
Elinor Monsell   219
Dame Ethel Smyth   223
Theodore Spicer-Simson   233
General Sir Ian Hamilton   237
General Sir Neville Lyttelton   243
Coole   246
Autograph Tree Lists   253
Notes   255
Bibliography   275
Index   282

ACKNOWLEDGEMENTS

Thanks to my wife Noreen, sons Patrick and David, and daughter Lisa. I would also like to acknowledge with grateful appreciation the National Library of Ireland, Dublin; James Hardiman Library, NUIG; and County Galway Library, Island House. Thanks also to the staff members of the various libraries: Kieran Hoare, Marie Boran, Mary O'Leary, Geraldine Curtin, Liam Frehan, Maureen Moran and Mary Kavanagh.

Thanks to all the media organisations who over the years have supported my work: Galway Bay FM, Raidió na Gaeltachta, *The Tuam Herald*, *Connacht Tribune*, *Galway Advertiser* and *Galway Independent*. Thanks to all those who have always given excellent publicity to my various books and other projects: Mike Glynn, Dave O'Connell, Judy Murphy, Brendan Carroll, Dave Hickey, Joe O'Shaughnessy, Stan Shields, Ronnie O'Gorman, Declan Varley, Tom Kenny, Keith Finnegan, Katie Finnegan, Peadar O'Dowd, David Burke, Jim Higgins, Declan Dooley and Máirtín Tom Sheáinín.

Sincere thanks to the following for all their support: Eamonn O'Regan, Angela Sheerin, Audrey Sheerin, Mike McDonagh, Karolina Pakos, Tom Joe Furey and Anne Maria Furey. Thanks also to the late Sheila O'Donnellan for her support. In grateful appreciation to James Harrold, Galway City Arts Officer, for his support. Thanks to Mary Waller, Mark Sweetman and

Noreen Henry for proofreading this work and making valuable suggestions: *go raibh míle maith agaibh*. Special thanks to Marita Silke for all her years of support and friendship. As with all of my work, I owe a great debt of gratitude to my constant friend Jacqueline O'Brien, for her long hours over many years of research, proofreading and support with this and many other projects.

COOLE PARK

I pass beneath the arching trees black with mystery,
Here Gothic and Romanesque combine
To form a fitting entrance to nature's palace,
Lying peaceful and sublime.
Beneath copper beech and elm I pace the rain-sodden earth,
Seven woods surround me, lakes and tumbling streams.
I follow the meandering ways, passing barely visible ruins
Of a house preserved in photographs or in an old man's
    dreams,
On the bending arm of a willow a pigeon swoons,
The gates of a garden of orchard greet me, outhouses stand,
Maecenas' head now silent and alone inside a crumbling
    door,
His bust once stood at the garden's end
His echoing voice once heard, now no more.
I pass the 'Autograph Tree' of etched memories,
Walking to the end of a garden to the graves of the dumb,
Looking back upon the narrow path I visualise
The founding of a theatre, the writing of a play or poem,
Afternoon conversation of the talented and the wise.
Traversing a similar path I make my way along
Over cobbled stones and acorns withered by the wind,
To the lake's edge, the sanctuary of the swan.

A nipping breeze shatters its reflection,
I stand and gaze upon its beauty and trees so tall,
All passing things, too soon a memory
But their existence assured for generations
To outlive us all.

W. N. Sheerin, 4 April 1975

Introduction

Between the late nineteenth and early twentieth centuries Lady Augusta Gregory welcomed numerous distinguished literary and artistic friends to her home in Coole Park. Many of these visitors were invited to carve their initials onto a wonderful 160-year-old copper beech tree in her walled garden, which became known as 'the Autograph Tree'. This book contains profiles of those signatories.

The book is also a history of the Irish Literary Revival told through the biographical accounts of those people, as many of them played significant roles in this very important event. The revival could be said to have started with the founding of a number of societies in the early nineteenth century to promote Irish language and literature. However, these were mainly academic and appealed only to scholars. The revival really came to prominence with the sudden emergence of a potent dramatic movement in the late nineteenth century.

At the time, there was little evidence to indicate that there would be strong support among the general public for the theatrical world and literature, given that many people were living in poverty and hardship, particularly in the west of Ireland. However, the country was also in the grip of political and social issues that sometimes became prominent and could arouse a patriotic passion in many people – for example, the 1898 commemoration of the

1798 rebellion. Strong Irish ideals and cultural traditions existed just below the surface, waiting to emerge.

Moreover, after the death of Charles Stewart Parnell, leader of the Irish Parliamentary Party, in 1891, many young people became disillusioned with nationalist politics and turned instead towards the cultural movement. They began to follow or become actively involved in the literary revival, which included and celebrated all aspects of Irish culture.

One of the central organisations of the revival, the Gaelic League, was founded in 1893 and spread quickly across the country, bringing with it a pride in the Irish language, music, dance and storytelling. People were reminded that Ireland was a land of ancient legends and it was important that these should not be forgotten.

One of the most important events that took place during the literary revival was the meeting of Lady Augusta Gregory and William Butler Yeats in 1896. This signalled the beginning of a lifelong friendship and a total commitment to the Irish theatre. The foundation of Irish literary societies in Dublin during this period was also important for the growing revival's success. These societies paved the way for the literary renaissance that erupted in Ireland over the following years, of which Yeats and Lady Gregory were a driving force. For example, they promoted the urgent need for a national theatre, as they were aware that there were a number of playwrights eager to showcase their work and in need of an outlet.

Of course, finance was necessary to make this dream a reality. Their plan was to request £300 from any prospective sponsors and assure them that Irish plays would be staged annually. They felt that these plays would bring passion to the stage and result in deeper thoughts of and emotions towards Ireland among the people. There was also an ambition to develop an Irish school of dramatic literature, as they believed that without this no new literary movement could succeed. They were confident that the Irish people would support the venture, as many of them felt misrepresented on the English stage, where they were depicted only as negative stereotypes. It was also intended to show the world that Ireland was the home of ancient idealism.

The appeal was successful and people from all levels of society supported the idea of an Irish theatre. However, their financial support was not required because Edward Martyn of Tulira stepped in and made a very generous donation to ensure the success of the venture. This laid the foundation for a society named the 'Irish Literary Theatre'. The project provided fertile ground for new and potential playwrights. The influence of Lady Gregory, Yeats and a new group called the 'Irish National Theatre' subsequently led to the foundation of the Abbey Theatre in December 1904. Through its productions, the Abbey became the potent voice of an emerging Irish nation and attracted some of the leading literary figures, artists, actors and actresses of the period. Accounts of these people and the events that shaped the early theatre in Ireland can be found throughout this book.

The biographical profiles that appear here do not follow an alphabetical order. They begin with Lady Gregory, and some of those closest to her, such as her son, Robert, and W. B. Yeats. These are followed by those connected to her mainly through the Abbey Theatre. The idea of recording names on the Autograph Tree began in the summer of 1898 when Lady Gregory invited

Yeats to carve his initials into its bark. Over the following years many more poets, writers and artists were also given this privilege: Jack Butler Yeats, John Millington Synge, Sara Allgood, Frank and William Fay, George William Russell, John Quinn, Augustus John, James Dickson Innes, George Bernard Shaw, Lennox Robinson, Sean O'Casey, George Moore, Douglas Hyde, Violet Florence Martin, Lady Margaret Sackville, the Countess of Cromartie, John Masefield, Robert Ross, Elinor Monsell, Dame Ethel Smyth and Theodore Spicer-Simson. Strangely, two soldiers, General Sir Ian Hamilton and General Sir Neville Lyttelton, were also asked to 'sign' the tree. With the exception of these last two, her reason for choosing the signatories is apparent: they were involved in art, literature and the theatre. The Autograph Tree acts almost like a 'who's who' of those involved in the artistic world during that time.

Writing this book proved rather difficult because a number of the personalities shared intertwining lives. It was important that each of the signatories should be profiled as separate individuals and that the profiles could be read independently of each other. Therefore, great care has been taken to ensure that each person remains central in their own profile, but also that the information included is not repetitive. However, it was equally essential to inform the reader of any connections between these people. There are some instances where aspects of individual lives are strongly linked, as with the Fay brothers. Both men were involved in the Abbey Theatre and worked closely together on many occasions. Another instance is the love affair between Lady Gregory and John Quinn; while this episode is mentioned in her profile, it is explored in more detail in his.

Another aspect of the profiles that needs to be taken into consideration is the amount of information available about the various individuals. Some of the personalities achieved greater distinction than others and thus there was more source material available to the author. For example, people such as Lady Gregory, W. B. Yeats, Shaw and O'Casey have been the subject of a number of books. In other cases there was much less information available.

It was while visiting Coole Park with my children and family friends over many years that I developed an interest in the names carved into the Autograph Tree. Thousands of people from all over the world flock to Coole Park every year and visit the now-famous tree. While enjoying the afternoon sunshine in May 2013, a friend observed the gentle movement of its branches and remarked how it reminded her of a peaceful ocean floor, with the leaves placidly moving to and fro like the ebb and flow of a tranquil sea. But it was the curiosity of my children that helped to trigger my own interest in the signatories, and so the idea of this book was born. It fills a unique and important void in Irish literary history because it captures the lives of all of these people in one publication.

The Autograph Tree is a living monument and a symbol of Irish culture and heritage. It emits an atmosphere of timelessness from the overburdened branches that shelter its carved bark, thus protecting the names of people who have gained international prominence in the world of literature and art. Coole Park is now celebrated around the world as the centre of Irish literary culture, and the Autograph Tree is the physical link with these people who have left Ireland with an extremely rich inheritance.

Augusta Persse
'Lady Gregory'

Playwright 1852–1932

Isabella Augusta Persse, or 'Lady Gregory' as she was later known, was born on 15 March 1852 at the family home, Roxborough House, Co. Galway. Her parents were Dudley and Frances Persse (*née* Barry).[1] She was from a wealthy background and was educated by a governess from an early age, as well as being influenced by their housekeeper, Mary Sheridan, who often told her stories of local folklore. While the rest of her family were not overly interested in literature, the young Augusta developed a strong interest in reading and creative writing.[2] She was described as a vivacious child with soft dark eyes and lustrous brown hair. She had thirteen siblings, but those closest to her were Gertrude and Arabella, who were a little older.

Growing up, Augusta preferred the outdoor life, which was mostly reserved for her brothers. The fact that she managed to have herself included in their activities would indicate that she was a strong-willed young girl. Her time with the boys was spent fox hunting and trapping rabbits and birds. She was also close to her brother Frank, who was two years her junior. She was shy when in the company of adults and sometimes depended on her sisters to conceal this shyness. It seems her father didn't have much time for Augusta and she reciprocated this lack of affection. Meanwhile, her mother was a fashionable lady dressing in the latest styles of the period and could at times display great courtesy, though she was also self-centred. Augusta differed from her mother, as she had a great capacity for warmth, love, kindness and friendliness, and a keen interest in books. Despite these qualities, her mother considered her a failure. Perhaps this was because she thought that reading books was of no great benefit to girls.

The fact that Augusta had more in common with her brothers than with her sisters throughout her teenage years didn't enhance her confidence when in the company of other young men. Perhaps this was because she spoke with a slight lisp. In 1875 she was chosen to accompany one of her brothers when he was sent abroad. He had been advised to spend the winter in Cannes on the French Riviera because of an illness. While there, Augusta often thought about marriage and wondered if it would be appropriate to marry someone out of affection and mutual respect, rather than love.

When Sir William Gregory had met Augusta as a child, he had told her mother that she was the prettiest of her daughters. Augusta met Gregory again, for the first time as an adult, while he was attending a cricket match at Roxborough in the summer of 1877. He was thirty-five years her senior, but was very attentive to her. This obviously impressed Augusta, as she met him on a number of occasions that summer. It was during this time that she was invited to Coole for what was likely the first time. There was a total contrast between her own home, which was associated with hunting and a degree of rowdiness, and Coole, known for its civilised manner and culture.

Despite the age gap, a relationship developed between Gregory and Augusta. By this time Gregory was very lonely, but he feared proposing marriage to her as he didn't wish to look foolish because of the age difference. In 1879 he loaned her a book entitled *Roderick Hudson*. When Augusta returned the book in January 1880, she placed a letter inside indicating that she would consider marriage. They communicated through writing and this was how Gregory made his proposal of marriage, which she accepted.[3]

Shortly before the wedding, Gregory wrote to Augusta concerning his tenants around Kiltartan:

> I am very glad indeed that the country people are pleased. Whatever naughty deeds I may have done I always felt the strongest sense of duty towards my tenants, and I have a great affection for them. They have never in a single instance caused me displeasure, and I know you can and will do everything in your power to make them love and value us.[4]

It would seem that Gregory was trying to ensure that she would not bring any bigotry to Coole, as he feared that she shared her mother's distaste for the Catholic religion. However, Gregory needn't have worried, as Augusta didn't agree with her mother's intolerance towards people of that faith. She merely objected to the Catholic Church because she felt it placed intolerable restrictions on people and more or less suppressed their free spirit.

Even as an adult, she was not close to her mother; in fact, one of the reasons she embraced marriage to a man so many years her senior was to escape the burden of having to look after her parents in old age. It comes as little surprise then that her mother's death at the Croft, Taylor's Hill, Galway on 23 March 1896 did not have much of an effect on Lady Gregory. If anything, it seemed to unshackle her. A year later she wrote about the importance of Catholic Emancipation and this was something she would not have done were her mother still alive. This could indicate that she had been controlled to some extent by her mother's domineering influence.[5]

The wedding of Augusta Persse and Sir William Gregory took place on 4 March 1880 at St Matthias' church in Dublin. Gregory took his new bride to the Continent on their honeymoon and introduced her to European aristocratic society, with whom he was well acquainted. They returned to Coole on 29 July 1880 and were received with the traditional welcome for a newly married Anglo-Irish couple. Members of the local clergy and the temperance band, along with a huge crowd, greeted them at Gort. A bonfire was lit at the gates of Coole and a welcome slogan was placed over the gateway. A month later, Augusta announced that she was pregnant. There were rumours at the time that the father of the baby was a local blacksmith named Seán Farrell. Some said that this gossip arose because they believed that Gregory was too old to father a child. However, this was highly unlikely.

The baby was born on 20 May 1881 and was christened William Robert Gregory, but he was always known as Robert. Typically, babies born into landed gentry families at that time did not interfere with the lifestyle of their parents and were normally handed over to a 'wet nurse' to be looked after. Therefore, shortly after the birth of Robert, his father insisted that the couple resume their travels. They left Coole soon afterwards and journeyed to London, where they attended the Queen's Ball. During their travels they stayed with some highly influential people in England. Gregory also planned a trip to Egypt for them later that year. This trip changed everything for Lady Gregory and it revealed her true sensuality.[6]

It is known that Lady Gregory had at least two lovers in her lifetime: Wilfrid Blunt and, later, John Quinn. Both could be described as men of the world, confident and experienced.[7] The first, Blunt, had been in the diplomatic service. He married Lady Annabella King-Noel and they had at least one daughter, Judith. Augusta met Blunt in Egypt during the winter of 1881–82. She didn't record her first impressions of him but later wrote that she admired his outspoken manner. Politically, she found herself supporting him and his views regarding local policies, sometimes in opposition to her husband.

It was during this time that Blunt and Augusta first kissed. While neither of them ever made direct reference to sexual relations in their writings, they did refer to the affair in different ways. Blunt, in his *Secret Memoir*, hinted at the liaison, writing that they found comfort in each other's arms and in each other's affection. Augusta wrote in her earliest sonnet that after kissing Blunt for the first time she realised she could become his lover. The intense pleasure that it brought her was marred by the guilt and fear of this forbidden love, which would suggest that it was a sexual affair. Although she tried to resist, she could not give Blunt up and was ultimately unrepentant – given the choice she would have allowed it to happen again. The only fear she had was of being discovered.

In the end, Blunt's wife became aware of the affair. She had ignored others over the years, but this time she challenged her husband. It is not known for certain if William Gregory was aware of the situation while it was going on, but after it ended he did encourage Augusta to write, as he felt she needed an outlet to release her energy.

In July 1891 Gregory began having breathing difficulties. By Christmas of that year he was more or less confined to his room. The couple had planned a trip to Algiers for the spring of 1892, but, because of the illness, his doctor advised them to go to Bournemouth instead. As his health continued to deteriorate, he confessed his undying love to Augusta. Sir William Gregory died on 6 March 1892.[8]

***

Following her husband's death, Lady Gregory found herself with the responsibility of managing the Coole estate. She was a practical and intelligent woman and set about the task professionally to try to ensure that it would pass on intact to her young son when he came of age. Lady Gregory also spent considerable time in London, as this was the centre of her social life. She was a committed unionist, but, being an open-minded woman, she adapted to change as time passed. She made an attempt to improve the situation for the inmates at the Gort Workhouse. Her suggestions included employing people to manufacture fishing nets and helping them to develop carpentry skills. While this seemed like a good idea, the local parish priest, Fr Jerome Fahey, didn't approve and so her plans never became a reality. She later became involved with a local convent school, where her idea for linen-weaving was taken on board. The girls were soon manufacturing products to designs supplied by Lady Gregory. These were exported to London, where they were sold as Irish Cottage Industry items. Over time, she became increasingly interested in Irish literature and indeed other aspects of life in Ireland.

By this period, things were changing dramatically for landlords and, indeed, their tenants, because of the introduction of new land acts. These acts compelled landlords to sell part of their land to tenants, who were being financially assisted by the government to buy the land. Some landlords resisted and this caused friction, which in some cases resulted in violence. Take, for example, the case of Lady Gregory's neighbour and friend Edward Martyn of Tulira, who paid the price for his indifference; or rather his steward did, when he was shot dead near the gates of Coole. This shooting caused much fear among the landed gentry, and Martyn had to have police protection for a time.

Lady Gregory accepted the changes being introduced. She must have been aware of the legacy of the landlord system when she later recorded in her journal: 'God knows many of our ancestors and forerunners have eaten or planted sour grapes and we must not repine if our teeth are set on edge – I would like to leave a good memory, and not a monument of champagne bottles.'

On 27 July 1896 Lady Gregory visited the home of Count de Basterot at Duras, on the Co. Clare and Galway border. It was there that she first met the poet W. B. Yeats. She took an instant liking to Yeats and, before leaving, invited him to visit her at Coole. Thus began thirty-five years of a warm, mutually beneficial, platonic relationship. This also turned out to be the most important meeting in the world of Irish literature, as the first seeds of the Irish Literary Theatre were sown that day.[9]

One cannot over-estimate the influence that Lady Augusta had over Yeats. She became not only his friend, but also his counsellor and confidante. Over the following years, Yeats spent almost every summer at Coole, and often visited her during the winter.[10] But their friendship also benefited Lady Gregory. Encouraged by him, she began collecting Irish stories and legends from people in the locality, and later based many of her plays and books on this material.

After a meeting with writer and nationalist Douglas Hyde, she formed a branch of the Gaelic League in the Coole district. Times were certainly changing for her. She was now venturing down a path which her family would never have approved of or envisaged. She also became a supporter of Home Rule, which would have given Ireland a degree of independence, and recorded an entry in her journal: 'I defy anyone to study Irish history without getting a dislike and distrust of England.'

She was by now committed to raising awareness of the rich culture of Ireland and continued to collect local folklore. These stories found an opening on the national stage through her books, some of which were *Cuchulain of Muirthemne* (1902); *Poets and Dreamers* (1903); *Gods and Fighting Men* (1904); *Kiltartan History Book* (1909) and *Kiltartan Poetry Book* (1918). Her most successful plays were *Spreading the News* (1904); *The Rising of the Moon* (1907) and *The Workhouse Ward* (1908).[11]

When the Abbey Theatre opened on 27 December 1904, with Lady Gregory's advocacy for a national theatre being one of the main reasons behind its foundation, she was unable to attend due to illness. However, she made a barmbrack that was two feet in diameter and sent it as a gift to be shared among the actors, actresses and staff at the opening-night celebrations. Incidentally, this was remembered on the Abbey's ninetieth anniversary when the theatre ordered a similar barmbrack from O'Connor's Bakery in Gort to have at their celebrations.[12]

Lady Gregory became further absorbed in the world of literature and art following the theatre's opening, surrounding herself with like-minded people. Over time more writers, poets, playwrights, actors and actresses began visiting her at Coole. Her home became a Mecca for these people and they found a wonderful and generous host at Coole. Lady Gregory loved Coole and its acres of foliage, and had a particular fondness for a large copper beech tree in her walled picnic garden. This became the Autograph Tree, as she began inviting her visitors to carve their initials into its bark.[13]

It was while touring the United States with the Abbey Theatre in 1911 that Augusta fell deeply in love with the American lawyer John Quinn, whom she had met earlier in Ireland. On her return home, she wrote some passionate letters to Quinn. She met him again during another visit to the United States the following year. (This relationship will be explored in more detail in the profile on John Quinn.)[14]

The Great War of 1914–18 proved to be a double tragedy for Lady Gregory, as she suffered two personal losses. First her nephew Hugh Lane was drowned in the sinking of the *Lusitania* in 1915 by a German submarine.[15] Her son, Robert, was then killed on 23 January 1918, after his plane was shot down.[16] Robert had been married to Margaret Graham Parry and they had three children: Richard, Anne and Catherine. Even though Lady Gregory was devastated by her son's death, the wonderful relationship she shared with her grandchildren somewhat consoled her.[17]

The secure world that Lady Gregory had known in her youth was changing. The political strife that followed the 1916 Rising led to the War of Independence in Ireland and culminated with a civil war. Lady Gregory's former home, Roxborough House, was burned down during the latter war, possibly because it was seen by many as a symbol of bigotry.[18] Throughout the early 1920s she struggled to hold on to her property; however, the upkeep of the house and land ultimately proved too much. Thus, in December 1927, she sold Coole to the Department of Lands and Agriculture, and it was agreed that she could lease back the house and gardens. One can hear the sadness in her when, in 1930, on the eve of her grandson's birthday, Lady Gregory recorded:

I used long ago to say I should like, I thought, to live until Richard's 21st Birthday. And it comes tomorrow. And I am still here in health and strength, and he is well and doing so well at Chatham! But it is a contrast to Robert's coming of age, with the gathering of cousins and the big feast and dance for the tenants. Coole is no longer ours. But the days of landed property have passed. It is better so. Yet I wish someone of our blood would after my death care enough for what has been a home for so long, to keep it open.[19]

While she accepted the changes in Ireland during the early part of the twentieth century, the death of her only son had undoubtedly been devastating. As the mother of a young child, the future had seemed secure and she envisaged that Coole would eventually pass on to Robert. However, the war changed everything, leaving her hopes and dreams in ruins. Shortly before her death, she had the Gregory burial vault in Kiltartan securely sealed. She then made arrangements for her own burial beside her sister Arabella in the New Cemetery at Bohermore, Galway.

Lady Gregory died on 22 May 1932. Upon hearing the news of her death, a devastated Yeats wrote that he had lost someone who had been his strength and conscience for almost forty years.

In the years following her death, Coole House gradually deteriorated. The lead was stripped from the roof, and the windows and doors fell into a ruined state for want of maintenance. In 1941 the Local Defence Force hoped to use the house as a field hospital for training, but it proved unsuitable due to its dilapidated state. It was decided to demolish the house in 1942 and the contents were sold at auction.[20]

Lady Gregory's contribution to Irish literature is immeasurable. She was a guiding light to some of the leading writers and poets of her time; an avid collector of folklore; a writer, poet and author of twenty-seven plays. Her legacy still lives on at Coole, as people from all over the world meet for the annual 'Autumn Gathering', where they celebrate the literary revival, of which she was one of the leading figures. One of the many great tributes paid to Lady Gregory was from playwright Sean O'Casey:

Living her own life with insistent intensity, Lady Gregory lived, at the same time, ardently, a life among the plain people. She knew Curley the Piper as well as she knew Yeats, and Ardrahan church better than Westminster Abbey ... Though far from being well-off, she gave of what she had and added a large part of herself to the gift.[21]

Robert Gregory

Artist and Pilot 1881–1918

Robert Gregory was born on 20 May 1881 and was the only child of Sir William and Lady Augusta Gregory. His parents sailed for Egypt when Robert was five months old, but when they returned to Coole, Lady Gregory developed a strong bond with him and they shared a love of animals. Although a wet nurse was employed by the Gregorys, Lady Gregory took care of Robert herself when he was ill. His father, on the other hand, was unable to tolerate any noise created by the child.

When his parents were travelling, Robert was looked after by his nurse and sometimes by the Persse family at their home in Roxborough, or by his maternal grandmother at Taylor's Hill, Galway, where she sometimes lived. During her travels, Lady Gregory always wrote to Robert and found it difficult to be away from him. By the age of seven he was old enough to travel with his mother, and she found him to be a delightful companion. He shared in all her activities and most important for them was the fun they had together.

In 1891 Robert was sent to Park Hill Boarding School in Lyndhurst, Sussex, which was a heartbreaking time for both of them, even though he fitted in well at the school and was a bright student. When his father died in 1892, Lady Gregory and Robert began spending more time together during the school holidays, both in Coole and London. In 1893 Robert was enrolled in Elstree School near London, where he progressed quickly. He later attended Harrow, which pleased his mother, as it was a well-disciplined school. Despite having an excellent school record, Robert didn't excel there and found himself at the lower end of the scale academically. He had been apprehensive when he entered the school, as he was the only new boy starting and did not know what was expected of him. Perhaps this was the reason for his poor performance. At the time, Robert had an interest in politics, but was still too young to become involved; instead he attended Oxford to study Classics.

Robert liked playing cricket, and while he was at home the sport became a ritual at Coole. Games were played regularly on the lawns around the house, where he formed a local cricket team.[1] Gort was a stronghold for cricket and this sport thrived, mainly under the patronage of the local gentry. Matches were organised between the other landed gentry estates such as Clonbrock. Venues in Galway city included Eyre Square and the Grammar School on College Road. A great rivalry developed between the various estates and villages, which helped contribute to some thrilling games. The golden era of Galway cricket was between 1870 and 1914, when the county produced no less than twelve international players.

Robert was an outstanding sportsman and excelled in this sport.[2] He became friends with Jack B. Yeats during this period, as they both enjoyed riding and playing cricket, and they also sketched together during Jack's visits to Coole. Robert's tutor in Oxford recognised that he was more creative than scholarly and informed Lady Gregory, who then enrolled him for art lessons. Nevertheless, he worked hard at his studies in Oxford and passed all his exams.

When he was twenty-one, the tenants at Coole celebrated his 'coming of age' in style. The roads were decorated with flags, and bonfires were set between Gort and Coole. He fitted into the role of a country gentleman very well and followed in the path of his ancestors, hunting, shooting and holding dinner parties.[3] Robert developed an even greater interest in the artistic world and attended the famous Slade School of Fine Art in London. It was there that he met a young art student named Margaret Parry. They fell in love and were married in 1907.[4] His best man at the ceremony was another artist, Augustus John.[5]

The couple spent much of their time abroad, but during summer holidays they would often stay at Mount Vernon, the family holiday home at New Quay in the Burren, Co. Clare.[6] This was a wedding gift from his mother.[7] Augustus John often joined them there and he was always accompanied by a number of women.[8] It was inevitable that Augustus John would become acquainted with Lady Gregory, and his being an artist and a friend of Robert assured him of an invitation to Coole.

Margaret and Robert began spending the winters in Paris and the summers between Coole and Mount Vernon. While in Ireland, Robert sometimes worked as a set designer for the Abbey Theatre and also captured the Burren landscapes on canvas. They had three children, all born in Coole: their first baby, Richard, arrived on 6 January 1909; Anne was born on 13 September 1911 and almost a year later Catherine made her appearance, on 21 August 1912.[9]

The couple continued to spend as much time as possible in Paris, where they did a great deal of painting, but they always enjoyed returning to the children and Coole. One night, while all the family were in Coole, Robert had a strange experience. There was an enormous chandelier that was lit by some fifty candles hanging in the middle of the dining room, which was used on special occasions. They decided to hold a séance after dinner, but became disturbed by the messages they were receiving and decided it was bedtime. Robert quenched all the candles before retiring, but was awakened early the following morning by a rather annoyed servant. She informed him that they could all have been burned to death as he had neglected to put out the candles. Robert followed her down to the dining room, where, sure enough, all the candles were still alight. He assured her that he had most definitely put them out and remembered the effort he had made to reach all of them. He was even more astonished when he noticed that none of the candles had burned down – they were still at the same level as they had been the night before – and the grease had not melted down from them.

Robert was a good boxer and an excellent horseman. He had a horse called Sarsfield, which he rode regularly in local point-to-point races, and the punters would always have a bet on him because of his successful record. His skills as a rider were certainly put to the test in one race, when the bridle became loose and all hope seemed lost for those who had backed him to win. He lived up to his reputation, however, when he kept the horse on course by using his legs and tapping the animal on either side of the face with the jockey stick. He went on to win the race, much to the delight of the punters. There is another story of him making an enormous jump over the wall surrounding Roxborough during a fox hunt. Astride the same horse, he rode onto a huge rock and from there leapt over the wall, landing safely on the other side. Robert schooled all of his horses himself at Coole.[10]

While he welcomed Jack Yeats to Coole as an old friend, there was sometimes tension between W. B. Yeats and Robert. Yeats was a regular visitor to Coole and stayed for long periods of time. Although Robert was generally very tolerant by nature, over the years he had come to dislike Yeats. The poet was, for the most part, responsible for this animosity, as he assumed a position that could be seen as head of the household. It didn't help that Lady Gregory also seemed to pay too much attention to Yeats' needs and comfort. Before one visit, Robert told Yeats to bring his own wine and two or three dozen bottles of sherry. This was certainly to make Yeats aware of Robert's feelings about the poet's obvious and selfish consumption of wine and sherry from the family cellar.

Robert continued to paint, taking much of his inspiration from the Burren and Galway Bay. In July 1912 he had his first exhibition in the Baillie Gallery in London. His second and more successful exhibition went on display in July the following year. Over time, his paintings showed continued improvement.[11]

However, all was not well between Robert and his wife. Margaret was devastated to discover that he had been having an affair with a young married woman named Nora Summers. Nora and her husband were friends of the Gregorys in London and were also regular guests at Mount Vernon.[12] When Robert confessed to Margaret, he assured her that the affair was over. He hoped that she would accept what had happened and that they could move on with their lives. Although hurt, Margaret believed him and tried to come to terms with the situation. However, in June 1915 Robert invited the Summers to Coole. During their stay, Margaret caught her husband and Nora together in a situation that she found disgusting. It was clear that the affair was not over and the Gregorys had a terrible row. Robert then told Margaret he was going to enlist for army service, as the Great War was raging in Europe at the time. She pleaded with him not to join up and even told Lady Gregory.

In the meantime, Gerald Summers too had found out about the relationship, so he challenged Robert and a fistfight ensued. It seems that after the affair was thus exposed, Robert stormed off and joined the Connaught Rangers.[13] In September 1915 he obtained a commission with the 4th Battalion Connaught Rangers, then stationed in London.[14] His daughter, Anne, later recalled the last time she saw her father:

He was killed when we were very young and I have only one visual memory of him. He was standing outside the hall door with Mamma and Marian [one of the servants], and they were all taking it in turns to wring the last drop of water out of a duster or something. I was watching from the nursery window above, and was quite upset when Mamma fell out of the competition early on, but then Dada and Marian went on and on against each other, and I don't know if anyone won, because I remember the Victoria [carriage] drove up then, and Dada got into it without a word. Marian made the sign of the cross, I remember, and Mamma just stood and stood looking after the Victoria and I don't think she waved and I couldn't see Dada looking back.[15]

Robert Gregory displayed immense courage during the war and was awarded the Military Cross and the Legion of Honour in the rank of Chevalier. During the course of his service, he transferred from the army to the Royal Flying Corps (RFC).[16] When the war had begun, aeroplanes were essentially a new and untested military machine mainly used for monitoring enemy troop movements. By the time Robert joined, however, they had evolved into fighter planes.[17]

He fitted in well and, it seems, was very happy serving in the military, as he saw it as doing his duty. The RFC had been supplied with a new aircraft, the F.E.8, which was fitted with Lewis machine guns. Robert flew on patrol missions over northern France in preparation for the Somme offensive, which was planned for 1 July 1916. He was careful when writing home not to worry his family and avoided making any mention of the suffering he saw. Over time his letters became shorter and his writing more careless and untidy. In January 1917, while he was on leave, his mother went to meet him and said that he looked good and she was proud of him. He was by then a flight commander with men serving under him.

Margaret was also helping the war effort by working in a munitions factory. The children were being looked after in Coole, with the two eldest, Richard and Anne, attending a local school. Despite the earlier affair, the couple spent time together and managed to visit some friends. A short time later, Robert returned to the Front. The weather in Belgium was dreadful, so he amused himself by organising some plays. George Bernard Shaw went to visit him there and later wrote that the weather was terribly cold and Robert was suffering from frostbite. As the war progressed, Margaret and Lady Gregory became increasingly concerned about him.[18]

On 23 January 1918 Robert, now a major serving with the 66th RFC, took off on a routine flight, but tragically his aircraft was shot down in error by the Italian Air Force and he was killed. His body was retrieved from the wreckage and his remains were buried in Padua Main Cemetery, Italy.[19]

At the time, Margaret was with the children and they were staying with Lady Gregory's sister in Dominick Street, Galway. When news reached Coole that Robert had been killed, Lady Gregory went there to tell Margaret. She arrived at night and, having told her daughter-in-law the dreadful news, sent for the children. Anne later remembered that it was terrible to see their mother so upset and crying. All she could do was put her arms around the children and tell them that their father loved them dearly. It was Lady Gregory who told them he was dead. Although the children didn't fully understand, they were crying and became terrified, saying the Germans would come to Galway and kill them all.

The family returned to Coole after a few days, as the children felt more secure there; it was really their home. One of them later said that 'No one could invade Coole. Coole was safe.'[20] The grandchildren became Lady Gregory's delight; she always loved having them at Coole, but more so after Robert was killed. Her thoughts were captured in her journal on 1 August 1919, when Richard arrived for a visit:

He was well, bright, and happy. It was just as Robert used to come. He was taken up for the first day or two with thoughts of cricket and talk of school. I read him a cricket story after he was in bed last night. It was that day 18 months ago the news from Italy had come [Robert's death]. It is great happiness seeing that room occupied, the little dark head lying where the little fair head used to lie in holiday-time long ago.[21]

The Ireland Robert Gregory had left was a very different place by the time the war ended. The 1916 Rising had taken place and in its wake came the rise of the Irish Republican Army (IRA). The War of Independence, which officially began in 1919, resulted in great insecurity for many landed gentry families.

Margaret Gregory experienced its terror and violence first-hand. She was the only survivor of an IRA ambush on a vehicle at the gates of Ballyturin House near Gort on 15 May 1921. Those killed were District Inspector Cecil Blake and his wife, Eliza, as well as Captain Cornwallis and Lieutenant McCreery of the 17th Lancers. Margaret managed to get out of the car and make her way to its rear. When the firing ceased a man armed with a rifle walked up to her, then led her back towards Ballyturin House and allowed her to go free.[22] At Coole, the children heard the whispered talk that something bad had happened and their mother had been involved. Upon her return, Margaret was so terrified that she couldn't sleep alone, so the children slept in the large four-poster bed with her.

A short time later she took them to London. This was the first time the children had been outside Ireland. However, they were very unhappy being away from Coole and Margaret allowed them to return to their grandmother. She didn't travel herself, but hired a woman to accompany them to Dublin, where Lady

Gregory met them.[23] Margaret eventually returned to Ireland and married Guy Gough of Lough Cutra Castle in Co. Galway. The couple also bought a house in Co. Dublin.[24]

Following the death of Robert Gregory, W. B. Yeats wrote a poem to honour his memory:

> *An Irish Airman Foresees His Death*
> I know that I shall meet my fate
> Somewhere among the clouds above;
> Those that I fight I do not hate
> Those that I guard I do not love;
> My country is Kiltartan Cross,
> My countrymen Kiltartan's poor,
> No likely end could bring them loss
> Or leave them happier than before.
> Nor law, nor duty bade me fight,
> Nor public men, nor cheering crowds,
> A lonely impulse of delight
> Drove to this tumult in the clouds;
> I balanced all, brought all to mind,
> The years to come seemed waste of breath,
> A waste of breath the years behind
> In balance with this life, this death.[25]

William Butler Yeats

Poet and Playwright 1865–1939

Life for William Butler Yeats began on 13 June 1865 in a pleasant house called Georgeville in the seaside suburb of Sandymount, Co. Dublin. His father, John Butler Yeats, was a barrister and later became a portrait painter, and his mother was Susan Pollexfen from Sligo. Yeats was one of four surviving children, the others being Jack (artist), Susan – known as Lily – and Elizabeth, who was always called Lolly. When Yeats was three years old, the family moved to Fitzroy Road, Regent's Park in London, though during his childhood he was taken on long summer holidays to 'Merville', his maternal grandparents' house in Sligo. This part of Sligo was immersed in ghost and fairy stories, and of course tales of the banshee. It was a great place for a boy with an enquiring mind and a vivid imagination.

During his school terms at Godolphin School in London, Yeats was incredibly lonely for Sligo and its stories, and he often daydreamed of the monsters and magic that he believed haunted the roads of Sligo. He later described Godolphin as an 'obscene bullying place' and always had a yearning to return to Ireland.

Eventually, in 1880, his hopes materialised when the family moved to a thatched house on top of the cliffs at Howth. Their new home and its surroundings influenced Yeats and his later stories, as that place too was rich in fairy and ghost lore. Yeats attended the Erasmus High School and would sometimes sneak out of the house at night to sleep in a cave. This strange behaviour may have been caused by his restless nature, as he was always on a quest for some solitary adventure.

In 1883 the family moved to Ashfield Terrace in the Dublin suburb of Rathgar, and the following year Yeats enrolled in the Metropolitan School of Art, where his father was an instructor. It was there he met the writer George Russell and the two men became friends.[1] Despite his success as a writer and poet, Yeats was not considered a genius in school; in fact, he was a comparative failure and later declined to sit any Intermediate Exams in university. Although the family was plagued by poverty during those years, Yeats decided that he was going to follow a career in literature rather than find a regular job that would bring financial security.[2]

In 1885 his first two poems, 'A Faery Song' and 'The Everlasting Voices', were published in the *Dublin University Review*. That same year, he met the old Fenian John O'Leary, who had just returned to Ireland having spent twenty years away due to a mix of prison and forced exile. O'Leary was a charismatic man and played an important role in Yeats' life at that time, acting as a substitute father figure. He was also an excellent and generous supporter of Yeats' work. O'Leary introduced Yeats to the work of the writers and poets of the Young Ireland movement. Many years later Yeats reflected on O'Leary, the man he considered to be the embodiment of romantic Ireland, when he penned these words in one of his most famous poems: 'Romantic Ireland's dead and gone,/It's with O'Leary in the grave'.[3] Yeats also wrote that he was greatly influenced by conversations with O'Leary and by Irish books he had lent or given him. During one of his visits to O'Leary's house, he met Douglas Hyde, who later became the first president of Ireland. On another occasion, he met the very talented poet Katharine Tynan.[4]

Yeats' mind craved a greater understanding of life, but the Church didn't appeal to him, so he joined the Contemporary Club, an organisation set up to provide a forum for Dublin intellectuals to express their opinions; it was a place where they could talk and debate on a wide variety of subjects to broaden their own horizons.[5] Yeats had a strong interest in the occult and was taken to his first séance by Katharine Tynan. This turned out to be a chilling experience for both of them. Yeats felt an evil presence in the room and reacted violently, disrupting proceedings and breaking the table. However, the experience didn't deter him from occultism. In 1887, when the family moved back to London, Yeats met magician MacGregor Mathers, and Madame Blavatsky, founder of the Theosophical Society. This worldwide organisation was founded in 1875 and its primary aim was to create a universal brotherhood of spiritual self-transformation without distinction of race. Yeats soon became a member of the society.

During this period, Yeats' literary activities began to gather momentum and he published *Fairy and Folk Tales of the Irish Peasantry*. Other works about this time included *Mosada* and 'The Madness of King Goll'. He was gaining a reputation as a poet and an authority on Irish folklore. He was continually drawn to Sligo and frequently visited his uncle, George Pollexfen.[6]

On 30 January 1899 Yeats met Maud Gonne for the first

time, when she called to his family home in London, all because the poet Ellen O'Leary, a sister of John O'Leary, had asked her to call on the Yeats family while she was travelling. This was a momentous occasion in the life of Yeats, but one that caused him many years of heartbreak and desperation.

He was stunned by Maud, whose beauty and political passion overwhelmed him. She was indeed a woman of extraordinary beauty and he could not suppress his powerful feelings towards her. Over time his heart yearned for Maud to such an extent that he immortalised her in some of his greatest love poetry. Yeats dined with her each evening during her stay in London. One evening Maud mentioned that she would like to take part in a play in Dublin. Yeats immediately offered to write a play for her. Over time he became her powerful ally, confidant and close friend, but never her husband, though it was something he wished for with deep emotion.

In November 1898 Yeats and Maud were in Dublin together, but staying at different hotels. Yeats awoke one morning after dreaming that Maud had kissed him. He met her for breakfast and she asked him if he had had a dream – he told her and she was silent for a few moments, then said that she had had the same dream. She added that a great spirit took their hands and, placing them together, told her they were married. She confessed to Yeats that she had a horror and terror of physical love and, while Yeats proved a persistent suitor, she would not entertain the idea of marriage, at least not to him. While they were both interested in the idea of a mystical marriage, a spiritual connection was never enough for Yeats and he continued to pursue her.[7] She refused three proposals of marriage between 1892 and 1899.

Following the last refusal, he spent the summer at Coole with Lady Gregory and this retreat possibly saved him from a nervous and physical breakdown.[8]

As mentioned earlier, his meeting with Lady Gregory on 27 July 1896 at the Count de Basterot's estate had a profound effect on his life.[9] At the time, Yeats and the poet Arthur Symons were touring Sligo and the Aran Islands, when Yeats decided to take Symons to visit Edward Martyn in Tulira Castle, Co. Galway. It seems that Yeats had been introduced to Martyn by the author George Moore while in London. Yeats and Symons were guests of Martyn and all three decided to visit the de Basterot estate on the same day that Lady Gregory arrived.[10] She had an extraordinary enthusiasm for literature and became more or less a surrogate mother to Yeats, consistently encouraging his work.

Coole became a home to him over the following years. Staying there gave him time to concentrate on his writing surrounded by the magic of its beautiful, lush woodlands. Yeats also continued to visit Maud Gonne whenever the opportunity presented itself, and her refusal to marry him did not diminish his affection towards her. Also in 1896 he met Olivia Shakespeare, novelist and playwright, who became his lover for a time.[11] At one stage, Lady Gregory told him not to give up on Maud, but to persevere until she agreed to marry him. However, Yeats replied that he was exhausted and had done all in his power to win her love.[12]

News of Maud's sudden marriage to Major John MacBride, who had fought against the British in the South African (Boer) War of 1899–1901, arrived one evening in February 1903 in a letter from Maud explaining her decision. It came just before he was to address a meeting in Dublin and, although stunned, he went ahead with the lecture. While he was congratulated on his performance and delivery, he could not remember anything he had said. The news had a devastating effect on him and he recalled this moment in his poem 'Reconciliation' six years later.

Yeats decided to go on a lecture tour of the United States organised by New York lawyer John Quinn, which he hoped would help distract him from the absolute emotional distress caused by the marriage. Although he was preoccupied by the loss of the woman of his dreams, he gave excellent talks throughout the United States and Canada, and his tour culminated with a powerful lecture delivered in Carnegie Hall. Quinn said afterwards that Yeats had made a greater impression on his audiences than any other speaker since Charles Stewart Parnell.[13]

One of the greatest achievements of the Irish Literary Revival was the foundation of the Abbey Theatre, which opened its doors to the public on 27 December 1904.[14] The first performances were *On Baile's Strand* by Yeats and Lady Gregory's *Spreading the News*.[15] Although trying to move on with his life, Yeats was still preoccupied by his feelings towards Maud Gonne. Her marriage to MacBride resulted in the birth of their only child together, a son, Seán, in Paris on 26 January 1904. She already had another child, Iseult, who was the daughter of her French lover, Millevoye. Despite this, Yeats continued to support her and remained an ally. This is clear from an incident that occurred in the Abbey Theatre in October 1906, when Maud Gonne returned to Ireland following her bitter divorce from MacBride. Many Irish nationalists supported MacBride and when Yeats took Maud to the opening night of Lady Gregory's play *The Gaol Gate*, someone shouted 'Up John MacBride', which was followed by others 'hissing' at her. Yeats was enraged and stood by her side, and, although he didn't react at that time, he carried the indignation for years. He later remembered this incident in his poem 'The Phoenix'.[16]

Following the execution of John MacBride for his role in the 1916 Rising, Yeats proposed marriage to Maud for the last time. She again refused and, some months later, he proposed to her daughter Iseult, with the same result.[17]

Many historians and indeed people with an interest in Yeats are consumed by one question: did he and Maud ever consummate their relationship? During a later interview with the poet's wife, Georgiana Hyde-Lees, Richard Ellman (an authority on Yeats) asked if there had been a sexual relationship between them. She was obviously aware of a liaison, as she replied by saying that she wouldn't have mentioned this, but confirmed that Yeats and Maud Gonne did have a brief affair in May or June of 1909.

The 1916 Rising inspired Yeats to write about the event. He didn't forget his old rival Major MacBride, and referred to him in his poem 'Easter 1916', recalling some of the accusations made against the executed rebel during the divorce proceedings: 'A drunken, vainglorious lout./He had done most bitter wrong/To some who are near my heart …'[18] Yet Yeats reluctantly gives him his due for his role in the uprising: 'He, too, has been changed in his turn,/Transformed utterly;/A terrible beauty is born.'

Marriage was at last on the horizon for Yeats when he proposed to Georgiana Hyde-Lees, whom he always referred to as 'George'. She was an English lady of great charm and culture from an upper-middle-class background, who had a modest income of her own. They shared a common interest in the occult and she admired his poetry. They married in a London registry office on 21 October 1917.[19] Maud must have continued to play on his mind, however, and the marriage might have ended rather abruptly but for the quick thinking of his new wife, who decided to enlist help from the spirit world – or at least this is what she told Yeats. One day, George began to write as if in a trance and Yeats believed that the message – 'With the bird all is well at heart. Your action was right for both' – was addressed to him from the spirit world, more or less blessing the union.[20]

While his feelings for George may have been different from the all-consuming passion he had for Maud, Yeats was pleased with the marriage. In a letter to Lady Gregory, he wrote, 'My wife is a perfect wife, kind, unselfish. I think you were such a young girl once. She has made my life serene and full of order.'[21] In 1918 Yeats took George to Ireland, and they lived in Dublin for a time. Their first child, Anne, was born on 24 February 1919, and their son, Michael, in August 1921. The family moved into number 82 Merrion Square in 1922.

In January 1923 Yeats accepted a seat in the Irish Senate, which was offered to him by the new Free State Government. Also in 1923, he was awarded the Nobel Prize for Literature. Over the following years the family lived in a number of locations, including Co. Galway, Dublin, England and on the Continent.

Yeats' home in Co. Galway during this period was a Norman tower house named Thoor Ballylee, near Gort, which had two cottages attached to the structure.[22] He had purchased the buildings from the Congested Districts Board for the princely sum of £35 as he felt that it was a wonderfully romantic setting, a perfect home from where he could write his poetry, surrounded as it was by the beautiful Kiltartan countryside. It was there he took his family for the summers, while also spending time at Coole.

Over the years, Lady Gregory had taken Yeats to various houses around the district, collecting folklore and stories. He had made good connections and knew the local people well, which was an added bonus when living in the area. George took over the running of the household and believed that part of her role in life was to ensure that nothing would interfere with her husband creating poetry. Their son, Michael, later remembered that his father was a very slow worker, even when it came to short poems. There were many deletions and amendments, and he considered five or six lines of poetry to be a good day's work. Upon finishing a poem he would have George type it up, but continued to make further amendments while looking over her shoulder. He also had difficulty with spelling and punctuation. Although he would set aside periods for work, he could start to compose any time or anywhere. The family were aware of the signs before these moments, as he would begin by making low humming sounds and his right hand would move as if beating time. They were all careful not to interrupt his flow of thought and George would tell the children not to make any noise while their father was working.

Yeats had difficulty in talking with children, even his own. George was concerned and put plans in place to ensure that he would spend more time communicating with them. On one occasion, she arranged for Anne, who was about fourteen years old at the time, to go into her father's study and spend half an hour talking with him. She hoped this would happen every day after dinner. Anne was unsure about what to say, but did try to get a conversation going, with little success. The third evening she tried a different approach and spoke to him about some English poet, but he reacted by almost lecturing her on the man's life. Ultimately, her visits to the study ended because of his inability to hold a general conversation with her. It was a similar story with Michael when he made attempts to engage his father in conversation. The situation must have changed with the passage of time, however, as many years later Michael wrote, 'The remote and distant figure of my childhood had been replaced by someone with whom I could talk on a basis of equality.'[23]

In 1928, because of lung congestion and influenza, Yeats moved to Rapallo in northern Italy with his family. He returned to Ireland the following year and paid his last visit to Thoor Ballylee. He also visited Lady Gregory. After she died in 1932, life was never the same again for Yeats. He wrote that she had been like a mother, a profound friend, and he could not comprehend the world without her.

Yeats continued to write, and produced some more excellent works including *The Winding Stair and Other Poems* and a new edition of his *Collected Poems*.[24] He also visited London and southern England during this period. In his book *W. B. Yeats*, author David Ross tells us that Yeats had two affairs while staying in England – one was with a young actress named Margaret Ruddock, and sometime later he established a simultaneous liaison with an attractive writer named Ethel Mannin. In January 1935 he went home to George, as his health was in decline, but he continued to write to both women. His old friend George Russell died that year and this made Yeats reflect on his own demise.[25] Shortly before his own death, Yeats wrote to a friend saying that he was happy and full of energy: 'It seems to me that I have found what I wanted. When I try to put all into phrase, I say, Man can embody the truth, but he cannot know it.'[26]

In August 1938, after his play *Purgatory* was staged, Yeats addressed the audience at the Abbey Theatre, possibly for the last time. Towards the end of that year, George brought him to Cap Martin in the Alpes-Maritimes, France. Surrounded by the beauty of the sea and mountains, and in the care of his wife, William Butler Yeats died of heart failure on 28 January 1939. He was buried in the little cemetery at Rocquebrune.[27] In 1948 his body was brought to Galway on an Irish naval vessel. The Irish government representative was Seán MacBride, minister for external affairs and son of Maud Gonne MacBride. Yeats was buried under the shadow of Ben Bulben at Drumcliff in Co. Sligo.[28] His gravestone bears the following inscription:

> Cast a cold eye
> On life, on death.
> Horseman, pass by!

Jack Butler Yeats

Artist 1871–1957

Jack Butler Yeats was born on 29 August 1871 in 23 Fitzroy Road, London. He was the youngest son of John Butler Yeats and Susan Pollexfen and a brother of William Butler Yeats. His father's family had land in Co. Kilkenny, but lost it through inferior business practices during the mid-nineteenth century. The family then settled in Dublin and later moved back to London. As a young boy, Jack was known as Johnny and, along with his brother, spent his early years living between Sligo and London. It was mainly because of financial difficulties that Susan brought the children on lengthy visits to their grandparents in Sligo. Their grandfather owned a number of ships, and young Jack developed a great love of the sea while being taken on voyages to Liverpool.

By the time he was nine years old, Jack had been sent to live on a full-time basis with his grandparents, possibly because of continued financial difficulties at home. His experiences in Sligo had a huge impact on his paintings.[1] He loved the Irish countryside, especially the area around Rosses Point, as it was close to the ocean and he was fascinated by the tall ships. He would spend hours sketching them and indeed creating his own images of the sailors who manned the vessels.

His interest in painting was influenced by his father, a portrait artist. It is noteworthy that, when they were children, his brother William displayed more skill as an artist, which caused a rivalry to form. The brothers carried some of this resentment into their adult lives and this was confirmed by author David M. Kiely when he wrote, 'How unfortunate for the literary revival, that old childhood rivalries prevent the brothers working closely together.'[2]

Jack was a diligent and competitive student with a flair for drawing from an early age. Unlike his older brother, he was a good-humoured child and got on very well with his grandfather, William Pollexfen, who spent time telling him stories of sea adventures and of pirates, which greatly excited and influenced the boy and later inspired a great number of his watercolours and paintings. Jack often travelled about the countryside with his grandfather on a pony and trap, listening to all his tales. Life in his grandparents' home gave Jack great comfort and security during those years, as it was a large house with servants.

In 1887 he returned to his family in London to enrol as an art student in the South Kensington School of Art. The family seem to have led a somewhat nomadic life in London, which must have been disruptive for the children. By Christmas 1887 they were living in Bedford Park and Jack was attending the Chiswick School of Art in that area. Between 1890 and 1894 he attended both the West London School of Art and the Westminster School of Art. He was also expected to contribute to the family finances during this period, which he found difficult to do, but he did manage to help by selling his drawings through a shop in Piccadilly. One of his first assignments as an artist was to paint characters from the Buffalo Bill shows then playing in London.

Jack didn't let family poverty cloud his sense of humour and his friendly nature ensured a wide circle of friends. The exception to the rule was his father, whom he very much resented, as he felt that he was the cause of his mother's growing ill health.[3] She was totally withdrawn and depressed as feelings of isolation overwhelmed her. Susan Yeats also suffered two strokes, and was left almost silent and forgotten within the household. Following her death in 1900, Jack was determined to have her remembered, so, along with his sister, Lily, he travelled to Sligo, where they had a memorial plaque erected to her memory. They felt that this was the place their mother always remembered with much happiness. The following words were inscribed on the plaque: 'To the Memory of Susan Mary, wife of John Butler Yeats and eldest daughter of William Pollexfen of this town. Born July 13th 1841. Died Jan. 3rd 1900. Erected by her four children.'[4] Jack was deeply upset by the death of his mother and believed it had been hastened by stress caused by the neglectful behaviour of his father. He felt that his mother had been worn out both mentally and physically by the insecure life imposed on her by her husband, so he ensured that his father's name was not included in the list of people who erected the plaque.

In 1889 Jack met Mary Cottenham White, affectionately known as 'Cottie', a student at Chiswick and an accomplished watercolour artist. They fell in love and were married on 23 August 1894. Following their honeymoon in Dawlish, they moved to a house in Chertsey. Cottie came from a relatively wealthy background and had her own income, which ensured the couple were not overly burdened financially. They moved to Strete, near Dartmouth, in the west of England, purchased an old cottage and barn overlooking the River Gara and converted the barn into a studio. Jack began sketching and produced watercolours on all aspects of life in the west of England, which formed almost his entire first exhibition in 1897, hosted in the Clifford Gallery in London. It was a huge success and his work was well received. One review stated that 'quite apart from the exquisite humour of these sketches, there is another reason which makes them quite remarkable and worthy of attention. They show an astounding capacity for grasping and retaining the impression of certain moments.' Jack also secured work as an artist for the *Illustrated London News,* a highly sought-after newspaper posting that attracted some of the best sketch artists of the day.

A short time later he returned to Ireland along with Cottie. He was a bit apprehensive about returning at first because he felt somewhat intimidated by his brother's literary success.[5] Still, upon his return he began working on a series of sketches and watercolours of life in the west of Ireland. In 1899 he held his first exhibition in Dublin and again this was a success. George Russell reviewed the work in *The* (Dublin) *Daily Express* and wrote, 'These sketches of the west of Ireland reveal a quite extraordinary ability in depicting character and movement.' It was Ruth Shine, a niece of Lady Gregory, who helped him with the exhibition, which was held in Leinster Hall, Dublin. Lady Gregory was excited about this exhibition and felt that his talent was lost by him living in Devon. In April of that year, she invited the couple to visit Coole, and as Jack was more relaxed than his brother, Robert Gregory enjoyed his company. It helped that they had a common interest in painting, horse riding and cricket. Having experienced Coole, Jack left with even more expanded horizons.[6]

While Jack could have benefited from his brother's influential friends, there was still a degree of rivalry and animosity between them that forced the artist to take his own path. Jack had initially shown an interest in being a dramatist and produced some plays for children's theatre, which were produced as 'Punch and Judy' shows, on a series of topics including pirates and smuggling. These were influenced by the stories of his grandfather. While these miniature plays seem to have been superior to W. B.'s work, he was overshadowed by his brother's growing reputation as a playwright, which may be part of the reason why Jack stopped writing plays and followed a career as an artist.

His motivation to paint was described by Hilary Pyle when she wrote that the problem for him was to choose between painting and writing as a means of communication. She said that Jack ultimately chose painting because he felt it was direct vision and greater than writing. Jack decided that painting would be his contribution to the Irish Literary Renaissance, so he entered the Gaelic revival movement founded by his brother and embraced the Irish tradition as an artist. It was said that he 'translated the essence of that tradition, and the life from which it emanated, the love of poetry and the spoken word, of landscape, of humour, of legend, of idiosyncratic character into his paintings'.[7]

His success as an artist took him to various parts of the country and he was continually building up a portfolio for his next exhibition. In 1904 Jack visited the United States and met Mark Twain, a man whom he greatly admired. He also met John

Quinn, the New York lawyer and friend of Lady Gregory, who purchased some of his work. Having returned to Ireland, Jack and his wife continued to visit the west of the country and always found a wonderful host in Lady Gregory.

Jack was a close friend of John Masefield, who was another visitor to Coole. In 1905 Masefield secured a commission for Yeats to compile a report on the congested districts of Galway, Connemara and Mayo. Noted playwright John Millington Synge also became involved in the project, recording the information while Jack captured the areas in his artistic work. The two men became close friends.[8] This connection led to a series of drawings for Synge's *The Aran Islands*, which was published in 1907.

Lady Gregory particularly loved Jack's paintings of the islands and wanted to see him paint across the west of Ireland. She once said to a friend while Jack was still living abroad, 'I grudge him to overpainted England and want him to keep in touch with our neglected west country … He paints peasant life with a kind of dramatic fervour.'[9]

The fact that the Yeats brothers were both members of the United Arts Club didn't change their relationship. The club was a centre for people who were interested in all aspects of the art world: music, writing, acting and painting. Other members included Synge, Padraic Colum and Percy French.[10] Many people in this circle admired Jack's style of art. In fact, Edith Somerville and Violet Martin had a shared conviction that through his visual expression in painting, Yeats was being theatrical in his work. They felt that he was expressing the theatre in the countryside rather than the countryside in the theatre. Jack believed that Irish life itself manifested a spirit of performance normally found in a theatre. In 'The Country Shop' he places the viewer inside the shop along with the customers and the items on sale, giving one the feeling and experience of actually being there.[11]

His sisters, Lily and Lolly, helped set up the Dun Emer Guild with Evelyn Gleeson, who moved to Dublin from London. The guild was a hive of traditional industry, producing a wide range of items using embroidery, weaving, tapestry and lace-making. Jack showed great interest in the guild and helped by advising and planning practical ideas for them. The business provided employment for a number of women and the premises was always full of writers, painters and intellectuals. A short time later, the sisters established the Cuala Press in Dundrum village.[12] Jack began producing hand-painted broadsheets for them. The sisters were also joined by their father for a short time before he left for the United States.

In the late 1900s Jack began painting in oils, but it took a few years for him to achieve his watercolour standards. In 1913 he was asked to exhibit his work in the Armoury Show in New York and one of his paintings to go on display was 'The Circus Dwarf', which had already been critically acclaimed in London the previous year.[13] His work 'At the Feis' was based on his time travelling around the west of Ireland, where he was influenced by storytellers and other people he met along the way. Another of his paintings, 'Man from Aranmore', was described as a classical portrait of an upright peasant – an idealised figure who epitomised a sturdy, self-reliant individual. The figure was also described as a man who was ready for the responsibilities of self-government. Also in 1913, George Birmingham published his book *Irishmen All* and the illustrations included some of Jack's work, namely,

'The Police Sergeant', 'The Lesser Official', 'The Publican' and 'The Politician'.[14]

In 1914 Jack was granted an associateship of the Royal Hibernian Academy and the following year he was elected a full academician. His work during this period reflects the politics and violence of the time, such as the Easter Rising. 'Bachelor's Walk in Memory' is a painting of a girl placing flowers in memory of the people who were shot dead during the gun-running that took place before the Rising.

In 1915 he suffered a nervous breakdown, though the cause is not clear. It lasted for two years. He later continued his political illustrations with works such as 'The Funeral of Harry Boland' and 'Communication with Prisoners'. Despite these artistic views of a troubled Ireland, Jack had no great interest in politics, although he did become a supporter of Éamon de Valera during the Civil War, in opposition to his brother, who supported the pro-Treaty side.

Jack appears to have travelled quite a lot during the 1920s, exhibiting in places such as London, Liverpool, Rome, New York and Pittsburgh.[15] He became close friends with author Sean O'Casey and a young poet named Lyle Donaghy, whom he met while visiting Lady Gregory in Coole. He had not been there for a few years and she was glad to see him. When he told her that he had republican sympathies, she felt closer to him politically than she was to W. B.[16]

Both brothers continued to exhibit the spirit of Ireland in their respective works, which is evident from the following description of Jack's later works:

We are still in the visible world of the west of Ireland, still among stormy skies and seas and rain-shrouded mountains; we see these, however, through eyes which have grown wild, not with the capricious energy of youth, but with the savage tenacity of age. A rout of new images intrudes: suddenly in the place of hills and bogs and the snugs of country taverns among itinerants and cutters of turf, we find ourselves in city streets or theatres or in some room full of books, and strange or familiar urban faces gaze at us through a glittering light.[17]

While he was celebrated in Dublin and around Ireland, he found it increasingly difficult to sell his paintings as the country was suffering financially. During the 1930s his art output decreased, but he filled this void by writing. He produced works in fiction such as *Sligo* (1931), *The Amaranthers* (1936) and *The Charmed Life* (1938).

On New Year's Day in 1942 his artwork formed part of an exhibition in the National Gallery in London, which raised his profile even more in both England and Ireland. Following the Second World War, his reputation reached new heights and he became one of the most revered artistic figures in Ireland. The demand for his work forced him to produce paintings at an extraordinary rate and there was no other Irish painter to match him. It is said that he was the greatest Irish painter of the first half of the twentieth century. His vast output covered every aspect of Irish life and reached out to an extremely wide audience.

However, the success of his work was marred by the death of his beloved Cottie in 1948. Jack lived on for another nine years and died in Portobello Nursing Home on 28 March 1957. Government ministers led by Éamon de Valera, as well as members of the opposition party, turned out for his funeral to Mount Jerome Cemetery in Dublin on 30 March 1957.[18]

Although it could be said that their father didn't provide for his children financially, he did pass on a love of art. Augustine Martin later wrote that it was no accident that the family produced 'not only Ireland's greatest poet but its greatest artist'.[19] As with many other artists, Jack's work became much sought-after following his death. While he walked somewhat in the shadow of his brother, he still left his own indelible footprint on the Irish artistic world and his work was displayed in the most prestigious galleries. The National Gallery of Ireland later dedicated an entire room to his paintings and the Crawford Art Gallery in Cork also houses some of his work. His paintings have been on exhibition alongside artists such as Picasso and Renoir. In his beloved Co. Sligo, the place of his artistic obsession and exciting childhood, his paintings can also be seen in the County Museum and Art Gallery.[20]

John Millington Synge

Writer and Dramatist 1871–1909

John Millington Synge was born on 16 April 1871 in Rath-farnham, Dublin. He was the youngest of five surviving children born to John Hatch Synge, a barrister by profession, and Kathleen, the daughter of Dr Robert Traill, rector in Schull, Co. Cork. They were a Protestant family with extreme anti-papal views and strong evangelical beliefs. The other children were Robert, Edward, Annie and Samuel. The Synge family were of Anglo-Irish origin and were big landowners in Co. Wicklow, where their ancestral home was Glanmore Castle.

In 1845 the family declared bankruptcy after reckless spend-ing of the estate finances. This forced some family members to leave home and earn their own living, so John Hatch studied law. He died of smallpox in 1872, before his son's first birthday. The tragedy had far-reaching consequences for Synge. As a youth as he was condemned to a life ruled by his religiously fanatical mother, and the children had to listen to her preaching hell, fire and damnation for sins against God.[1]

The family moved to Orwell Park in Rathgar shortly after the death of the father. He had left them with an income of £400 per annum. Synge's education began at home with a private tutor, though he was later sent to Harrick's Classical and English

School in Dublin. As a child, Synge was frail and prone to illness, which resulted in poor attendance at school, but most summer months were spent on extended family holidays in Greystones. As Synge matured, his ill health didn't deter him from taking part in outdoor activities. He loved the open-air life and nature, and joined the Dublin Naturalists Field Club. Over time he became a keen walker and also liked to cycle about the countryside, particularly around Wicklow, as he enjoyed meeting the so-called 'kings of the road' (vagrants and tramps) and also members of the old farming communities. He was fascinated by the manner in which they spoke and believed that these people could represent the final stages of a vanishing Gaelic language.

He also developed an interest in flora and fauna, which led him to read *The Origin of the Species* by Charles Darwin.[2] He was fourteen years old at the time and his enquiring mind created much controversy in the family. His newly found education resulted in him turning away from religion and this led to constant arguments with his devout mother. Although Synge was influenced by Darwin, he never lost his belief in God and 'sought the Creator in places where his family would not have cared to look'.[3] He also developed an interest in Irish folklore and read widely on the subject. His knowledge of ancient Irish legends and the conflict between the pagan and Christian ideas played a part in his later writing, which was perhaps his way of analysing and informing the reader of his own family conflict.

His brother Edward had managed to acquire property in Cavan, Mayo and Wicklow, and was a landlord during this time of unrest in Ireland. He was obviously a harsh landlord, as Synge disagreed with his brother's strong-arm tactics when it came to evicting tenants. His past experiences in meeting people on the roads and around the countryside played a part in his opinions.[4]

In 1889 Synge began attending Trinity College Dublin and Irish was among his chosen subjects. He was awarded a prize for his *Diarmuid and Grania* text and graduated three years later with a BA degree. The Gaelic revival that was sweeping across Ireland engulfed many like-minded people with a pride in Irish history and culture, and through the Gaelic League Irish people found a way of expressing their nationalistic views in literature and music.[5] This was the world that Synge found himself being absorbed into during this period. He was musical, playing the piano and flute at the Royal Academy of Music. He also played the violin and even composed some works, and thoughts of a musical career were ever-present in his mind, but this dream was not realised because of his reluctance to appear before an audience.[6]

After he graduated in 1892, Synge set off for Germany to continue his studies. In 1894 he moved to Paris, where he hoped to teach English. It was there, two years later, that he met W. B. Yeats. This later proved to be a pivotal encounter for the Irish Literary Revival.[7] Synge had stayed for a time on the Aran Islands and spoke about his experiences in this ancient landscape. Yeats advised him to return there, saying, 'You will write your satirical masterpiece.'[8] Synge said that if he were to live in such a wild Atlantic place for any length of time it would be the cause of his death. Yeats simply replied, 'Not before you have written your masterpiece.' Yeats was right and had great confidence in Synge's ability.

Having returned to Ireland in 1897, Synge noticed a growth on his neck. It was the first sign of Hodgkin's disease. Some months later, he had an operation to try to have it removed; it was only a temporary measure, however, and he continued to suffer from the disease.

In May 1898 he went back to the Aran Islands and, although he was ill, the remoteness didn't deter or frighten him. He spent much time on Inishmaan and during the following six weeks, and on subsequent annual visits, he studied the Irish language and listened to the stories of the islanders. He was captivated and inspired by the islands and the people, with their unremitting struggle against the elements.[9] By now Synge had lost his hair through the illness that continued to plague him and he had a wig fashioned from his own hair so people wouldn't notice. He was described as a strong-looking, well-built man with broad shoulders, and was approximately five foot eight inches tall. He had an expression of sadness on his face and looked drawn because of the illness.

Synge was captivated by the women of the islands and recorded, 'I have noticed many beautiful girls whose long luxuriant lashes lent a shade to wistful eyes.' Focusing on one particular girl, he said, 'Her face came with me all day among the rocks. She is Madonna-like ... The expression in her eye is so overwhelmingly beautiful that I remember no single quality of her colour.'[10]

A local man, Pat Dirrane, acted as a guide for Synge during his time on the islands. When Synge later published *The Aran Islands*, he gave a picture of the everyday life of the islanders from both his and Dirrane's points of view. A friend, Francis MacNamara from Doolin, often joined him on the Aran Islands and sometimes Augustus John and George Bernard Shaw also visited. Synge felt at times that it was almost impossible to acquire reliable information on the island, not because the people were uncooperative, but rather because they were clannish and their kinship was important to them.[11] However, through his connections with Pat Dirrane and some other local people who were willing to support him, he learned about the legends and traditions of the islands. He had a particular interest in the old Gaelic poems and would sometimes make his way to the highest point of Inishmaan and sit by a little stone enclosure, known today as 'Synge's Chair'. It was here that Synge contemplated his own life and the lives of the islanders.[12]

On 27 June 1898 Synge visited Coole for the first time. The invitation arrived in the form of a letter from Yeats, who said that Lady Gregory would like him to stay with her at Coole for a few days. Synge was delighted, not realising that the invitation was actually from Yeats alone. Yeats had written to Lady Gregory and told her that Synge would be an ally in the literary days ahead. When his train pulled into Gort station, Lady Gregory was there to collect him. When he informed her that he was collecting the folklore and stories on the islands, she was annoyed, even jealous, and considered him an outsider trespassing on her dominion in Co. Galway. Nevertheless, she felt that his stay on the Aran Islands had agreed with him and thought he looked well, with a good colour on his face. The outdoor life on the islands had improved his health.

Despite her feelings about him collecting folklore, Lady Gregory soon found herself warming to Synge. He was somewhat uncomfortable at Coole among the art treasures and lavish furnishings that seemed alien to him, particularly after experiencing the simple way of life on the Aran Islands. He missed them, their people and the Irish language. Synge was difficult to draw into conversation and, for the most part, spoke only when asked a question. Lady Gregory later said that she found him to be a comfortable guest, good-humoured, gentle and a good listener.[13] This meeting was important, as it eventually helped in connecting him with the Abbey Theatre.

Synge's play *The Shadow of the Glen* was staged in Dublin in 1903. It was a portrayal of a loveless rural marriage which some believed was a slur on Irish women, and while it was set in Wicklow, it was inspired by a story that Synge was told in Aran.[14] The play basically tells the story of a young woman trapped in an unhappy marriage to an elderly husband who discovers that she has taken a lover and banishes her. She is then abandoned by her lover.[15] The story was too realistic for many people, including Arthur Griffith, who wished to see a more romantic portrayal of Ireland, and a row developed between Maud Gonne and W. B. Yeats, as she believed that the play was forced on the theatre because it had not been submitted to the reading committee before being staged. She obviously didn't attend, as she wrote to Yeats saying that she heard it was a horrid play and would not take any responsibility for it appearing in public. The fact that Maud Gonne didn't like Synge possibly didn't help matters. Her ill feeling towards him was caused by earlier comments he made regarding Irish freedom. Synge said that England would never give this freedom until an independent Ireland could be proven a reliable friend, and he also felt that Maud Gonne was too spiteful when it came to politics.[16] She was not a woman to forget such comments. Regardless of her opinion, the play was proclaimed by many to signal the arrival of the astonishing talent of Synge.[17]

After another visit to Coole, he left for the Blasket Islands.[18] It was said that Synge was the first of the literary and scholarly visitors to arrive in this ancient place. He was made welcome and enjoyed his time there recording information and stories about the island. While some people believed that Synge wrote carefully and was sensitive about island culture, others from the island took offence at his work. He wrote about a young married woman who made him feel welcome by frying rashers and making tea and described her as follows: 'She was a small beautifully-formed woman, with brown hair and eyes – instead of black hair and blue eyes that are usually found with this type in Ireland – and delicate feet and ankles that are not common in these parts, where women's work is so hard.'[19]

On 4 February 1905 *The Well of the Saints* opened in the Abbey Theatre, but it didn't attract the audiences expected. Lady Gregory had travelled to Dublin for the play and was disappointed that Synge didn't join the others in the Green Room after the play. The following night she asked him where he had been, saying they thought he had committed suicide. She felt that he was disappointingly slow to take responsibility for his play, which is possibly what triggered such an offending comment.[20]

During this period Synge's life was changing; he was falling in love. It had all begun during rehearsals for *The Well of the Saints*, when Synge was introduced to Molly Allgood, a sister of actress Sara Allgood, who was starring in the play. She had asked Sara to try to arrange an audition for her. Molly had not reached her eighteenth birthday, while Synge was close to thirty-four at the time. She was anxious to make an impression on Synge, who was by then the most controversial dramatist in Dublin.

Romantic feelings developed for both of them during that year; Synge decided to give Molly the part of Cathleen in *Riders to the Sea* and worked closely with her. She responded admirably to his coaching and took the stage name 'Máire O'Neill'. However, he was careful to conceal his feelings for her from other members of the cast and indeed the staff at the Abbey Theatre.[21]

In September 1905 he was summoned to a meeting at Coole because George Russell was announcing some proposed constitutional changes in the theatre. Synge was appointed as a director of the Abbey Theatre along with Lady Gregory and W. B. Yeats.[22]

In January 1906 his love affair with Molly began with a passion, but brought complications. Synge was described by many people as a perfect gentleman and he would not invite Molly to his apartment alone. They met instead in public venues. He delighted in taking her for walks around Wicklow, the countryside he had loved since his childhood. While Synge's feelings were strong, he was not happy with her inadequate education and working-class background, which he wished could be changed. Despite their differences, however, the romance continued to blossom and soon people became aware of the liaison. Yeats and Lady Gregory were against the relationship, but were unable to challenge him on the matter as Synge was by then too powerful in the world of theatre.

The fact that Molly was a Catholic was another concern for Synge, should he ever have to introduce her to his mother. However, the two women met in November 1906 when he took Molly to Glendalough House in Co. Dublin at her request. His mother was impressed by the charming manner of the young actress. She may not have accepted Molly as a future daughter-in-law, but she certainly extended a warm welcome to her.

Molly continued to cause Synge some frustration as he found it difficult to control her in the way he would have liked and even her erratic letters annoyed him. Moreover, he was jealous of her being in the company of other actors. Despite these annoyances, he loved her deeply and the romance continued. Molly meant everything to Synge; to him she was life itself, full of youth and energy. Coupled with this somewhat strange relationship, he had to deal with a body racked by illness. He was suffering from bronchitis, asthma, influenza, hay fever and, of course, the ever-present Hodgkin's disease. He was also struggling to finish his most difficult play to date. Telling Molly of his struggle, he added, 'that accursed *Playboy*'.[23]

It was while he was in the Aran Islands that he found the inspiration for his most famous work, *The Playboy of the Western World* (1907). The story is based on a man named William O'Malley, from Callow in Connemara, who in 1872 made his way to Inishmaan having accidentally killed his father during a fit of rage. He hid in Doonconor, an old fort on the island, until local people helped him escape to the United States.[24]

Because it was centred around such a terrible crime, the play caused huge protests during opening week in the Abbey Theatre. Lady Gregory informed Yeats by telegram – he was in Scotland at the time – that the audience was appalled at the use of the word 'shift', which referred to a long-obsolete female garment that lay close to a woman's skin. While this word provoked riots, there were much deeper causes. Many people were angered because they felt that Synge was ridiculing Irish people with his use of language. He was also criticised for the manner in which he used the words 'God' and 'bloody'.

Some people truly believed that the play was a slander on Ireland. One member of the Gaelic League, Ayamonn O'Farrell, was enraged, describing it as a woeful, wanton play that was the most bitter enemy of Ireland. The trouble continued throughout the week, as the Abbey directors refused to stop it being staged. Despite all the protests, the play continued and the audiences had to be controlled by policemen occupying the aisles in a bid to keep order.[25] *The Playboy of the Western World* even caused riots in America several years later, but it was to many people the masterpiece that Yeats had hoped to see from Synge.

This play also filled the theatre for the first time, giving credence to the notion that there is no such thing as bad publicity. In a sense, Synge had prepared the way for Sean O'Casey, who would later suffer the same indignation at the hands of angry audiences. According to Micheál Mac Liammóir, Synge was the first and last dramatist who combined the quality of the 'Yeatsian hope for a poetic theatre with the grim, earthly and violent sense of comedy that outraged the fools and turned the heads of wise men'. [26]

When Yeats returned to Dublin, he called for an open forum in the theatre to discuss *Playboy*. Although a supporter of Synge, Lady Gregory didn't like the play. During the discussions that followed, Yeats strongly defended both play and playwright, causing one observer to say that they had never witnessed anyone fight as hard to justify *Playboy*. Despite all of its problems in Ireland, the play went on to be a success when it toured England.[27]

In April 1908 Synge suffered a relapse of ill health while

visiting his mother, who was convalescing from an illness at the time. She was shocked by his appearance and he told her that he was growing steadily weaker and could not sleep until the early hours of the morning because of pains in his stomach and back. By this time he and Molly were living together and his mother had accepted the relationship. She had grown to like and respect Molly to such a degree that even marriage would have been acceptable. However, Molly was aware that this would not happen because of the illness, and Synge obviously knew that death was close when he asked her if she would be attending his funeral. Molly told him that she would not be there because she could not tolerate seeing him dead while others lived.

He was admitted to Elpis Nursing Home in Dublin while struggling to finish another play, *Deirdre of the Sorrows*, but it was not to be. Handing the unfinished manuscript to his brother, Robert, who was visiting him, Synge said that posterity would never know how perfect the completed play would have been. Sometime later he was set to have surgery for another Hodgkin's-related growth on his neck, but the doctors ultimately decided that this would be futile. The stream of visitors and even the nurses were greatly distressed by his appearance, as they loved his gentle manner and ease of conversation. One of the nurses discovered a book wrapped in brown paper on his locker. It was the Bible, which he had been reading secretly. 'God have mercy on me, God forgive me,' the nurse heard him say as she watched over him.

On the morning of 24 March 1909, John Millington Synge passed away peacefully and was buried in Mount Jerome Cemetery. His funeral was attended by some of the most famous playwrights, poets, actors and actresses of the day. Molly Allgood didn't attend; she mourned for her lover in private.[28] It was later said, 'His creative years were not many, but in them he made masterpieces that will be admired as long at the theatre exists.'[29] Following his death, Molly collaborated with Yeats and Lady Gregory to finish *Deirdre of the Sorrows*.

By 1910 Molly was sharing an equal status with her sister in Abbey Theatre productions. However, she never shared the bond her sister had with Lady Gregory, as Sara was one of Lady Gregory's favourite actresses and the only one to be invited to Coole on a regular basis. Molly married twice; her first husband, in 1911, was George Herbert Mair, who died in 1926. Molly married Arthur Sinclair five months later. That marriage lasted five years and ended in divorce. Molly died in Basingstoke on 2 November 1952.[30]

Sara Allgood

Actress 1883–1950

Sara Allgood was born on 31 October 1883 in Dublin. She was the second daughter of George and Margaret Allgood. Her father was a printing compositor and her mother worked in the second-hand furniture business. Sara was educated in the Marlborough Street Training College in Dublin.[1] While her father was a staunch Protestant and Orangeman, her mother was described by author Marian Broderick as a feisty Dublin Catholic. Sara had seven siblings and among them was her younger sister Mary, more commonly known as Molly. While their father saw the children as Protestant, Margaret secretly raised them as Catholics.

Following the death of her father, Sara trained as an upholsterer to help support the family.[2] Their mother obviously had a great influence over the children, as they were all drawn towards nationalist organisations. Sara joined Inghinidhe na hÉireann (Daughters of Erin), which was founded by Maud Gonne. She was not alone in her nationalist ideals, as her brothers joined Sinn Féin shortly after it was founded.[3]

Sara developed a reputation as a singer and was also described as an aspiring actress with an excellent ability to recite poetry. She had a natural flare for the stage, which brought her to the attention of some of the top names in the business, including

Lady Gregory and W. B. Yeats.[4] In 1903 William and Frank Fay, who were noted in the Dublin theatrical scene, began training her for the stage and encouraged her to become a member of the Irish National Theatre Society. Her tuition under the Fay brothers paid off and the long hard hours of intense training helped Sara develop her own natural talent. A year later she made her first appearance on stage in *Twenty-Five,* a play by Lady Gregory. In December 1904 she played Mrs Fallon in *Spreading the News,* also by Lady Gregory, at the opening night of the Abbey Theatre. Some of her early roles include Princess Buan in Yeats' *The King's Threshold* and Cathleen in Synge's *Riders to the Sea.* She had a powerful stage presence and an excellent voice, which led to her becoming the undisputed leading lady of the theatre company.

She continued to work with the Irish National Theatre Society, which was acclaimed both at home and abroad, and over the following years she took centre stage in a variety of important roles. She developed a close and lifelong friendship with Lady Gregory, who supported her throughout her career, even though some people intimated that Sara only developed this friendship because of the social benefits she would gain from such a close connection.[5] However, such sentiments could well have been formed from jealousy. Mary Colum maintained that Lady Gregory behaved like a grand duchess, treating people as if they were her subjects, and that she remained somewhat aloof from most people – with the exception of Sara Allgood and Sean O'Casey. As far as Lady Gregory was concerned, she had found an actress in Sara who would complement her plays and contribute greatly to the success of her work.[6] It was an unlikely friendship, given that they were from totally opposite backgrounds. Never-theless, Sara was the only Abbey Theatre actress invited to Coole Park on a regular basis, and it would have been during one of these visits that she signed the Autograph Tree.[7]

Sara played Cathleen again in 1909 and her role was so convincing that George Bernard Shaw said that it was enough to make a man do something foolish. Journalists shared his view of her outstanding performance. While reviews in *The United Irishman* didn't have favourable comments for a later production, *Spreading the News*, the paper did praise Sara for her role as Bartley's mother, saying that she lived through every minute of the part.[8]

Despite those who felt that Sara had developed the friend-ship with Lady Gregory purely to promote her acting career, she worked extremely hard in rehearsals and when performing. She was determined from the beginning to reach her full potential and made the stage her home. While she played some comic roles, she excelled in tragedy. As a true professional actress, she could transform herself on stage and capture the audience. Sara was also much admired by other actresses, and one of the leading ladies of stage during this period, Máire nic Shiubhlaigh, described her as wonderfully gifted. She went on to say that her sad, expressive dark eyes and her magnificent contralto voice rivalled those of the great Sarah Bernhardt.[9]

Sara's sister, Molly, also joined the Abbey Theatre, but she changed her name to Máire O'Neill to avoid being confused or overshadowed by Sara. The fact that both sisters chose the same profession caused rivalry between them throughout their careers. Molly also trained with the Irish National Theatre Society and was said to be a mischievous, rebellious young woman, and almost bewitching. Her romantic relationship with Synge was frowned upon by Sara.[10]

Given her reputation as an actress, it seems strange that Yeats made an attempt to have Sara replaced in 1907 with someone he considered a more professional, 'English' actress. This potential replacement, Miss Darragh as she was known, was in fact Irish, and the fact that her salary was in excess of those of the other women in the company caused a lot of resentment. However, Yeats' expectations of Miss Darragh becoming a leading light in the Irish theatre failed and business carried on as normal. The irony was that a number of years later, Sara Allgood was in the position where she could command her own salary.[11]

In 1908 Sara found herself as stage manager in the theatre following the departure of the Fay brothers, both of whom left for the United States. This was a position that demanded professional management skills and experience. It proved a tough task for her and she was somewhat erratic in the role. Although she worked long hours, she still needed help from Yeats to run the theatre efficiently.[12]

She must not have remained in this role very long, as she helped open the Gaiety Theatre in Manchester that same year. She also found herself touring Stratford with the *Measure for Measure* production by William Poel. Having attended the play, Yeats commented that her appearance as Isabella was magnificent, rich and passionate. In 1914 she spent a season in the Liverpool Repertory Theatre, and the following year she delighted her audience playing the lead comic role in *Peg o' my Heart*.[13]

A short time later, she toured Australia and New Zealand

with the same play, staring opposite actor Gerald Henson; the two fell in love and were married in Melbourne in the autumn of 1916. The tour continued and the couple were very happy together, with both enjoying much success in the theatre. Sara became pregnant, but sadly their baby, Mary, died an hour after her birth in January 1918. Further tragedy struck in November 1918 when Henson died during the influenza pandemic that was sweeping across many areas of the world. Despite these bereavements, Sara continued the tour of Australia and New Zealand for another eighteen months and then returned to Ireland, where she received a warm welcome from her fans in Dublin and of course in the Abbey Theatre.[14] She then made her way to London, having been invited to play Mrs Geoghegan in Lennox Robinson's play *The Whiteheaded Boy*. In 1920 she played Mrs O'Flaherty in George Bernard Shaw's play *O'Flaherty V.C.*

In 1924 Sara gave such a memorable performance as Juno in Sean O'Casey's play *Juno and the Paycock* that it was said she made Irish theatrical history.[15] Before the production opened, actor Gabriel Fallon, a close friend of O'Casey, said, having seen the rehearsals, that it seemed a strange, baffling mixture of comedy and tragedy. He felt that one could not say with any degree of certainty if it would be successful on stage. Despite being an experienced professional actress, Sara sometimes struggled during rehearsals. She did have some difficulty in reading her script, on occasion referring to 'Joxer Daly' as 'Boxer Daly'. However, she was chosen for the part because of her powerful performances, and her reputation was such that she was often called the tragic queen of the Abbey. She made the role of Juno her own and following opening night, Fallon wrote that he was stunned by the tragic quality of the third act, which was played magnificently by Sara Allgood. Sara was splendid in this role, which made her the natural choice to play Bessie Burgess in *The Plough and the Stars*, but she had been released from the Abbey at the time and was committed to travelling to London with *Juno and the Paycock*, which was booked for the Royalty Theatre.

Although a confident actress, Sara could be sensitive to certain remarks or comments, even if she caused them herself. On one occasion, after actor Cyril Cusack joined the company, he was standing in the wings and Sara asked him if he thought she was fat. He replied 'no', but when she pursued the question, he admitted that she was 'plump'. At the moment, and much to his relief, she was called on stage, but she never spoke to him again. She had more reason to fall out with Sean O'Casey some years later, when he was asked during a photo-call in London to pin a shamrock on Sara's breast. He refused, saying, 'You can have it if you want it, but it's pinning it on her arse I'll be and not her breast.'[16] This may have been because she had more or less shunned actress Eileen Carey Reynolds, to whom O'Casey had shown favouritism in an earlier play.

Sara continued to perform in London during the 1920s and also toured the United States. Her role as Mrs Henderson in *The Shadow of a Gunman* was described as being 'truly unforgettable'.[17]

Sara had, by this time, aspirations of performing before cinema audiences. In 1930 Alfred Hitchcock released his film version of *Juno and the Paycock* and Sara repeated her role as Juno, but some said that she 'looked past her prime and showed little grasp of screen acting'.[18] Nevertheless, she moved to Hollywood in 1940 and sacrificed her theatrical work to pursue a film career.

She starred in some fifty films, among them the first British talkie, Alfred Hitchcock's *Blackmail*. She was nominated for an Academy Award as best supporting actress in 1941 for her role in John Ford's film *How Green Was My Valley*. In 1945 she became an American citizen. Sara died of a heart attack on 13 September 1950 in Woodlands Hills, California, and is buried in Culver City.[19]

Sara Allgood had an exciting theatrical career and played many outstanding roles both at home and abroad. Her exceptional performances in some plays made audiences believe that the parts had been written for her alone. The success she experienced in her career was through hard work, helped by the early tutoring she received from Frank and William Fay.

Frank Fay

Actor and Theatre Producer 1870–1931

Frank Fay was born on 30 August 1870 at 10 Lower Dorset Street, Dublin. He was the eldest of four children born to William, who worked for the civil service, and Martha Fay (*née* Dowling).[1] According to one source, the family were originally from Galway and had changed their name from Fahey to Fay.[2] Frank had a passion for the theatre from an early age and immersed himself in books on the subject. His younger brother, William, shared this passion and they later worked together in the theatre business. Frank's perfectionist nature and special flare for elocution were of great benefit to him in the world of theatre.[3]

Frank was educated in Belvedere College, Dublin and his subjects included shorthand and typing, which helped him secure a position as secretary with an accounting firm in Dublin.[4] His work there must not have been very satisfying as he, along with William, decided to attend the Dublin Dramatic School. They immersed themselves in study to ensure a successful theatrical life, and their aim was to reach professional tutor standards in order to train others. According to the playwright Lennox Robinson, their first performances were in rather worthless plays, but they gained valuable experience until the time when they eventually became involved in the production of more committed national

Irish plays. Naturally, they were delighted with this move into more serious material. It is a tribute to their dedication and ability that over the following years their work became as important to the Irish theatre as that of Yeats and other leading dramatists.[5]

Frank Fay was strongly nationalist and this brought him into contact with men like Arthur Griffith. He was appointed as drama critic for Griffith's nationalist newspaper *The United Irishman*. It was in this role that he developed confidence in his own ideas on how a theatre should be managed. Given his nationalistic leanings, it is no surprise that he was very much in favour of Irish language plays being staged, even though he didn't have a good command of the language himself. However, he soon realised that this would not be commercially successful because the audiences were mainly English-speaking and would not fully understand the performances.[6] Yeats was not in favour of the idea either, as he felt that it was in the best interests of the Abbey to satisfy audiences.

Fay was an admirer of the French theatre and asked the author George Moore to help the cast in developing different Irish accents when reading verse, as he wanted performers to speak realistically on stage.[7] Although the idea of a total Irish language theatre was a non-runner, Fay was deeply committed to the revival of Irish drama and believed that it was time to make the Irish accent and dialect an expression of the Irish character, even when speaking English. He didn't want the Irish language or accent being used on stage to provide laughter, like the 'stage Oirish' stereotype you would often see in foreign productions.[8]

When the Irish Literary Society staged *Diarmuid and Grania* by Yeats and George Moore, two notable English actors – Frank

Benson and Edward Elgar – were approached to play the leading roles, as both Yeats and Moore believed that these actors would raise the production standards of the play. However, the idea of having them play Irish roles proved a failure and Fay was very critical, saying that to have this play written in English and using such actors was intolerable. He also said that even amateur Irish actors could have given the play more meaning than the experienced English professionals. As if to prove his point, he referred to the one-act play *Casadh an tSugáin*, written by Douglas Hyde and directed by William Fay, which accompanied *Diarmuid and Grania* on the same night and proved more successful.

Frank's reputation as an acting coach was a great asset to him, and he insisted that his students should attend the theatre with him on all possible occasions. It didn't matter how good actors were, or indeed their status in the world of theatre, provided they put in a serious effort under his tuition. He rigorously put them through their paces and painstakingly examined each performance. It seems he had one rule: to ensure all his students gave their best effort on stage. Despite his ability, the Abbey only offered him fifteen shillings a week, which was the equivalent of a domestic servant's wages at that time. It would seem that Fay was more interested in producing professional performances than in making any financial gain.[9]

His position with *The United Irishman* gave him a means of promoting his own strongly nationalist views. This can be seen in his attack on Yeats in May 1901 regarding his ideas for the theatre and work as a dramatist. The idea of Yeats using English actors was a major cause of concern for Fay, and he came on strong, saying that there was a 'herd of Saxon and other swine fattening on us. They must be swept away into the sea with the pestilent breed of West Britons with which we are troubled, or they will sweep us there.'[10] The following year, Fay published an article promoting the idea of a national theatre company to act as a nursery for Irish drama and literature; this subsequently materialised in 1902 with the foundation by William Fay of the Irish National Dramatic Society, which was eventually absorbed into the Abbey Theatre. Despite Frank's earlier attack on Yeats, the poet publicly recognised the Fays' contribution, saying that the national theatre owed its existence to the brothers.[11]

It was George Russell who first introduced Yeats to the Fay brothers. It is clear that Russell played a fundamental part in the careers of both brothers. In fact, Lennox Robinson mentioned that Russell played a more important role in their careers than Yeats.[12] In spite of Frank's previous unkind words about Yeats, he agreed to produce *Cathleen ni Houlihan* for the poet and Lady Gregory. The play was to be performed in St Theresa's Hall, Dublin in 1902.[13] It made sense for the brothers to consolidate their position with Yeats and Lady Gregory if they wished to become leading figures in the Irish Literary Revival, and by doing so it was inevitable that they would be invited to Coole.[14]

Despite this form of networking, the brothers were certainly not afraid to voice their opinions if they felt that a play was unsuitable, regardless of the playwright or their reputation within the theatre, as can be seen in a 1902 letter from Frank Fay to Yeats when he rejected Lady Gregory's play *Twenty-Five*:

> In my brother's opinion *Twenty-Five* would not suit us. He thinks
> the dialogue excellent, but does not think an Irish peasant, however

hard up, would play a stranger for his money like old Michael does ... the play in country districts might incite emigration, on account of the glowing terms in which America is spoken of. I may say that myself I quite agree with this verdict.[15]

While Frank Fay was a low-sized man, being under five feet six, this certainly didn't interfere with his confidence or acting ability before an audience. He was an excellent tragic actor with a powerful voice, which made audiences sit up and take notice of him, and because of this he seemed much larger than his physical size. He starred as Cú Chulainn in Yeats' *On Baile's Strand* when the Abbey Theatre opened in December 1904. It was said that as an elocution teacher he could not be equalled, and he believed elocution was a vital part of his stage work as it ensured clarity to the theatre audience. People were entranced by the quality of his voice on stage, so much so that Yeats later dedicated his play *The King's Threshold* to Fay's vocal ability.

While Frank had a close relationship with his brother throughout his career, this was sometimes turbulent and volatile, sporadically coming to blows.[16] The pressure that they placed on themselves to ensure that their plays were professionally produced perhaps caused the occasional strong difference of opinion and subsequent physical confrontations. They both took their work very seriously and worked hard for the sake of the theatre. Frank was largely responsible for creating the economic style of production for which the Abbey became famous.[17]

Frank was sometimes quick-tempered and prone to fits of depression. Nevertheless, he continued his acting career and played Shawn Keogh in Synge's *The Playboy of the Western World* in 1907. Over the following year, the brothers lost much of their influence in the Abbey and had disagreements with Yeats over methods of theatre production, so they resigned from the Abbey in January 1908. This may also be the reason why two months later they were suspended from the Irish National Theatre Society.

Frank then toured the United States with his brother, before making his way to England, where he travelled around the country taking part in Shakespearean productions. During this period he was approached by two men, Thomas MacDonagh and Joseph Plunkett, both of whom later signed the Irish Proclamation and were executed as leaders of the 1916 Easter Rising. They offered him a position as actor-manager of an Irish theatre company (Theatre of Ireland), which it seems he turned down.

Frank became involved with a woman named Freda, known as 'Bird', and they were married in 1912. The couple lived in Upper Mount Street, Dublin and had one son, Gerard, who later became a popular writer. By 1918 Frank had obviously settled his differences with the Abbey Theatre and Yeats, as he took part in two of the poet's plays, *The Hour Glass* and the aforementioned *The King's Threshold*. He was credited for having created the style of acting for which the Abbey Theatre is internationally recognised and which has influenced many other schools of acting. By 1921 he was teaching elocution and directing plays in local colleges, which financially sustained him.[18] He also gave private acting lessons in the traditional Abbey style in his Upper Mount Street flat. It is a testament to his ability that the acclaimed actor, and later critic, Gabriel Fallon took advantage of this tuition.[19]

His wife predeceased him, leaving Frank devastated, and he died on 2 January 1931, some say from a broken heart. He is buried in Glasnevin Cemetery. His teaching influenced genera-tions of actors and actresses, leaving the Irish theatre with a rich legacy.[20] In the years that followed, people remembered the talent of the Fay brothers and would speak of them with great admi-ration.[21] However, it is unfortunate that in the modern world of stage acting, the brothers are somewhat overlooked by the general public. Many people think of Yeats, Robinson and Lady Gregory regarding the foundation of the Irish theatre, but Frank Fay played a major role in this achievement and his contribution in those early years was immeasurable.

William George Fay

Actor and Producer 1872–1947

William George Fay was born in Dublin on 12 November 1872 and was the brother of the aforementioned Frank Fay. From an early age he was interested in the theatre and his first performance was in the play *Eileen Oge*, which was staged in Queen's Theatre, Dublin.[1] Although Fay became an electrician, his heart was set on a career in the theatre. He was a confident young man with a high opinion of himself, who believed that he could make things happen and had a particular talent for comedy.[2]

The formation of the Ormonde Dramatic Society by the Fay brothers in 1892 proved successful for them and they played in many venues around Dublin city and county. They had remarkable success in teaching and their students included Sara and Molly Allgood, Joseph Kerrigan and Dudley Digges. In 1902 William helped form the Irish National Dramatic Society, which was the first Irish company dedicated to Irish plays. This brought him close to George Russell, Yeats and Lady Gregory, and the following year he joined with them in forming the Irish National Theatre Society.[3] The founding of these societies provided a venue for young, talented people to perform before public audiences. This is evident from a letter written by its secretary, Frederick Ryan, regarding Fay's Dramatic Society:

As I believe Mr Russell has told you, the Irish National Dramatic Society which Mr Fay organised has been placed on a more definite basis, and has rented a Hall for twelve months, capable of accommodating 200 people. This gives a permanent prospect of carrying on the work and in every way preferable to spasmodic performances.[4]

The first play performed by the society was *The Laying of the Foundations*, followed that same night by *The Pot of Broth*. They weren't very successful, as can be seen from the following extract taken from the diary of W. A. Henderson, who was involved in the production. However, it seems that Fay came to the rescue of the latter piece:

> Those who were present on a bitter October night, in a draughty ill-lighted hall and without fire, will not forget the experience – the first performance by the Irish National Theatre Society … The play was *The Laying of the Foundations* in two Acts by Fred Ryan. At 8 o'clock three knocks noted the rising of the curtain. There were many defects; the scenery was poor, and the stage very small. The play did not make amends. It was a drama of musical wrong-doing and drain-pipes, after the fashion of Ibsen. Then followed *The Pot of Broth*. A poor farce, only bearable by the funny acting and freaks of W. G. Fay. One wonders that Mr Yeats would put his name to such a production.[5]

It was during this period that Lady Gregory invited the Fay brothers to Coole. They were well respected for their ability by all involved in the theatre business. The National Theatre Society worked hard, but finance was required to ensure its survival. Following the performance of his play *The King's Threshold* in 1903, Yeats appeared before the audience and appealed for financial support to carry on the work of the society.[6] He was hoping for subscriptions, no matter how small, but to his astonishment a woman named Annie Horniman came forward and said, 'I will give you a theatre.'[7] She was the English heiress of a wealthy tea merchant and a confirmed spinster, who had a total intolerance towards sex and would react wildly against any such relationship between members of the cast or staff in the theatre.[8] Unlike Yeats, William was not overly surprised by her offer and subsequent investment, as she had mentioned earlier to him that she had been thinking about this for some time.

William later recorded that during this period there were two theatre fires. One occurred in England, followed by a disastrous fire in the Iroquois Theatre, Chicago, which caused great loss of life. The local authorities across the United Kingdom began to tighten up on theatre regulations and thus one of the oldest Dublin entertainment houses, attached to the Mechanics Institute and commonly known as 'The Mechanics', closed. Fay reacted quickly and set about having the premises assessed; he also secured financial estimates on how much it would cost to carry out the necessary alterations to have the building reopened as a theatre. He then sent all the details to Annie Horniman, along with his letter of appeal for a new theatre. Her reply was positive and she returned to Dublin immediately to begin working on the project, which resulted in the foundation of the Abbey Theatre.[9] William began managing the Abbey in December 1904.[10] Meanwhile, Annie Horniman provided an annual subscription towards the running of the theatre, which under her patronage became a limited company.[11]

William's brother, Frank, joined the Abbey Theatre as the stage manager and speech tutor, and together they brought much experience to the business.[12] Lennox Robinson recognised their talent, saying that their rehearsals of *Deirdre* 'proceeded with growing mastery and enthusiasm' and that all the performers learned each other's part for the sheer love of it. In fact, within a few years they had built up a company of actors, including Arthur Sinclair, Fred O'Donovan and Sydney Morgan, that could equal any theatre in Europe.[13] Sara Allgood attributed her success to William Fay. Speaking of his tutoring, she said that one of his most admired qualities was the stillness he instilled in people, and he was responsible for the strange repose and movement of the actors on stage that astonished even the English and American critics. Allgood also stated that 'it was Willie Fay's brilliance' that earned for them a place in the spotlight: 'He didn't let us move a muscle or stir a foot unless it was desperately necessary: he knew damn well we were able to do it, and thus the cast remained motionless, mystic and wonderful.'[14]

One of the women William met through the theatre business was a nineteen-year-old actress named (Anna) Brigit O'Dempsey, the daughter of Thomas O'Dempsey, a lawyer from Enniscorthy in Co. Wexford. They fell in love, were married in 1906, and had one son.[15] Married life didn't interfere with William's work in tutoring or acting, and he even found time to play a leading role in Synge's *The Playboy of the Western World*. At the closing stages of the play, many people in the audience began hissing and voicing their anger, not because of his ability on stage but, as mentioned earlier, because the content of the play caused much trouble in the theatre.[16]

Overall, life at the Abbey Theatre was far from smooth, as various disagreements arose due to internal politics.[17] Yeats had ambitious plans for the Abbey and believed that the works of Shakespeare and Greek tragedies should be part of the schedule. He felt that the Fay brothers were not qualified enough to train actors for these classical roles. Moreover, William Fay, who was already overworked, was often called away from rehearsals to attend business meetings, and this may have been construed by some members of the cast as neglecting the real business of 'acting'. There were also complaints from staff members that he could be rude to the actors and sometimes even alienate them. The situation was not helped by the fact that Annie Horniman had, by this period, taken a dislike to Fay and his brother and promised £500 per annum if a new manager was appointed.

While Yeats was in favour of having an English manager appointed, Lady Gregory didn't want to see the Fay brothers forced out of the Abbey and would have preferred to see Annie Horniman leave the theatre rather than the Fays. However, William agreed to step down as stage manager and a young inexperienced man named Ben Iden Payne was appointed in early 1907. Some of the directors didn't agree with his appointment and Payne's management was short-lived; he left the company after just six months.

With Payne gone, William Fay found himself back in control again. In December 1907 he complained about a lack of discipline among the actors and outlined a series of proposals to Yeats. He wanted more power when negotiating contracts and also control in the case of dismissals. Yeats reported the situation to Lady Gregory, and although she felt that Fay was now incompetent, she was unsure about who could replace him. Again she didn't want to see him driven out of the business and hoped that he would resign. The turning point for her came when Fay programmed *The Gaol Gate* for Galway. This outraged her because she had not been consulted about the play being staged there. She felt it would be contentious in that city because of events surrounding a workhouse boycott that had occurred in the city. She now agreed with Yeats, who was trying to persuade the actors to resign on the grounds of poor management. The strategy worked and as a result both Fay brothers resigned on 13 January 1908.[18]

However, there were other factors at work in the lead-up to their departure. George Moore was critical of many people involved in the Abbey, including William Fay. He had an article entitled 'Stage Management in the Irish National Theatre' published in a new journal called *Dana*, saying that Fay didn't know the ABC of staging. Moore's article created much of the animosity towards Fay, which was part of the reason Annie Horniman was determined to have the brothers forced out. In a personal attack, she referred to William as a dirty little Catholic and former electrician. It seems that she made these remarks while visiting Coole with Yeats. Moore obviously had second thoughts about his comments when he later said that Fay was to be admired for his success.[19]

The resignation was in reality a clash of personalities: the Fays versus Yeats and Lady Gregory, who did not want to relinquish power to William Fay after he had requested total management and production control. Fay felt that there was too much interference from the directors and wished to end this situation. It is difficult to determine who was right or wrong, but perhaps both sides were at fault to some degree.

Unlike his brother, William Fay never set foot on the Abbey Theatre stage again. He later wrote about his ambitions for the theatre and his views of what happened: he had from the beginning seen the National Theatre as the possibility of a real art movement and was led to believe that the Abbey directors shared this vision. He gave credit to Annie Horniman, saying that she had certainly shown her commitment through her financial support. He felt the lavish, high-flowing expressions of the English press had been too heady for Yeats, Synge and Augusta Gregory, as they 'imagined we had arrived when we had only started'. Fay believed that the theatre company could produce plays that would not be rivalled, much less excelled. His idea was to create a company that would be capable of performing any type of play and include all levels of society in prose or verse. While it would be a difficult task, he believed that it could be accomplished by degrees and experience. He said that even with the excellent material at their disposal, it would take at least ten years before they could boast of having a real art theatre.

Fay had placed his proposals and ideas before the directors and said that he would not move forward with these plans unless he was given the powers as a manager and producer. He had added that they could continue along the current path if they were content to produce 'peasant plays', which ultimately resulted in stagnation and closure when there were 'no more pots to boil and no more news to spread'. He was soon made aware of the directors' stance when, a few days later, Lady Gregory informed him that they were not willing to make any changes. She asked what he was going to do about it. Fay later said, 'I did the only thing that was left to me – I resigned on the spot.'[20]

The people he mentioned – Synge, Yeats and Lady Gregory – all had a hand in undermining him as manager. There were some who saw these directors as relicts of a self-styled colonial regime as all three of them were Protestant and there was a perception that they were the landlords, while the actors and staff were the peasantry.[21] Despite their differences and conflicts, Yeats had great admiration for the work of the Fay brothers. Writing about William just before his resignation, Yeats gave the impression that Fay resigned on relatively good terms. One can see that Yeats seemed genuinely regretful that Fay was leaving the Abbey when he wrote:

We are about to lose our principal actor. William Fay has had enough of it, and we do not wonder, and is going to some other country where his exquisite gift of comedy and his brain teeming with fancy will bring him an audience, fame and a little money. He has worked with us now since 1902 when he formed his Company to carry on the work of the Irish Literary Theatre, and feels that he must leave to another man the long laborious battle. We have his good wishes, and he will return to us if at all possible to play his old parts for some brief season, or seasons, and may possibly join us for a London or American tour. We believe that William Fay is right to go and he will have our good will and good wishes with him, though we have lost in losing him the finest comedian of his kind in the English-speaking stage.[22]

As previously mentioned, the Fay brothers travelled to the United States. William secured a position with Charles Frohman as theatrical manager, and his work included producing a number of Irish plays that were staged in New York and Chicago. He gave his first performance in New York as the tramp in *The Pot of Broth*. Through his work in the United States, William found that he could promote Irish plays and talent. From there he travelled to London, where he began a strong career on the English stage. While most of his work was in the West End, he also travelled throughout England, delivering many memorable performances in *The Merry Wives of Windsor*, *The Merchant of Venice* and *John Bull's Other Island*.

In 1914 he became chairman of the Actors' Association, a position he held until 1918, and at the end of the Great War he was producing a number of plays for the army and navy. In 1919 he was appointed as stage director with the Aldwych Theatre; a year later he became a producer for the Nottingham Repertory Theatre and toured with his own theatre company. The following year, he appeared in the silent film *The Dangerous Moment*. In addition to all of these engagements, he produced plays at other theatres in England throughout the 1920s.

Outside of his dedication to the theatre, he was keen on landscape painting. He also found time to write, and in 1930 published *A Short Glossary of Theatrical Terms*. It was the first of four publications, the last being *The Fays of the Abbey Theatre: an Autobiographical Record*, which appeared in 1935. During this period he became further involved in the cinema, making such films as *The Blarney Stone* (1933); *The Last Curtain* (1937); *This Man is Dangerous* (1941); *Spellbound* (1945); and *London Town*

(1946). In 1947 he gave what was perhaps his best performance, as Father Tom in *Odd Man Out*. However, by this time he was unwell and died from a combination of illnesses at his home in Wood Green, North London on 27 October 1947, leaving an enduring mark on the Irish theatre.[23]

George William Russell

Journalist, Poet and Economist 1867–1935

George William Russell was born on 10 April 1867 in William Street, Lurgan, Co. Antrim. He was the youngest of the three children of Thomas and Marianne Russell (*née* Armstrong), the others being Thomas and Mary. His father worked as a book-keeper for Bell & Company; the family were devout Church of Ireland members and lived on Lord Lurgan's estate. When he was four years old, Russell was sent to the local model school and, from the beginning, he was described as a bright, gentle and artistic pupil.

When George was eleven, the family moved to Dublin, where his father had accepted a position with an accountancy firm. George began attending Dr Power's School in Harrington Street and remained there until 1882. Because of his artistic endeavours he was sent to the Metropolitan School of Art in Dublin to give him an opportunity to develop his skills. He also enrolled in Rathmines College and was well liked by the other students and noted as a good-humoured teenager.

During a visit to his relatives in Armagh, Russell began to have supposedly supernatural experiences in the form of visions, which sapped his confidence, and he became somewhat withdrawn. In October 1883 these experiences manifested themselves in his artistic expression when he began taking evening classes in art. During class he would sometimes paint his interpretations of eternity, rather than complete the projects assigned to him. It was during this period that he became friends with Oliver Sheppard (artist), John Hughes (sculptor) and W. B. Yeats.[1] Closer to Yeats, perhaps because the young poet also had an interest in the occult, Russell had a lifelong influence on him, the two often composing work together.[2] Russell chose to be called Æ, the first two letters in the word 'aeon', because he wished to remain unknown and obscure and avoid drawing public attention to himself. He seems to have become preoccupied with pagan rather than Christian beliefs. He continually saw visions that he would mould into verse.[3]

Through his connection with Yeats, Russell was invited to literary gatherings, but remained independent in his views. His first published article, 'The Speech of the Gods', was co-authored with Charles Johnston of the Theosophical Society and appeared in Madame Blavatsky's *The Theosophist* in December 1887.

Russell withdrew from art school, turned to meditation and began an in-depth study of spiritual manuscripts. He had a particular devotion to sacred Indian literature, an interest that remained with him throughout his life. In 1890 he accepted a position as a clerk in Pims Drapers in Dublin. He joined the Theosophical Society, an organisation formed to advance the idea of spiritual principles. A few months later he became part of a small community of like-minded spiritual people, known as the 'Household', who were living in Upper Ely Place. While this move isolated him from wider society, it stimulated his creativity.

In October 1891, in the *National Observer*, Yeats published a pen sketch based on Russell and entitled 'An Irish Visionary'. This was later republished in *The Celtic Twilight*, a collection of essays, sketches and anecdotes focused on Irish myth and folklore.

In 1892 Russell began to paint a series of murals depicting the pilgrim soul on its journey. Following allegations of fraud against a friend, William Judge, regarding his psychic ability, Russell defended him in a pamphlet called 'To the Fellows of the Irish Theosophist'. This was printed along with *The Irish Theosophist* weekly journal. Russell became a regular contributor to this journal and had poems and articles published. His work came to the notice of Charles Weekes, a man of great enterprise who set up his own publishing company. This helped to give Æ a wider audience.

Prompted by Yeats, Russell joined the Irish Literary Society in Dublin. Russell had developed a stammer during his first supernatural experience and under the guidance of James Pryse, the American theosophist, he began a programme of meditation that helped him overcome this problem. In 1897 the Household disbanded and Russell moved back in with his parents in Monkstown.[4]

During that same year he accompanied Yeats on a visit to Lady Gregory in Coole. Yeats had described Russell to Lady Gregory as being wild, something between a peasant, a saint and a sensual-type person. This made her a bit apprehensive about meeting him. However, she took an instant liking to Russell and later said that he was a gentle, quiet man, who was apparently more in dread of her than she was of him. As he shared information about his life, she felt that they had much in common regarding personality and the manner in which they conducted themselves. She was pleased that Yeats and Russell were friends and encouraged both men to pursue mystical experiences. She took them to see a megalithic tomb across the lake near her home, where both claimed they saw a purple-clad druid.

Over time Russell developed a close bond with Lady Gregory and both of them encouraged Yeats to aspire to his full potential as a poet. Russell obviously trusted her, as he confided his own insecurities and his poetic ambitions. She in turn reassured him about his capability and encouraged him to persist in his work.[5]

In 1897 he published 'The Future of Ireland and the Awakening of the Fires', a pamphlet announcing a new age for the country. In May of that year he launched *Ideals in Ireland; Priest or Hero*, which was an attack on the domination of the Catholic Church. He had a great fascination for Standish O'Grady's work on mythological history. He was continually writing to Yeats during this time, keeping him informed of his opinions on various issues and news items, and he also kept in contact with Lady Gregory. It was during this period that he signed the Autograph Tree.

Russell's noted work, *The Earth, Breath and Other Poems*, which was published in September 1897, was well received by the general public. A month later he began writing articles for *The Internationalist*, a journal that was intended to replace *The Irish Theosophist* after it went out of business. By this time he was fanatical in his beliefs in the spiritual world and was intent on harnessing its power. He was offered a position as an editor for the theosophists in the United States. When Yeats became aware of this offer, he immediately set about trying to persuade him to stay in Ireland. With the support of Lady Gregory, he arranged a meeting between Russell and Horace Plunkett, founder of the Irish Agricultural Organisation Society, which resulted in Russell accepting a position with the Congested Districts Board. The work was hugely challenging and meant he would have to travel extensively throughout the west of Ireland.

His busy life forced him to resign from the Theosophical Society in March 1898, which allowed him time to concentrate on his other work. By this point he was caught up romantically with Violet North, an English lady and theosophist who was also involved in literature. They were married on 9 June 1898, but it seems that Russell took only an hour away from his work for the ceremony. Their first baby, Bryan, was born in January 1899, but died in childhood. Following the birth of their second son, they decided to name him Brian also, with a slight change of spelling. They had a daughter in June 1901, but unfortunately she only lived for a month. Another baby, Diarmuid, was born in November 1902, bringing great joy to the Russell household.

In 1901 Russell's essay 'Nationality and Imperialism' appeared in *Ideals in Ireland* and caught the attention of George Moore, whose work had appeared in the same volume. Moore arrived in Dublin shortly afterwards and the two men became friends. However, Russell was critical of both Moore and Yeats when they collaborated in the production of *Diarmuid and Grania*, as he felt it was not a true representation of the ancient Irish legend. In fact, Russell wrote his only play, *Deirdre*, to demonstrate the manner in which he felt it should have been portrayed. He had begun to take a deeper interest in the Irish literary movement, which pleased Yeats and Lady Gregory. After the formation of the Abbey Theatre, Russell declined an offer to become its president, but was involved.[6] He helped in drafting its constitution and formed a reading committee with Yeats, Arthur Griffith, Maud Gonne and some others to stage new works by emerging playwrights. When Synge's play *The Shadow of the Glen* appeared before the committee in 1903, they decided against it as they felt that it was not in keeping with national sensibilities. However, Yeats forced it through despite the opposition, which resulted in Russell resigning because he felt that the committee was not acting in a democratic manner.[7]

He then became a business advisor to Dun Emer Press, with whom he had published *The Nuts of Knowledge; Lyrical Poems Old and New* in 1903. A year later *The Divine Vision and Other Poems* appeared under Macmillan publishing, and his other works during this period include *The Mask of Apollo and Other Stories* (1905), *By Still Waters: Lyrical Poems Old and New* (1906) and *Some Irish Essays* in the same year. He was also known for his artistic work and began to exhibit his paintings to supplement his income.

Having lived in a number of locations around Dublin, the family moved to Rathgar Avenue in 1906. Over the years, Russell earned an enduring reputation for supporting and encouraging young writers, and his home in Rathgar became a clinic for advice on many aspects of culture and literature. These meetings took place on Sunday afternoons and continued while he had his health.[8] He was appointed editor of *The Irish Homestead*, which dramatically increased his workload. His output with this weekly journal was extraordinary: he produced articles and columns on current affairs, agriculture, technical advice and cultural issues over an eighteen-year period. His work with *The Irish Homestead* also enabled him to continue his support for young writers.

One of the young writers he helped was James Joyce. Having read sections of Joyce's novel *Stephen Hero*, Russell invited him to submit an article to *The Irish Homestead* for publication. Joyce agreed and a number of articles followed. However, as time went by, Russell felt that Joyce's work was not in keeping with his idea of fiction and asked him to cease sending articles. Their relationship became strained and Joyce later ridiculed Russell in the satirical ballad *The Holy Office*, which made matters worse, as Russell responded with some harsh comments of his own. However, these feelings obviously mellowed over time. In 1927 Russell signed a document against the pirating of Joyce's *Ulysses*, a book that he had dismissed during their time of feuding.[9]

Russell was not shy when it came to voicing his opinion. He had intervened and challenged Yeats on theatrical and publishing issues on several occasions. Russell felt he could state his mind regarding the poet's work because he knew him so well. However, Yeats didn't like being criticised and began to resent Russell.[10]

Over time Russell became one of the most recognised journalists of the day. His *Collected Poems* (1913) went into five editions and ten reprints. His work reflected political and social issues of the day, and in 1913 he became a strong supporter of James Larkin, James Connolly and the Irish Transport and General Workers' Union during the 'Great Dublin Lock-Out'.[11] This is the term given to a major industrial dispute involving approximately 20,000 workers, which lasted from August 1913 to January 1914. Central to the dispute was the workers' right to unionise. In an impassioned open letter to the press, when

William Murphy and his Dublin United Transport Company refused to employ members of the union, Russell accused the Dublin employers of failing to consider any solution except their own, saying, 'You determine deliberately in cold anger to starve out one-third of the population of this city, to break the manhood of the men by the sight of the suffering of their wives and the hunger of their children.' During a speech he gave at the Albert Hall in London, Russell declared that the majority of workers in Dublin were among the most obscure myriads who were being paid between five and twenty-five shillings a week, and added that these people were the true heroes of Ireland.[12] He also produced three so-called masterpieces on the subject – *To the Masters of Dublin*, *The Tragedy of Labour in Dublin* and *The Dublin Strike* – which earned him great respect among the general public. He had not been in contact with Yeats since his resignation from the Abbey Theatre, but his writings and stance once again brought the two men together.[13]

Murphy eventually forced most of the workers into submission, and in a letter to the press, which Russell addressed to the 'Four Hundred Masters of Dublin' (the main employers), he said, 'You may have succeeded, but the men whose manhood you have broken will loathe you, and will always be brooding and scheming to strike a fresh blow ... It is not they – it is you who are blind Samsons pulling down the pillars of social order.'[14] It is interesting that James Larkin introduced Russell to the writer Sean O'Casey in Liberty Hall as 'another rebel'.[15]

Being a non-violent man, Russell was against the Great War when it broke out in 1914. He was also astonished at the Easter Rising of 1916, and made his feelings public through his writing.

Although a pacifist, Russell still admired the courage of men who sacrificed their lives in the cause of Ireland, whether this was in the streets of Dublin or in Flanders' fields. He believed that all Irishmen were equal, regardless of their political or religious values. As far as he was concerned, even the invasions and plantations of Ireland, however morally unjustifiable and cruel, were justified by biology, as he believed that the invasion of one race by another was an ancient way of rejuvenating people.

Russell could champion both sides of the political divide in Ireland and this can be seen from the following extract:

> No one has more to give than life, and, when that is given, neither Nationalist nor Imperialist in Ireland can claim moral superiority for the dead champions of their cause ... We are all one people. We are closer to each other in character than we are to any other race ... I myself am Anglo-Irish, with the blood of both races in me, and when the rising of Easter Week took place all that was Irish in me was profoundly stirred, and out of that mood I wrote, commemorating the dead. And then later there arose in memory the faces of others I knew who loved their country, but had died in other battles. They fought in those because they believed they would serve Ireland, and I felt these were no less my people. I could hold them also in my heart and pay tribute to them. Because it was possible for me to do so, I think it is possible for others; and in the hope that the deeds of all may in future be a matter of pride to the new nation.[16]

He continued to write as Ireland descended into violence and chaos. He was seriously concerned and upset by the Black and

Tans' attacks on a number of cooperative creameries and mills in 1920–21, as some were destroyed, and it was believed that the police were also involved in some of the attacks. Russell published a letter in *The Irish Homestead* castigating those involved:

> … creameries and mills have been burnt to the ground, their machinery wrecked; agricultural stores have also been burnt, property looted, employees have been killed, wounded, beaten, threatened, or otherwise ill-treated. Why have these economic organisations been specially attacked? Because they have hundreds of members, and if barracks have been burnt or police have been killed or wounded in the lamentable strife now being waged in Ireland, and if armed forces of the Crown cannot capture those actually guilty of the offences, the policy of reprisals, condoned by the spokesmen of the Government, has led to the wrecking of any enterprise in the neighbourhood, the destruction of which would inflict widespread injury and hurt the interests of the greatest number of people. I say this has been done without regard to the innocence or guilt of the persons whose property is attacked.[17]

Following the ratification of the Anglo-Irish Treaty in January 1922, Russell declined an offer of a position in the new senate, but he did accept a post as editor of the pro-Treaty *Irish Statesman* newspaper. This newspaper helped him to promote a new generation of writers, such as Oliver St John Gogarty, Patrick Kavanagh, Monk Gibbon and Frank O'Connor. His work in poetry also continued, despite a hectic commitment as an editor, and his achievements and dedication were recognised by Yale University in 1928, when they honoured him with a DLitt.

This was followed a year later by Trinity College conferring him with the same degree. When the newspaper fell into financial difficulty in 1929, he travelled to the United States in a bid to raise money to ensure its survival, but, despite his best efforts, it closed in April 1930.

Later that year the Irish Free State awarded Russell £800 as a retirement settlement. He then travelled to the United States, where he spent time lecturing. From there, he went to London, where he published *Vale and other Poems* before returning to Ireland in May 1931.

His wife died on 3 February 1932, having developed cancer. Over the following year a number of his friends also died, including Lady Gregory, George Moore and Horace Plunkett. He lost another friend, Kingsley Porter from Donegal, who drowned the very day that Russell arrived there to spend some time with him.

Russell had always been confident that a 'new spiritual' Ireland would emerge from the old when the country settled down after the years of strife. However, he was disillusioned by the reality of what he felt Ireland had become: a country with strict religious restrictions.[18] He was also against the power that Éamon de Valera had gained over Irish society. It was not the Ireland that he had envisaged and, writing to Yeats, he said, 'Dublin is depressing these days. Ireland seems to be in my age like a lout I knew in boyhood who had become a hero and then subsided into being a lout again.'[19]

He sold his home in Rathgar and, having given away most of his belongings, left for the United States in 1933, as he had been invited there as an advisor to the secretary of agriculture.

His personal work continued and he produced *The House of Titans and Other Poems*. When he became ill, he made his way to Bournemouth in England, where he was admitted to the Stagsden Nursing Home suffering from bowel cancer; he died on 17 July 1935. His remains were returned to Dublin for burial in Mount Jerome Cemetery.[20]

John Quinn

Lawyer, Art Collector
and Patron 1870–1924

John Quinn was born on 24 April 1870 in Tiffin, Ohio, in the United States. He was the eldest of eight children born to James William Quinn, from Co. Limerick, and Mary Quinlin, originally from Co. Cork. His father was a baker and ran a thriving business near Fostoria, where John attended high school. He enrolled in Georgetown University and graduated in law in 1893, then in 1895 he was awarded a similar degree from Harvard. His ambitions brought him to New York, where he eventually emerged as one of the city's leading financial lawyers.

Quinn was interested in the arts; he became friends with many artists, writers and poets of the day and is remembered as a patron of the arts. This support mainly consisted of purchasing and commissioning works. He was also one of the pioneering figures involved in collecting and promoting modern art, and he acquired a substantial collection over the years. He was a tall, thin man with a commanding presence and was said to be classically handsome with lively blue eyes. He went bald while he was still young.[1]

He first arrived in Ireland in 1902 and attended *Feis Ceoil* in Killeeneen, Co. Galway. The feis was being held in honour of the long-deceased blind poet Anthony Raftery. Also there that day were Lady Gregory, W. B. and Jack Yeats, and Douglas Hyde, all of whom he met. He was already aware of Jack Yeats' paintings and had thought about becoming a patron of Irish culture as he was impressed by poetry, plays and legends. It was felt by those involved in the literary scene that he could offer an unbiased opinion on these subjects because he was an 'outsider' and avoided petty or political differences between artists and writers. Quinn became immersed in this artistic world and was welcomed by all those present that day. When Lady Gregory invited him back to Coole along with the others, he was delighted. He was very impressed by the house and intrigued by the other guests, and before leaving Coole on that first visit, he signed the Autograph Tree. Upon returning to New York, he began corresponding with Lady Gregory and started to promote Irish plays.[2] The meeting was also very beneficial to Jack Yeats as Quinn began purchasing his paintings.

Quinn was delighted by his visit and acted almost as an ambassador for Irish culture, helping promote a wider awareness of its richness in the United States. One method he employed was organising tours of the United States, like the one for W. B. Yeats in 1903, which earned the poet some $3,000. The following year, he organised an American exhibition of the works of Jack Yeats. In 1905 he arranged a tour for Douglas Hyde, which highlighted the importance of the Gaelic League. That same year he convinced the organisers of the Irish Industrial Exhibition being planned for Madison Square Garden to include craftwork from Ireland, and loaned over seventy paintings from his own collection to the organisers. In 1906 Quinn opened his own law practice in New York, which proved very successful and resulted in him substantially raising his support for the arts.[3] His assistance was sought outside the world of art and literature as well – while in Ireland he had also been introduced to George Russell, and on a visit to his home Quinn met Maud Gonne for the first time. Maud maintained the usual charming façade and avoided questions relating to her husband, Major John MacBride, and their failing marriage. On 25 February 1905 Maud, being determined to end the marriage, filed for divorce and then sought advice from Quinn. This was the beginning of a long friendship.[4] When he returned to the United States, Yeats wrote to Quinn on her behalf to ensure his support. Correspondence continued between them over the following years.[5]

Quinn was extremely helpful to many Irish playwrights, and in 1907 he defended John Millington Synge's *The Playboy of the Western World* against the public backlash it received after its premiere. He admired Synge and had become a good friend of the playwright; however, because of his stance on the play, Quinn received much criticism from John Devoy, the American Clan na Gael leader. He had also befriended John Butler Yeats, father of the poet and artist, and even though he was against the idea of John Yeats emigrating to the United States in 1908, he financially supported him when he arrived.[6]

In 1909 Quinn travelled to Paris to visit Maud Gonne and W. B. Yeats. By this time Quinn had a mistress, Dorothy Coates, and a rift developed between the poet and Quinn because the latter believed that Yeats had seduced Dorothy. Maud Gonne advised Yeats to try to clear up the matter as Quinn was extremely important to the Irish theatre in America. She also warned Yeats not to inform Lady Gregory as it might only exacerbate the situation. Yeats claimed he had not made advances to Dorothy Coates and that his behaviour had been misunderstood or his intentions exaggerated on her part.[7] However, it was many years before the two men communicated again, even though Quinn continued his support of the Irish theatre.

During the 1911–12 Abbey Theatre tour of the United States, Quinn again defended Synge's *Playboy*. Lady Gregory had also travelled with the tour, and Quinn, who had enormous respect for her, looked after all her needs and placed his staff at her disposal. She was a regular guest at his luxurious Central Park apartment, which was decorated with some of the finest contemporary European art, and he introduced her to members of the leading society in New York. Quinn was also protective of her and after she received an abusive letter because of *Playboy*, Quinn hired private detectives and instructed the federal postal authority to trace the letter. However, the person who wrote it remained anonymous despite Quinn's best efforts.

As Christmas 1911 approached, Quinn was rarely away from Lady Gregory and, although she was eighteen years older than him, she fell in love and an affair became inevitable. He took her Christmas shopping and bought her an expensive gold watch. He was careful never to mention the argument with Yeats. It was something he had left behind without dwelling on what may have happened, since Yeats had denied the accusations.

After Lady Gregory returned to Ireland in the spring of 1912, love letters were exchanged. Although they had agreed to burn the letters after reading them, Quinn neglected to do so. He was also corresponding with a woman named May Morris at that time and it seems he had stronger feelings for her. Despite the women in his life, he never married – he was a confirmed bachelor who valued the freedom of his way of life. Over time, his letters became fewer and were not as intense as Lady Gregory's. While she still entertained hopes of a deeper relationship, perhaps even marriage, she shows a growing awareness that he didn't love her as she loved him. In one of her last letters she wrote, 'I am afraid the real ring is certainly gone with the *Titanic*', meaning there was no hope of a relationship. This was a comment that brought Quinn much relief.[8] Lady Gregory later wrote to Augustus John, another signatory of the Autograph Tree, saying that perhaps she was better off without a ring.

Quinn's interest in Irish culture seems to have diminished somewhat in the aftermath of the Abbey Theatre tour. Some believe that it was because of the controversy over Synge's play, but might it have been because of the affair with Lady Gregory? However, he continued collecting art, showing particular interest in French artists, and accumulated a fine collection of notable works by painters such as Henri Rousseau, Matisse and, indeed, Picasso, among others. His manuscript collection included works by T. S. Eliot, Ezra Pound, Joseph Conrad and James Joyce.[9]

Quinn was a generous man not just in his support for the arts, but also to charitable causes. Between 1910 and 1911 plans were put in place to raise funds to feed 250 of the poorest children in Dublin. Having received a letter from Maud Gonne in January 1911, he replied immediately and sent a donation with a promise of another to follow. During the Great War, Quinn made financial donations almost every month and sent the money to Maud, who served for a time as a Red Cross nurse.[10] He had also sent her support for the workers during the Dublin Lock-Out. Quinn continued his close connection with her and she confided in him, which was evident following the 1916 Rising when she wrote to him explaining how her husband, Major John MacBride, was among those executed. She also sent him accounts of what had happened in Ireland.[11] While Quinn supported the idea of Home Rule for Ireland, he condemned the uprising. Nevertheless, he sought clemency for Roger Casement after he was sentenced to be hanged for his role in the Rising.

In 1918 Quinn was diagnosed with cancer and had to undergo surgery, from which he recovered. His connection with Yeats was renewed when the poet dedicated *The Trembling of the Veil* to him in 1922.[12] James Joyce was another Irish literary connection of his. Although he didn't actually meet Joyce until 1923, Quinn had been in contact with him earlier when he purchased his manuscripts.

In 1918 Joyce's *Ulysses* had begun appearing in serial form in the American journal *The Little Review,* which was edited by Margaret Anderson and Jane Heap. Anderson realised from the beginning that this was going to be the finest work that she would ever publish, but the contents of the July–August 1920 issue offended some people and the New York Society for the Suppression of Vice brought charges of obscenity against Anderson and Heap. In 1921 the editors enlisted Quinn to represent them in court, and although he had little time for the magazine and disliked the two women, as he felt that they exploited artistic talent – something he was very much against – he took the case and was determined to win. He feared a negative outcome might prevent the book from ever being published.

Quinn's tactical defence was straightforward and simple in

the extreme. He claimed that *Ulysses* was disgusting rather than erotic – it was therefore not obscene in the actual meaning of the word under the law. He was confident that this strategy would work, but, despite putting up a good argument, he failed to convince the presiding judges. When Joyce heard the outcome of the case, he was upset by Quinn's strategy, as were others, because they believed that an opportunity to challenge the censorship board had been lost. Anderson and Heap were found guilty and fined $50 each and prohibited from publishing any future extracts from the book. (It has since been suggested that Quinn's argument influenced the ban on the novel being lifted in 1933.)[13]

By 1923 Quinn was feeling unwell again. The cancer had returned. At the time of his illness, he was in a relationship with his secretary, Jeanne Foster. She was now his constant companion and supported him as the illness progressed. Although his relationship with Lady Gregory had changed following the 1912 tour, he had continued to write to her from time to time. He informed her of his illness and hinted that it was caused by a liver tumour, but reassured her that it was benign. By early July 1924 he had deteriorated to such an extent that he was hardly aware of Jeanne's presence. He was unable to read any letters from Ireland, which had previously always grabbed his attention. John Quinn died on 28 July 1924.[14]

Much of his art collection was auctioned off after his death and the remainder was sold under the terms of his will. Some of his autographed letters from influential people were housed in the New York Public Library. His unsold manuscripts were later acquired by the Indiana University.[15] His death signalled the end of a great personal support to the Irish literary and art world.

Augustus John

Artist 1878–1961

Augustus Edwin John was born on 4 January 1878 at Rope Walk Field in Tenby, Pembrokeshire, England. He was the third of four children born to Edwin and Augusta John (*née* Smith); the other children were Thornton, Gwen and Winifred.[1] The family had a house in Broad Haven on St Bride's Bay, and the children spent the summers there being looked after by two aunts. They loved being there, as they had great freedom with both aunts more or less allowing them to do as they pleased. They really enjoyed going to the seaside, which was almost on their doorstep, and explored the entire area in a wickerwork pony-trap they called the 'Hallelujah Chariot'.

One day young Augustus witnessed another child falling from a hobby-horse at a carnival and, on seeing the child's mouth covered in blood, he went into a dream-like trance. It was a traumatic experience that stayed with him for some years afterwards, and he often fell into bouts of silence during which his father would make apologies for him. While walking along the shore with his father one day, Augustus claimed that he saw a phantom island. He called to his father and pointed to the island, but his father merely muttered something and quickened his pace. As Augustus looked towards the island again it had vanished. He always believed that it was Tír na nÓg, the mythical land of the young.

His mother died when he was about six and the family moved to Tenby.[2] His father never remarried and soon after the death of his wife gave up his practice as a solicitor and became a recluse, though it seems he continued to work in a private capacity. He was rather a shy man and this caused him social problems – he made very few friends. The children lived in a loveless and somewhat restricted household. They were warned never to venture out on market days as the gypsies might kidnap them; however, Augustus hoped that he would be taken, as he longed for the freedom of open spaces. The gypsies later became one of his favourite artistic subjects and he once told a colleague that he had become one of them.

His early education was a bit haphazard: he received tuition from a governess and at Greenhill School, and later went to St Catherine's in Tenby.[3] While attending Greenhill, Augustus suffered the wrath of one of the teachers for being, as he said himself, out of order during drill. The teacher punched him on the side of the head and knocked him senseless, which resulted in deafness in one ear; he later said that a cricket ball did the same for his other ear.

During classes, Augustus had a habit of sketching some of the teachers, but he had to be careful as being caught meant punishment. One day, while he was sketching the head master, his subject discovered what he was doing. Having looked at the drawing, the man smirked and then proceeded to attack Augustus viciously with an ebony ruler. On another occasion, Augustus was caught by a teacher who was in the habit of sneaking up behind the pupils and suddenly hitting them on the back of the head with a ruler if they weren't doing their school work. When Augustus became a victim of one of these surprise attacks, he reacted by landing a punch on the teacher, sending him across the classroom. His father was informed and Augustus received a caning from him. But it wasn't too severe as his father's heart wasn't really in the punishment.

Augustus was aware of the path he was going to follow from a young age and recorded, 'I was an unsatisfactory type of fellow, moody and unpredictable, with no sense of figures nor respect for the value of money; it was certain I would never be any good in serious business; perhaps Art might be just the thing for me, since it involved irregular hours, few social obligations and no arithmetic.'[4] His interest in art brought him into contact with E. J. Head, from whom he received drawing lessons. Head realised that Augustus had artistic potential and, in 1894, asked the boy's father to allow him to attend the Slade School of Fine Art in London.

Augustus proved to be a rather shy, neat and diligent student. He would spend time visiting the National Gallery and was fascinated by the work of the old masters. His sister Gwen also attended Slade and became an artist, but was somewhat over-shadowed by her brother.[5] Slade formed part of the University of London, where students were first introduced to the Antique Room, which housed many classical sculptures. Both men and women used the studio. Augustus John later said that Slade abounded in talented and highly ornamental girl students. He also said the men were shabby and seemed far less talented. One of the students that he became good friends with there was William Orpen from Dublin.[6]

In the summer of 1895, Augustus was injured in a diving accident off Giltar Point near Tenby. He smashed his head on a submerged rock and his recovery was slow. By the time he returned to art school, his personality had changed totally. He was now a wild, bearded, anarchical young man, in total contrast to his former persona. He worked at a feverish pace and in general lived his life in the same manner. In a short period of time he produced an amazing amount of drawings that were described as remarkable for their fluent vigour and spontaneity. His fellow students were amazed at his output and expert hand. It was said that having dived into the sea and smashed his head, he had emerged from the water a 'bloody genius'. It was also said that he was a great man of action into whose hands the fairies had stuck a brush instead of a sword. The American artist John Sergeant said of his early drawings that they were beyond any work he had seen since the Italian Renaissance.

While at Slade, Augustus met Ida Margaret Nettleship, a fellow student and the daughter of the artist John Nettleship. They were married on 24 January 1901 and, following the marriage, moved to Liverpool, where Augustus took up a position in an art school and also pursued work as an etcher. During his time in Liverpool he met John Sampson, a gypsy scholar and a man who also loved adventure, and they became lifelong friends. After the birth of Augustus and Margaret's first child, David, in 1902, the family moved to London. Over time, they had four other children, Casper, Robin, Edwin and Henry.

In 1903, along with William Orpen, Augustus founded the Chelsea Art School and he was elected to the New English Art Club. Also in 1903, he met Dorothy McNeill, who was employed as a secretary with a local firm. She was destined to become his 'Dorelia', his female inspiration and subject of some of his best-known paintings – and of course his lover. Augustus eventually had four children with Dorothy, namely Pyramus, Romilly, Poppet and Vivien. He produced *The Smiling Woman* between 1908 and 1909 with Dorelia as the subject. This work, which established him as an oil painter, was purchased by the Contemporary Art Society and later presented to the Tate Gallery, thus becoming the first of his paintings to be included in the National Collection. Between 1903 and 1907 he spent a lot of time between Dorothy in London and Ida in Paris. While living in the French capital in 1907, Ida became ill, and she died a short time later from puerperal fever. Following her death, Henry, still an infant, was taken by Ida's family and reared by them. Dorelia began looking after the other children, along with her own, which eventually led to her bringing both families together in Alderney Manor, near Parkstone in Dorset. This arrangement gave Augustus the space and time to travel and pursue his career as a painter.[7] He was described as a man of extreme independence in speech and action: 'his championship of gypsies and of sundry unpopular causes, the common conception of John defines him as a man in rebellion against the established order of things; above all against traditional culture'.[8]

His first visit to the west of Ireland was at the invitation of Francis McNamara, a poet, philosopher and economist with whom he had become acquainted and who lived in his ancestral home in Doolin, Co. Clare. They would often frequent a she-been in Ennistymon where they listened to old Irish stories and watched people dancing. It was there that John met a woman named Mary Shannon, whom he said was remarkable, but 'no longer in her first youth'. McNamara told him that she was a priestess with some cult and as John was leaving she said to him, 'Good-bye now, ye'll remember me when ye'er betwixt the sheets.'[9]

The men visited the Aran Islands and John was very impressed with the islanders, saying that they were a polite and dignified people. He said that they spoke the best Irish he had heard, which would indicate that he was familiar with the language, or perhaps he was comparing it with the Gaelic spoken in parts of Wales. He added that their English was of Elizabethan style, being slow and ornate. During his time there, John seems to have gained a great knowledge of the history and traditions of the islands and, like many visitors, he stated that the women in their traditional dress were very pleasing to his eye. He was amazed at the self-sufficiency of the islanders and saw them as survivors of an ancient civilisation.

John later received an invitation from Lady Gregory to visit Coole – it was Robert Gregory who prompted the invitation because of his friendship with the artist. Before he left England, William Orpen advised him to contact a friend of his, Oliver St John Gogarty. John was hungry upon arriving in Dublin and found a restaurant where he had a meal. Having served him, the waitress joined him at the table and enquired about his reason for visiting Ireland. They had a pleasant conversation and John found it difficult to leave her – while he has been accused of being a philanderer, it would also seem that some women were drawn to him. However, he had to meet Gogarty and left. Over the following days, Gogarty took him around Dublin, introducing him to many like-minded people. He really enjoyed his time in Dublin, saying that he was never better entertained. Most of the people he met had a connection to the Abbey Theatre. However, it was soon time for him to once again make his way west, and thus he boarded the Galway-bound train.

John was unwell when he took the journey west. He later remembered arriving at Coole Park in poor shape: 'I might indeed have applied to Lady Gregory for first aid, but I knew of nothing in her store capable of subduing the frightful cough which now plagued me.'[10] John was so unwell for the first few days at Coole that Lady Gregory became concerned. George Bernard Shaw was staying there at the time as well and asked his chauffeur to take John to a chemist in Gort. He later said that the 'concoction' he received began working almost immediately. Perhaps an over-indulgence of alcohol while staying in Dublin was partially to blame for his condition?

When he was back on his feet again, Robert Gregory brought him horse riding over the following days. John also enjoyed listening to Shaw as he sang and played the piano. However, he sometimes found conversation with the author irritating for no apparent reason. He completed three paintings of Shaw, one with his eyes shut, as he was in the habit of falling asleep. Shaw kept one of the paintings himself and presented another to the Fitz-william Museum in Cambridge. The last one was later given to the Queen of England. John also did some sketches and portraits of Lady Gregory, Robert and Margaret Gregory and their son Richard. He also completed images of Yeats.

John spent many hours boating on the lake at Coole, saying that he had only 'Yeats' swans for company'. Yeats walked the gardens every morning and John, observing him on one occasion, said, 'He looked every inch a poet of the twilight.' When he was leaving, Shaw offered to take John to Dublin by car, and John was delighted as he would see more of the countryside and its people, which always pleased him.[11]

John's drinking habits do not seem to have affected his work, at least not as a young man. An example of this was when he was asked to paint the Madonna on a stained-glass window for Act II of one of Sean O'Casey's plays. The following is a description of the scene after he arrived in the theatre drunk. Wearing a great black hat cocked over his forehead, John sauntered down the aisle. He climbed unsteadily onto the stage and surveyed the scene in silence:

> The artist slowly moved towards the window frame lying on the stage, took up Alick's stick of charcoal and made a firm stroke on the oiled silk. He worked as though possessed and for more than two hours he never looked up. Cochran, Sean, Alick (the scene painter) and I and the crew watched in fascination. At last he was done. He moved to the side of the stage and stood waiting. Without a word, two stagehands lifted the window piece and placed it in position. The master electrician connected the cable and the lights for act 2. And there shone the Madonna of *The Silver Tassie* ... We cheered Augustus John. He did not hear us; he just stood there looking at his scene. He was pleased with it. He left, swaying slightly.[12]

By 1914 John was feeling a bit distant from the art world. His deafness was gradually getting worse and he was becoming depressed.[13] He tried to enlist in the army, but was refused because of a knee injury he had sustained during one of his escapades in Ireland, which he described as his 'grasshopper days'. He later went to a bonesetter for treatment, but then damaged the other knee while jumping over a fence.[14] In 1917 he found employment with the Canadian forces as a war artist and found himself on the Somme and Vimy Ridge, where he created a number of memorable cartoon portraits of soldiers. Being an artist, he was allowed to keep his facial hair and many said that he bore a strong likeness to King George V. His most appealing war image, *Fraternity*, later formed part of the Imperial War Museum collection in London. It portrays one soldier giving another a light for a cigarette, but it was in fact a scene from a postcard rather than something he witnessed at the Front.[15]

It is believed that he visited Galway sometime during the war, where he was arrested as a spy when he was observed at the end of Nimmo's Pier. He was released a short time later, when able to prove that he had no German connections. There is also a story in Galway that John painted at least one lady nude in a local hall on Prospect Hill.[16]

He travelled to Paris after the war and met James Joyce and his wife, Nora Barnacle from Galway. He completed a number of drawings of Joyce, who posed for him frequently. Before John left Paris, Joyce presented him with a copy of the French-translated *Ulysses*.[17]

John was not simply a portrait and landscape artist, however; he also completed many drawings and cartoons. His immense cartoon entitled *Galway* covered nearly 400 square feet, and incredibly he completed this work in just one week. It was later said that few living artists could work as swiftly and that he could produce masterpieces almost without effort.

In 1924 he won first prize at the Pittsburgh International Exhibition with a portrait of Guilhermina Suggia, the celebrated cellist, which ended up in the Tate Gallery. In 1928 he was elected to the Royal Academy, but he was drinking heavily and this was now seriously affecting his work. With his talent in decline, he travelled throughout Europe, Jamaica and the United States in an unsuccessful attempt to recapture his former ability. He returned to London's West End, where he continued to paint, but not as he had done in previous years; from that time until his death John's work was exhibited in the Dudley Tooth Gallery in Bruton Street.

He was awarded the Order of Merit in 1942. During the 1950s he attempted to create a huge work celebrating what he referred to as the 'pilgrim mystery of the gypsies', but was unable to complete the painting. On 17 September 1961 John made his way to central London to take part in a demonstration against the development of nuclear weapons. He was in his eighty-fourth year and seriously ill, so he waited in the National Gallery for the protest to start. When the demonstration began he walked to Trafalgar Square to join the protesters. This was the last stand of the rebel artist.

On 31 October 1961 Augustus John died of heart failure at Fryern Court and was buried at Fordingbridge. His passing signified the end of an era. His reputation as a painter slipped following his death and this allowed his sister Gwen to emerge from under the shadow of a brother who had always admired her work.[18] Writing about Augustus in 1945, John Rothenstein, the director and keeper of the Tate Gallery, stated:

Men of genius are rarely simple ... Most of the best painting of our time is the product of the wise and intensive cultivation of moderate talent; Augustus John's on the other hand might seem to arise from the prodigal cultivation of an egregious talent. That this artist is a man of genius posterity will scarcely question, though it may well speculate as to the degree to which his genius has been fulfilled.[19]

James Dickson Innes

Artist 1887–1914

James Dickson Innes was born on 27 February 1887 in Greenfield Villas, Murray Street, Llanelli, Wales. His parents were John and Alice Innes (*née* Rees) and they had two other sons, Alfred and Jack. James was educated locally and later attended Christ College in Brecon. Upon leaving college in 1904, he continued his education, studying at Carmarthen Art School, and in 1905 won a scholarship to the Slade School of Fine Art. While there, he met Augustus John, and the two students became good friends. Innes studied under Philip Wilson Steer, who had a strong influence over his work. While still a student, Innes began exhibiting his work in the New English Art Club. He had a studio in Fitzroy Street, London, where he gained valuable experience experimenting with colours and techniques.

Innes went to France in 1908 and travelled throughout the country until finally arriving in Collioure, a small town on the Mediterranean coast near the Spanish border. This area had a lasting influence on his art and his use of colour. However, his time there was cut short when he became ill with consumption and was forced to return to England. From there, he travelled to St Ives in the company of his mother to recuperate.

Following his recovery, Innes again set off for France and

this time he made his way to Paris, where he set up a studio and began to paint vigorously. His everyday life was quiet and this continued until he met a woman named Euphemia Lamb in a street café. She was the wife of an artist named Henry Lamb. This encounter changed his life, at least for a time, as they were immediately attracted to each other and Innes fell in love. He told her of Collioure, and a short time later he took her there. Following this liaison, Innes returned to London in 1910. A year later he held an exhibition of his watercolours. Many of these paintings were completed during his travels to Collioure and they went on display in the Chenil Gallery. It seems that he remained in contact with Euphemia during this time.

While in London he renewed his friendship with Augustus John and they decided to meet in Wales at a time convenient to each of them. The idea of meeting was to explore and paint together in Innes' home country.[1] The following is a description of Innes and his style of painting by Augustus John, which he recorded many years later:

> His early efforts reflect his admiration for Wilson Steer. Later his style took on a more poetic colouring with a growing insistence upon pattern which compensated to some extent for his faulty drawing. He himself cut an arresting figure: a Quaker hat, a coloured scarf, and a long black overcoat, set off features of a slightly cadaverous cast, with glittering black eyes, a wide sardonic mouth, a prominent nose and a large bony forehead, invaded by streaks of thin black hair. He carried an ebony cane with a gold top, and spoke with a heavy English accent, which had been imposed on an agreeable Welsh substratum.[2]

Innes had a romantic vision of mountainous country and was obviously very comfortable in such settings. The two artists seemed to complement each other. John was inspired by Innes, who created images of the mountains, while the former added the figures.[3] A short time later Innes invited John to meet him at the home of his parents in Llanelli. Innes planned for them to visit an inn that he had discovered earlier in the Arenig valley, just north of Bala. However, when John arrived he had already left. Nevertheless, his parents made John feel welcome and invited him to stay that night.

The following morning John made his way to meet Innes in the Arenig valley, beneath a mountain of the same name. Innes was captivated by Mount Arenig and felt that it was in a sense his spiritual home. The mountain had fine contours and shaped features; its rock consisted of porphyry and it rose steep and dark behind the Migneint moorlands. The plan was not simply to paint in the area, but also to climb the mountain. However, before doing either they needed to settle into their accommodation at the inn. The innkeeper was a man named Washington Davies.

The road to the mountain led across moorland, which was all part of the experience. Innes rarely returned in the evenings without having a couple of paintings completed – he was painting vigorously, but this did not interfere with the quality of his creations. John later said that perhaps these paintings were hastened because Innes may have seen them as some type of votive offerings to the mountains he loved with an almost religious fervour.

Despite Washington's excellent service – he fed them Welsh mutton in the evenings and would sometimes entertain them by playing music and dancing jigs – they wanted to move closer to the landscapes they were painting, and Innes found a cottage close to a little brook where their temporary home looked out on Mount Arenig. They bought some furniture and made it as comfortable as possible. After a time, they decided to return to their respective homes, but their experience was such that they went back to the Arenig valley the following year. Some evenings were spent over a few drinks in a local establishment. One night, Innes met a girl who was working in the White Lion pub in Bala. He was attracted to her and struck up a conversation. They began dating and he would sometimes take her boating on the nearby lake.[4]

One day Innes decided to climb Mount Arenig, his sacred mountain. There was a deliberate purpose in his decision as he took with him a casket of Euphemia Lamb's letters and, upon reaching the summit, buried them under a cairn. His motivation for carrying out such a ceremony is not known for certain; was this perhaps his way of saying goodbye to the past? Or did he feel that the letters were sacred also, and that depositing them on the mountain meant they would somehow be absorbed into its spirit?[5]

During their time in Wales, the artists visited another town called Corwen. While having a drink in a local inn one night, they met a gypsy family whose surname was Florence. One of the young women, Udina, was very beautiful, and both men were deeply taken by her. According to John, they both secretly established an 'understanding' with her and she flirted with each of them – she certainly knew that she had captured their attention. The men were staying in a small town nearby, in a premises owned by a man named John Samson. Before retiring that night, Udina told them that she would be leaving with her family the following morning. The two men left the premises reluctantly to return to their rented apartment, as it was closing time and there was no more drink available. When John awoke the following morning, Innes was missing and could not be found. John guessed immediately that Innes had gone back to Corwen as he wanted to see the gypsy girl alone before she left the area. Even though, by the time he got there, she had already departed, Innes would not give up and set out immediately to try to catch up with her. Just before he reached Ruthin, another small town en route, he was overcome with fatigue. His health hadn't been good and his body could not withstand the pressure he had placed on it. He collapsed on the roadside and was found sometime later by a passer-by, who took care of him until he recovered. Augustus John later said that neither he nor Innes ever saw the girl of their dreams again.[6]

Following their successful sojourn in Wales, the two men decided to spend some time painting in the south of France together. While working there they met Australian artist Derwent Lees, who gained much of his experience and inspiration from his gifted companions.[7] Innes and John also learned from each other. For example, it was in Wales that Innes began to work with oils, rather than watercolours, influenced by John. After a time, Innes again made his way back to Collioure, the town where he found so much comfort. He returned to London towards the end of 1911, and contributed to a number of exhibitions. However, health issues again affected his lifestyle, which was complicated even further by the fact that he was not really taking care of

Exterior of the Old Abbey Theatre, 1913.
(*Courtesy of the Abbey Theatre Archive*)

The Abbey Theatre
logo designed
by Elinor Mary
Monsell.
(*Courtesy of the Abbey
Theatre Archive*)

Portrait of Frank Fay by
John Butler Yeats.
(*Courtesy of the Abbey
Theatre Archive*)

W. G. Fay as The
Beggarman in the
1905 Abbey Theatre
production of *A Pot of
Broth* by William Butler
Yeats. (*Courtesy of the
Abbey Theatre Archive*)

William Butler Yeats
(*Courtesy of the Library of Congress,
LC-DIG-ggbain-00731*)

Augustus John
(*Courtesy of the Library of Congress,
LC-DIG-ggbain-35692*)

George Bernard Shaw
(*Courtesy of the Library of
Congress, LC-USZ62-7904*)

John Millington Synge
(*Courtesy of the Abbey Theatre Archive*)

Máire O'Neill (Molly Allgood) as Pegeen Mike in the world premiere of *The Playboy of the Western World*, Abbey Theatre, 1907. (*Courtesy of the Abbey Theatre Archive*)

himself. During this period, Innes became friends with Lord Howard de Walden, a man who had developed a strong interest in the arts. Although struggling at times, Innes was determined not to let his health interfere with his life or work and travelled to Spain with de Walden to complete some work.

It was following this trip that Innes and John arrived in Ireland in 1912. Innes had been invited to Coole by Lady Gregory and John was to accompany him.[8] During this visit, the artists visited Galway city and while there they had the idea of purchasing an old mill; however, the mill that interested Innes was very dilapidated and it seems water poured in across the ground-floor rooms. There were far too many repairs required to restore the building, so they decided against the idea.[9] During his stay at Coole, Innes signed the Autograph Tree. He also attended the Galway Races in Ballybrit, which were, and still are, a major attraction for people from all over Ireland and indeed abroad. However, between travelling and work, Innes had seriously over-burdened himself again. His health was failing and he collapsed at the races. He was taken to Coole, where he was cared for by Lady Gregory until arrangements were made for him to return to London. There, he recovered enough to begin working again and held a very successful exhibition in the Chenil Gallery. The finance raised through this exhibition enabled him to travel to Morocco and the Canary Islands in a bid to restore his health in those warmer climates.

However, it was not to be and his health continued to decline. Innes eventually had to be brought back to England by one of his brothers and taken to his mother's home in Brighton, but all efforts to nurse him back to health were in vain. He needed professional care and was admitted to a nursing home in Swanley, Kent. James Dickson Innes died on 22 August 1914 at just twenty-seven years of age.[10]

There was a suspicion that Innes was acutely aware of his own mortality and was working feverously to try to achieve as much as possible in the time available to him. This is mentioned in the following comments recorded after his death:

> James Dickson Innes, a painter with a passion for pure, vivid colours and for mountains. Innes had an original and lyrical vision, and his passion for mountains, those of his native Wales or of the South of France for preference, burned with an intensity often found among men who are conscious of having much to do and little time to do it in.[11]

George Bernard Shaw

Dramatist, Writer and Socialist 1856–1950

George Bernard Shaw was an Irish dramatist, literary critic, socialist spokesman and leading figure of the twentieth century. He was born on 26 July 1856 at 3 Upper Synge Street, Dublin, the youngest of three children and the only son of George Carr Shaw and Lucinda Elizabeth Gurly. His sisters were Lucinda and Agnes.[1] Shaw's father had a corn mill business which was not very successful and his drinking habits only made matters worse. His marriage to Lucinda was troubled from the beginning, as her family was against the union. It seems that he also had mental problems and once threatened to throw young George (known to his family as Sonny) into the Grand Canal while taking him for a walk. It was an unhappy household and Shaw grew up in a loveless home environment; even his mother had little affection for her children. The more Shaw tried to impress her, the more she snubbed him, and the children were more or less abandoned to servants who were underpaid and totally unfit to look after them.

The children received an elementary education from a private teacher. George showed a talent for writing from an early age and began to write letters for their illiterate servants. Both parents considered themselves to be part of a Protestant Ascendancy society and didn't want their son mixing with children whom they perceived to be from a lower-class background. Shaw was reminded of this continually.

Music was the only pursuit that gave the family enjoyment. His mother was an excellent singer and held musical evenings for friends. Shaw developed an interest in music and learned to play the piano under the professional tuition of George John Vandeleur Lee. He also attended Sunday school, where he received a strong scriptural education, but one wonders why he was sent there as his parents were not at all religious; in fact, his mother was an atheist.

Shaw began attending Wesleyan Connexional School when he was eleven, and while there he referred to himself as a dunce; however, he could be very clever when subjects interested him. He was later sent to the Central Model School, a non-sectarian establishment. He detested his time there and eventually refused to attend; he was then transferred to the Dublin English Scientific and Commercial Day School.

The Shaw family had access to a friend's seaside house in Dalkey, Torca Cottage, and young Shaw loved this place with its view of the sea and the Wicklow Mountains. He developed a keen interest in literature and began reading on a variety of subjects. He loved the works of Charles Dickens and was greatly influenced by him, and on his return to school began writing his own stories using a character from the great novelist. Unfortunately, Shaw's formal education soon came to an end as his father could no longer afford to keep him in school. Although he had ambitions to further his education, Shaw had to find work to help support the household. In 1871 his uncle, Richard Shaw, secured a position for him as a clerk in Uniacke Townshend's estate agent office. Shaw was an excellent worker and was quickly promoted. Over time he gained a vast knowledge of the business and found himself as chief cashier officer at the age of sixteen. It was around then that his mother took her daughters to England, leaving her husband and son in Dublin. It seems her reason for moving was to follow the music instructor, Vandeleur Lee.

While Shaw was proving successful at work, he still clung to his ambitions regarding music and art, but above all he wanted to be a writer. He wrote a letter to the press, which was published in *Public Opinion* on 3 April 1875. The letter was about two celebrated American evangelists, Shankey and Moody, who were attracting huge crowds during their visit to Dublin at that time, and he more or less denounced the preachers because of the influence they were having on some people. This caused arguments at work and he was reprimanded for writing the letter. By now he was seriously contemplating his ambition in becoming a writer and confided in a family friend, Matthew McNulty. Although his employer offered to increase his salary, he was not tempted and resigned from the firm. He was happy with his decision, but on that same day, 31 March 1876, his sister Agnes died of tuberculosis.[2] He travelled to London and found work in journalism, but could not support himself on the salary, so he depended to a large degree on his mother financially. He wrote a number of novels, including *Immaturity, An Unsocial Socialist* and *Cashel Byron's Profession,* but publishers initially rejected them. However, *Cashel Byron's Profession* was eventually published with some success.

He became a socialist after an encounter with the American

land reformer Henry George, and he read the works of Karl Marx, which had a huge impact on his political views. He joined the Fabian Society, a middle-class socialist debating group, shortly after it was established in 1884, and became editor of the society's publications.[3] He was of the opinion that the majority of people were incapable of forming their own judgement on matters, and believed that people rejected communism because they were seduced and brainwashed by capitalist regimes.[4] He also began reviewing books for *The Pall Mall Gazette* and secured employment as an art critic with *The World* through a friend, William Archer. Although somewhat shy, Shaw managed to overcome this by acting as an orator, speaking in Hyde Park and at the Royal Albert Hall, and in the years that followed he became renowned as an excellent lecturer.[5] While his work as a critic continued, he also found success as a writer of a number of witty, intelligent plays.[6]

In 1895 Shaw met Charlotte Payne-Townshend, a wealthy Irishwoman with left-wing ideals, and recruited her for the Fabian Society. He was already in a relationship with Florence Farr at the time, but this soon ended. Charlotte was to prove a great support to the future playwright. When he became ill from a foot complaint in April 1898, she was on a world tour, but upon hearing the news she returned immediately to London to look after him. He had to have surgery, which left him hobbling around on crutches for a time. The relationship matured and they were married on 1 June 1898 in Strand District Registry Office in London. While it was common among some members of their social circle for husbands and wives to allow each other sexual freedom, Charlotte didn't offer such liberties to Shaw. In fact, she was very jealous of any relationships with other women.[7] Shaw's marriage to Charlotte provided him with financial security, which allowed him time to concentrate on his writing.[8]

He wanted to see his work performed in Ireland, but was critical of certain aspects of his home country. After one visit to Dublin, Shaw indicated that little had changed in the city since his youth, saying he found the 'same old flies, on the same old cakes in the same old shop windows'. He added that the only saving grace for Dublin were the Abbey Theatre and Hugh Lane's Museum of Modern Art.[9]

According to one source, the Abbey Theatre rejected his play *John Bull's Other Island* for its opening night in 1904. Yeats and Lady Gregory thought it was too strange, dangerous and impractical for an Abbey production.[10] However, another source states that it was rejected two years later. Some said that the reason for the rejection was that they simply couldn't find an actor capable of playing the character Broadbent. Shaw believed they refused his play because they feared it would enrage nationalists. He said the play was by an Irishman about Ireland and was original and sympathetic to the people. One of his admirers told Sean O'Casey to read the play, stating that 'the Ireland you think you know and love will vanish before your eyes'. He also said that Shaw was 'the cleverest Irishman the world knows'.[11] Shaw affirmed that his play was too clear-sighted about Ireland, and that there were no banshees or leprechauns to appeal to Yeats. While there was a mutual respect between the two men, Shaw disliked Yeats' dreamy imagination of magical worlds. Yeats, on the other hand, believed that Shaw wrote too much like a journalist.

However, Lady Gregory liked Shaw's style and there was an immediate rapport between them when they met. While she didn't agree with him on common political or philosophical grounds, they did agree on Home Rule for Ireland. His opinion about England's apparent superiority over Ireland was rather witty. Shaw believed the reason was simple, saying that an Englishman would do anything for money, but an Irishman would do nothing for it. He began exchanging letters with Lady Gregory. He liked her style as a playwright and it was through their friendship that he became a fan of the Irish theatre. He also felt that she was very close to what he perceived as an ideal woman. He said that while she was not tall or strikingly good-looking, Lady Gregory was 'sympathetic, intelligent, tender and humorous'.[12]

John Bull's Other Island was accepted in 1907 by Harley Granville-Barker for the Royal Court Theatre in London, where it ran successfully and finally established Shaw as a serious playwright. The British prime minister went to see it four times and King Edward VII laughed so hard that he broke his seat. It was followed by a string of successes, including *Man and Superman, Major Barbara* (both in 1905), *The Doctor's Dilemma* (1906) and *The Shewing-up of Blanco Posnet.* The latter was later staged in Dublin because Lord Chamberlain deemed it too blasphemous for England.[13] The play was set in the American Wild West in a violent, corrupt and sexist setting. Although the English censor's rulings did not apply in Ireland, they still had to be overcome before the play could be performed there.

Lady Gregory proved a tremendous support in having the play staged as there was much opposition; even the authorities in Dublin Castle were against it being performed. However, Lady

Gregory arranged several meetings with the castle authorities and the censorship board and her efforts proved successful. When the play finally opened in 1909, the hall was packed and people were not at all shocked, but rather burst into applause and cheers after the closing scene.[14] There had been rumours that if the play went ahead, the Abbey Theatre would be closed down, but the threats did not deter the people involved and the opposition ceased after the play opened. This was seen by Patrick Pearse as a victory over the English censorship authorities.

Shaw became a regular visitor to Coole during this time and it seems the length of his visits was determined by the amount of luggage he had with him.[15]

After the birth of her grandchild Catherine, Lady Gregory prompted her daughter-in-law Margaret to ask Shaw to be godfather, but he refused, saying in a humorous manner that it was not in the baby's best interest. Lady Gregory later dedicated one of her works to him, saying that he was the gentlest of her friends. Shaw was not a demanding guest, but proved entertaining to her and the grandchildren, and she liked having him at Coole. Writing to Yeats, she said he was extraordinarily light in hand and there was a sort of kindly joyousness about him. There was great respect between them and she often referred to Shaw as 'our Irish Shakespeare'.[16]

Lady Gregory's granddaughters, Anne and Catherine, loved to see Shaw arriving, as he would always play games with them before bedtime. Their favourite game was 'Hunt the Thimble' and they were amazed at how he would always find the thimble quickly. This went on for some time and the children became suspicious, so they decided to keep a special eye on him as they hid the thimble. To their utter disgust they caught him cheating: instead of covering his eyes fully while they were hiding the thimble, he was peeping out through his fingers to see where they were placing it. The girls were highly offended and declared to their grandmother that her guest was a cheat, but she laughed so hard that tears ran down her face. Having returned to his home in England, Shaw wrote a letter of apology to the girls.

On another occasion, during the Great War, foodstuffs were rationed and the family at Coole decided to play their part. You could spread either butter or jam on a slice of bread, but not both. The girls were flabbergasted to see Shaw spread butter on one side of the bread and then turn it over and spread jam on the other side. His argument was that he wasn't actually having it together.[17]

In 1915 Shaw completed his play *O'Flaherty VC*, which was conceived at Coole, and he said that the ending would make *The Playboy of the Western World* look like a patriotic rhapsody. Some said his play was an attack on nationalism. Shaw also visited the Western Front during the war and met Robert Gregory.[18]

It was a turbulent time in Ireland, not just because of the war, but also because nationalist tensions were running high. On Easter Monday in 1916, the Rising broke out in Dublin and much of the city was destroyed. The leaders soon faced firing squads and, while Shaw had little tolerance for nationalism, he obviously understood their ideals and was among those who protested against the executions. The following is an extract from the letter he wrote:

My own view is that the men were shot in cold blood, after their capture or surrender, were prisoners of war, and it was therefore,

entirely incorrect to slaughter them ... Until Dublin Castle is
superseded by a National Parliament and Ireland voluntarily
incorporated with the British Empire, as Canada, Australia, and
South Africa have been incorporated, an Irishman resorting to
arms to achieve the independence of his country is doing only what
Englishmen will do, if it be their misfortune to be invaded and
conquered by the Germans in the course of this present war ...
The shot Irishmen will now take their places beside Emmet and
the Manchester Martyrs in Ireland. The Military authorities and
English Government must have known they were canonising their
prisoners.[19]

Shaw continued to write over the following years and some of
his other works included *Heartbreak House* (published in 1919,
produced in 1920), *Saint Joan* (1923), *The Apple Cart* (published
in 1928, produced in 1929) and *Too True to Be Good* (1931). His
1914 play *Pygmalion* was later produced as the musical *My Fair
Lady*, and in 1925 he won the Nobel Prize for Literature.[20] In
1931 Shaw visited Russia, where he met with Stalin. While
he was a committed communist, he was equally comfortable
in the drawing rooms of an aristocratic household. Speaking
of the Russian leader, Shaw once said, 'What does a bit more
slaughter matter – as long as true socialism is the result. After all,
Stalin was not unique in history.'[21] This comment is an example
of how Shaw couldn't refrain from making statements on the
international stage. Another example was after the Second World
War broke out in 1939 and there was a threat that the Irish ports
might be taken by the British. Ireland claimed neutrality and the
Irish-American magazine *The Nation*, being cynical, published

an article showing a German submarine passing along the Irish coast displaying a sign that stated, 'God bless Eire's neutrality – until the Fuhrer gets here'. The following is an extract from a statement by Shaw on neutrality in which he also made reference to Éamon de Valera's stance on the Treaty:

> If I were in Mr Churchill's place I should put it more philosophically. Instead of saying I will reoccupy your ports and leave you to do your damnedest, I should say – My dear Mr de Valera, your policy is magnificent but it is not modern statesmanship. You say the ports belong to Ireland; that is what you start from … Local patriotism with all its heroic legends is as dead as a doornail today. The ports do not belong to Ireland; they belong to Europe, to the world, to civilisation, to the Most Holy Trinity, as you might say and are held in trust by your Government in Dublin. In their names we must borrow the ports from you for the duration. You need not consent to the loan, just as you did not consent to the Treaty.[22]

This infuriated de Valera and he denounced Shaw.

On 12 September 1943 Charlotte died, having battled with illness for some time, and Shaw received an enormous amount of letters sympathising with him. He missed her greatly and felt very much alone in the world. Even in mourning and old age, however, his wit never left him. During an interview for his ninetieth birthday, the reporter said that he very much hoped that they could do the same for his hundredth, to which Shaw replied, 'I don't see why not, you look healthy enough to me.'

The end came for George Bernard Shaw four years later, after a fall sustained while pruning flowers in the garden of his home, in Ayot St Lawrence, Hertfordshire. He was taken to hospital where he slipped into a coma and died twenty-four hours later, on 2 November 1950.[23] He was cremated and his ashes were spread in the garden, appropriately named 'Shaw's Corner', along with those of his wife.[24]

Shaw left an enormous legacy in plays and literary manuscripts, which, when assembled, amounted to over forty volumes, and there was also a vast collection of other papers. It is believed that as an adult, he wrote some ten letters every day. His work is housed in special collections in universities across the world. He generously endowed the National Gallery of Ireland in his will and is remembered globally as one of the most outstanding figures of the twentieth century.[25] Shaw was highly respected across diverse and sometimes contrasting societies. His work was also admired in China and, in 1956, the Chinese government invited Lennox Robinson to deliver a centenary lecture on the topic of George Bernard Shaw.

Lennox Robinson

Playwright and Director 1886–1958

Lennox Robinson was born on 4 October 1886 in Castletreasure, near Douglas in Co. Cork, the youngest of the seven children of Andrew and Emily Anne Robinson (*née* Jones). The family moved to Kinsale in 1895 and seven years later they settled in Ballymoney in Co. Cork. Lennox suffered from ill health as a child, so his formal education was affected and, with the exception of a few years in Bandon Grammar School, he was mainly tutored at home. He was an intelligent boy with a wide interest when it came to reading, and he also liked music.

Despite his lack of a formal education, Robinson secured a teaching post at a preparatory school in Wellington, Shropshire, England. However, this move was short-lived as he was dismissed for incompetence after one term. Having returned home, he began editing a magazine called *Contributions*. In August 1907, in the Cork Opera House, he attended performances by the Abbey Theatre group, who were touring around the south of Ireland. Robinson was struck by the magic of the theatre. Yeats' play *The Hour-Glass* and Lady Gregory's *The Rising of the Moon* had a profound effect on him and he decided to write his own play, *The Clancy Name*. He clearly had a talent for playwriting, as the play was accepted by the Abbey and was ready for production by October 1908.

In 1910 Yeats arranged work for him with George Bernard Shaw in London and he gained a comprehensive knowledge of the overall theatre business. Yeats obviously saw potential in Robinson, as he offered him the post as manager of the Abbey Theatre that same year, which Robinson gladly accepted. He was also later given the added responsibility of producer-director at the Abbey.[1] Despite these appointments, Lady Gregory never really trusted his judgement. While Yeats believed that Robinson would become a great dramatist, she was not overly impressed by his style. Nevertheless, Robinson became a great supporter of her later work and this alone would have earned him an invitation to Coole.

Shortly after taking up the position as manager, Robinson became the target of the Abbey Theatre patron Annie Horniman because he didn't close the theatre on the death of King Edward VII in May 1910. She believed this to be a political insult to England as every other theatre in Britain and Ireland had closed as a mark of respect. However, there was no political malice in this action – Robinson had simply been unsure about closing the theatre. Yeats was in France, so Robinson sent a telegraph to Lady Gregory for advice on the matter. Although she replied telling him to close the theatre, the communication didn't reach him in time and he allowed a matinée performance to go ahead. The fact that Robinson sent the telegram to Lady Gregory was not taken into consideration by Horniman.[2] She threatened to withdraw her financial support for the theatre if an apology from Robinson and the directors was not published in the Dublin newspapers. Lady Gregory agreed and issued a public apology. However, Horniman rejected this, saying that it was inadequate.[3] Robinson wrote to

Yeats explaining the situation and said, 'I knew the Abbey had been carried on from the beginning as a purely artistic venture. I knew that its policy was to ignore politics.'[4] Yeats would not issue a second apology and informed Horniman that there was no place for politics in the Abbey Theatre. Horniman was actually of the same opinion regarding politics and the theatre, but she felt that the decision by Robinson had been political and so withdrew her financial support that same year.[5]

Her decision didn't have an immediate effect on Robinson or his position. In fact, he took on more responsibility and began organising tours of the United States between 1911 and 1914.[6] His final tour, in 1914, proved unsuccessful as a financial venture and Robinson resigned as manager. Lady Gregory felt that by this time he was unreliable and negligent and, writing to Yeats, she said that his judgement always seemed to fail him just when it was needed most. He was also reluctant to take her advice on certain issues. She was determined that he should not be allowed organise another American tour.[7]

Robinson joined the Irish Volunteers in Cork, but resigned following the split in the movement. He tried to enlist in the Munster Fusiliers when the Great War broke out, but was rejected because of poor eyesight. His brother Arthur was accepted into the British forces and was killed during the war.

A year later, in 1915, Robinson began working as a librarian for the Carnegie Trust, which was in the process of establishing a network of public libraries around Ireland.[8] He continued writing during this period and gained much success in 1916 with *The Whiteheaded Boy*, which was the last play produced by the Abbey Theatre before the Easter Rising. A year later, Robinson published his only novel, *A Young Man from the South*, and in 1918 he published *Eight Short Stories*.

That same year he became a founder member of the Dublin Drama League and directed some of the plays produced by this group, which attracted a new audience in Dublin. It has been said that they paved the way for the foundation of the Gate Theatre. In 1919 Robinson returned as manager and production-director of the Abbey Theatre, despite Lady Gregory's doubts about his ability. He was appointed as a member of the Abbey board of directors in 1923, to a post that had been vacant since the death of John Millington Synge. Robinson worked hard and managed to pull the Abbey out of the doldrums until it secured a government subsidy in 1925.[9]

On 9 September 1924 the inaugural meeting of the County Galway Library Committee took place in Galway County Courthouse. The meeting was supported by the Carnegie Trust and was chaired by Robinson, representing the Trust. The chairman of Galway County Council, Éamonn Corbett, was appointed chairperson; Lady Gregory and Professor Howley shared the vice-chairperson position and Samuel J. Maguire became the first county librarian.[10] A short time later, Robinson was dismissed from the Carnegie Trust amid some controversy over a short story he had published. Throughout this period he continued to write plays, such as *The Round Table* (1922) and *The White Blackbird* (1925), and in 1926 he established a school of acting and was for many years one of its teachers.[11]

Also in 1926 Sean O'Casey insisted on Robinson directing his play *The Plough and the Stars*. Rehearsals began in early January, but there were problems with the cast, as some of them didn't want to use words they believed to be rude on stage. Actor Gabriel Fallon blamed Robinson for the actors' stand and accused him of being jealous of O'Casey and of wanting to sabotage the play. Fallon also said that Robinson had chosen a weak cast, which had caused the problems. However, O'Casey didn't agree and mentioned in a letter to Sara Allgood that Robinson had read the last act during a lecture he gave in Liverpool University and felt it was splendid.

Robinson was drinking heavily at this time, but this didn't seem to affect his work. He was also prone to sudden outbursts of anger. One example of this occurred when O'Casey approached him offering advice on the sound effects in the theatre and Robinson flew into a rage, shouting, 'Oh, shut up. For Christ's sake, man! I've got enough to do to deal with the cast.'[12] Despite his drinking, actress Siobhán McKenna had a very high opinion of Robinson as a director. She said that he was 'very underestimated, very inconspicuous, but he had a wonderful way of bringing out the best in any part, and didn't mind where you moved or sat', and that he allowed actors a degree of freedom on stage, possibly to find a position where they felt most comfortable. This was not something the Abbey agreed with, but Robinson overruled any opposition and was allowed to direct plays in a manner that suited him. While Robinson and O'Casey were friends, the relationship was strained at times and, following a visit to Coole when O'Casey was not very complimentary of Lady Gregory and also mentioned her lisp, Robinson was annoyed and reminded him that she had made him comfortable in her home.[13]

Lady Gregory often travelled to Dublin to meet with actors and staff at the Abbey and sometimes took her grandchildren along. It was a great adventure for them meeting the various playwrights. Their memories of these visits are interesting. Yeats, they said, was not overly friendly and would only bid them good morning. The children were also not terribly impressed with Robinson and felt that he didn't really like them as he never spoke with them. Their memory of him was that he was very tall and looked rather like a ghost.[14]

Robinson went on a lecture tour of the United States in 1928, but it was not financially successful. Having returned to Ireland he began a relationship with Dorothy Travers-Smith, who worked as an artist and set designer at the Abbey, and they married on 8 September 1931. Robinson continued to drink heavily and was also suffering from depression, but despite these problems he continued writing and editing, and managed to achieve the high standards required by the theatre. In fact, he edited Lady Gregory's journals in 1946.[15] By this time, Coole was all but a distant memory; the manor house had disappeared and the only indication of the many writers, poets and artists who spent time there was the Autograph Tree. Robinson made an attempt to write Lady Gregory's biography, but abandoned the idea soon afterwards. It seems that O'Casey advised him on the matter, saying that it was difficult enough to write an autobiography, but to write a biography would prove even harder. Robinson then settled for editing her journals instead.[16]

In 1948 he became a founder member of the Actors' Church Union, a body on which he served as president and vice-president. That same year, he was awarded an honorary DLitt by Trinity College Dublin in recognition of what the college authorities considered his diverse achievements. In 1951 he published the official history of the Abbey Theatre and in 1953 was appointed honorary patron of the All-Ireland Amateur Drama Council.

The end came for Lennox Robinson on 14 October 1958, when he died of heart failure in Glensilva Nursing Home, Dublin. Following his funeral mass, he was buried in the grounds of St Patrick's Cathedral, Dublin.[17] Gary O'Connor, in his biography of Sean O'Casey, said that Robinson had served O'Casey faithfully as a friend and an enemy over many years.

Sean O'Casey

Writer and Dramatist 1880–1964

Sean O'Casey was born in Dublin on 30 March 1880. The family were of a lower-middle-class Protestant background and lived in 85 Upper Dorset Street, Dublin.[1] He was the youngest of five surviving children born to Michael and Susan O'Casey (*née* Archer).[2] The family occupied rooms in a large rented house, where it seems that Michael – who was a clerk in the Irish Church Mission – was the principal tenant. It has also been suggested that he was a sub-landlord letting out rooms to other families.

He would not educate his children through the free national school system; instead, he insisted on them attending a fee-charging central model school, as they would be in the company of middle-class students. Michael died in 1886, when Sean was just six years old and, following his death, the family found themselves living in dire poverty.[3] In addition to this, Sean was left almost blind from trachoma and he normally wore a peaked cap to protect his inflamed eyes.[4] His education was seriously affected, but his older sister, Isabella, who was a schoolmistress, ensured that he received some degree of instruction, and he was largely self-educated, with wide-ranging interests when it came to reading.[5] Many years later, O'Casey told Lady Gregory that he didn't attend school until he was sixteen years old and could not read or write until that time, and she was deeply impressed by this admission. His remarks were possibly a bit flippant: he probably meant that he could not read academic works until that time, as the fact that Isabella tutored him at home and his wide interests when it came to reading would contradict his admission to Lady Gregory. He was a great admirer of Charles Stewart Parnell, who was an important figure in the O'Casey household, indicating that he was introduced to nationalist ideals at an early age.

O'Casey was described as a thin, lanky youth with a mass of hair that his mother was always trying to brush back from his forehead. When he was fourteen, he began working in the wholesale chandlers business of Hampton and Leedon in Henry Street. Because he was a Protestant, the manager employed him immediately on a salary of 3s 6d per week.

There was an interest in the theatre among the family members and they constructed a stage in the sitting room where, together with neighbours and friends, they began to host plays. By the age of twenty-three, O'Casey was extremely well read and could have found employment on the clerical staff of most companies. On the advice of an old school friend, George Middleton, he began working for the Great Northern Railway of Ireland.[6] His nationalist interests were strong and, even after a hard working day, he would attend Gaelic League meetings in the evenings. He joined the Drumcondra branch of the league in 1906 with the intention of learning the Irish language.[7] Through this organisation he was given the first opportunity to have his work published, by writing for their journal, and he began signing his name as Sean, rather than John as he was known up to that time.

A year later he joined the St Laurence O'Toole GAA Club and became a founder member of the organisation's pipe band. O'Casey was drawn to the labour movement and in 1911 became a member of the Irish Transport and General Workers' Union. During the 1913 Dublin Lock-Out, O'Casey was appointed secretary of the Women and Children's Relief Fund.[8] He was also chosen as a section leader in the Irish Citizen Army. He had great respect for James Larkin, the labour leader whose vision of justice for people was to allow them time to enjoy the beauty of life. This prompted O'Casey to write that this was a man who would put a flower as well as a loaf on the table.

His political views must have become more militant as between 1912 and 1913 he was sworn into the Irish Republican Brotherhood (IRB) by the rebel leader Tom Clarke. A contemporary remembers O'Casey at this time as being a tall, short-sighted man with an intelligent, sardonic face and small red-rimmed eyes that stabbed all the beauty and sorrow of the world in bursts of anti-English rhetoric. Despite his involvement in the IRB, he took no part in the 1916 Rising because he believed that the leaders of the uprising didn't have the workers' interests at heart, and he bitterly resented James Connolly for bringing the Irish Citizen Army into the revolt. O'Casey roamed the streets of the capital during the Rising and recorded the destruction of the General Post Office:

In the sky the flames were soaring higher, till the heavens looked like a great ruby hanging from God's ear. Now it was above them locking away the roof from over their heads, and they were too weary to go on trying to put it out. Their faces were chipped into bleeding jaggedness by splinters flying from shattered stones and brick ... their leaders, before a wall of flame, standing dignified among them, already garlanded for death. They had helped God to rouse up Ireland.[9]

The Abbey Theatre refused his play *Profit and Loss* that same year and later rejected four more: *The Harvest Festival, The Frost in the Flower, The Crimson in the Tri-Colour* and *The Seamless Coat of Kathleen*. It was April 1923 before they finally produced one of his works, *The Shadow of the Gunman*, which played for three nights in the Abbey.[10] Lady Gregory was obviously not impressed with this play, but she didn't prevent it from being staged, saying that they should let him see how bad it was. However, as time went by, she became a strong supporter of O'Casey's work. She recorded in her journal that *Juno and the Paycock* was a wonderful and terrifying play of futility, irony, humour and tragedy. Of *The Plough and the Stars* she wrote that it was an overpowering play and added that all others would seem shadowy in comparison.

All three of these plays were set in Ireland's turbulent years of violence between 1916 and 1922, and they troubled many nationalists. *The Plough and the Stars*, described as the third of his masterpieces, caused uproar when it opened and it seems that the president of the Gaelic League had to leave the theatre before the second act because of a fit of nausea. O'Casey was surrounded in the foyer by an angry mob shouting abuse at him and the police had to be called.[11]

Nationalist feelings were high and the men who had fought in the Rising were national heroes. The problem was that some militant republicans believed the play ridiculed the men of 1916.

Cumann na mBan were so incensed that they organised a protest outside the theatre and threw rotten fruit at the actors. Some members of the audience even invaded the stage and Yeats was called on to address the howling crowd, but failed to pacify them, and it was only when the police arrived that order was restored. Perhaps Yeats describing O'Casey's play as a work of genius didn't help matters.[12]

The reaction to the play highlighted disillusionment among many activists of the Rising and War of Independence, who believed that the new Ireland being created by the men taking power lacked any trace of the idealism that had been central to the nationalist cause. But O'Casey's work was simply an attempt to show the lives of working-class people in Dublin during the Rising. In one scene, the Tricolour is taken into a pub frequented by prostitutes and there is a suggestion that the men of 1916 were drinking there. The message of the play is that nationalism had no relevance for the working class.

Among those who took offence to the play was Hanna Sheehy-Skeffington, who was very articulate and challenged O'Casey to a public debate organised by the University Republican Society. An angry crowd turned up for the debate and much abuse was levelled at O'Casey. While the insults offended, he acknowledged that this lady was very clever and upright, and that she raised the controversy above the level of abuse.

However, his words for Maud Gonne were very different as she had attacked his plays. She attended the debate and O'Casey wrote, 'Here she sat now, silent, stony; waiting her turn to say more bitter words against the one who refused to make her dying dream his own … her deep-set eyes sad, agleam with disappointment;

never quite at ease with the crowd, whose cheers she loved, the colonel's daughter still'. [13] He was hinting at her English military background and the fact that her role as a 1916 widow was always clouded in controversy, particularly given her divorce from the 1916 martyr MacBride. O'Casey had a total dislike for upper-class women who took up the Irish cause, and this could also be seen in his resentment of Countess Constance Markievicz, which had led to him resigning from the Irish Citizen Army many years earlier.[14]

In June 1924 Lady Gregory invited O'Casey to Coole. She met him at Athenry station and they travelled to Gort by train. He wondered at her composure sitting in a third-class carriage, unaware that this was how she usually travelled. Some twenty-five years later he wrote that she sat there in all her elegance, well at ease among the chattering crowd of common people. He enjoyed walking with her and was impressed at the way she listened to the stories of the people they met and sang songs with them. He described Lady Gregory as 'a sturdy, stout little figure soberly clad in solemn black, made gay with a touch of something white … Her face was a rugged one, hardy as that of a peasant, curiously lit with an odd dignity, and softened with a careless touch of humour in the bright eyes.'[15]

While he had strong opinions on social classes and was easily upset when it came to people with power or authority, O'Casey respected her. For her part, Lady Gregory extended courtesy to him and accepted without question his comments and views even after a refusal to take tea with her in the Green Room. When they were alone in the evenings she would read to him from *The Dynasts*, Thomas Hardy's epic story of the Napoleonic War.

However, O'Casey found it difficult to remain awake on these occasions. She also expressed her deep sorrow and loneliness at the loss of her son Robert and nephew Hugh Lane during the war.

O'Casey only stayed a week at Coole and later wrote that he was never really drawn to the woods because he felt they were gloomy. He paid a second visit to Coole in August 1925 and among the other guests were Jack B. Yeats and his wife, Mary. Lady Gregory had received a copy of *The Plough and the Stars* from Lennox Robinson, which she read aloud to her guests over two evenings. O'Casey later wrote that it was rather embarrassing to hear Lady Gregory reading the play, particularly the 'saucy song sung by Rosie & Fluther from the second act'. Nevertheless, he wasn't overly concerned as he felt that Lady Gregory was an exceptionally broad-minded woman.[16]

One of the housemaids, Marian McGuinness, was not at all happy with O'Casey being a guest at Coole. It seems that he would not wear a collar and tie and this was a cause of concern for her. At one time, she exclaimed, 'Great playwright is it. I'll give him great playwright. What right at all has a man to come to Coole without a tie on his collar, nor a collar on his shirt.'[17] This was not a lack of respect for Lady Gregory; it was simply how he dressed.

O'Casey carried treasured memories of Coole and was always grateful for Lady Gregory's support. She gave him more encouragement than any of the Abbey directors as she liked his strength of characterisation. He also inspired her and was the embodiment of the success of the Abbey at that time. Unlike many other visitors to Coole, O'Casey noticed the people who worked there and when writing to Lady Gregory, he would sign off by sending them his best wishes.[18]

Lady Gregory's grandchildren remembered clearly the day Sean O'Casey carved his name on their 'magnificent copper beech tree'. Many years later, Anne Gregory wrote that it was to this tree, with its long straight trunk, that 'Grandma brought all the important people who stayed at Coole, to carve their names'. Anne showed them the names of 'GBS' and 'Augustus John', and they actually watched as O'Casey carved his name into the tree. She said that 'He was very good at it and said that he had had a lot of practice, as he had often carved his name on the door of his tenement flat in Dublin.' They said that after he returned to Dublin, O'Casey wrote a letter to their grandmother thanking her for the kindness at Coole. He said that he had visited the parks in Dublin and was trying to identify trees and remember the names of the various species that she had shown him. O'Casey admitted that he hadn't found any trees that were as fine as the ones in Coole.[19]

In 1926 O'Casey won the Hawthornden Prize for *Juno and the Paycock*, and it was while he was in London to collect his award that he met George Bernard Shaw and Augustus John. Shortly after, John painted a portrait of O'Casey. The latter also met Eileen Reynolds, a singer and actress who worked under the stage name Eileen Carey and took part in the London production of *The Plough and the Stars*.[20] He was attracted to Eileen and asked her back to the house where he was staying in Trafalgar Square. The landlady, Mrs Sparrow, made tea and prepared something to eat for them. It seems that every time O'Casey made advances towards Eileen, Mrs Sparrow appeared asking if they wanted more tea or milk, or needed the table cleared, so the couple eventually gave up and went for a walk in Hyde Park. Eileen was involved with another man at the time, but found herself increasingly attracted to O'Casey, who paid her a lot of attention and charmed her with his comments, saying he had rarely seen a 'lovelier face or figure anywhere in this world'. The relationship deepened and they fell in love, but Eileen's mother was against the union because she felt that O'Casey was closer to her own generation. Although both of them wanted to get married, they were nervous about the situation, and even when Eileen became pregnant, her mother continued to try to prevent the marriage. Despite this objection, they married in London on 23 September 1927. Their honeymoon was spent in Ireland and he took her to visit old friends around Dublin before they returned to live in London, where O'Casey felt at home.[21] Although he was twenty years older than his wife, they had three children: Brecon was born in April 1928; Niall in January 1935 and a daughter, Shivaun, in September 1939. The family moved a number of times until they eventually settled in Totnes, Devon.[22]

O'Casey's decision to live in England was really a self-imposed exile because the Abbey Theatre had refused his play *The Silver Tassie*. This rejection stunned O'Casey, but he had alienated himself from many sectors of Irish society. He had written the history of the Irish Citizen Army, which enraged many nationalists when he stated that the real hero of the Easter Rising was Francis Sheehy-Skeffington and not the executed leaders. The Catholic Church was also very hostile towards O'Casey because of his portrayal of the clergy in *Juno and the Paycock*. He felt the clergy manipulated Christianity and mocked them by saying they were blind to the humiliation of man in destitution. 'Didn't they [priests] prevent the people in '47 from seizing the corn, and they starving?' asks Captain Boyle in *Juno and the Paycock*. 'Didn't they down Parnell; didn't they say that hell wasn't hot enough nor eternity long enough to punish Fenians?' These comments didn't sit well with many people in Ireland.[23]

The decision to reject *The Silver Tassie* was three-fold as it turned out: Lennox Robinson disliked certain sections; Lady Gregory thought it was fragmented; and Yeats felt that O'Casey had abandoned his subjects – the working class of the country. They advised him to make changes and at first he was willing to revise the play, but then Lady Gregory unwisely sent him the letters containing the comments from the others and O'Casey was highly insulted. He took the criticisms as a total censure of his play and made up his mind never to return to Ireland. A year later the play went into production in the Apollo Theatre in London. While visiting London, Lady Gregory went to see the play and had some regrets about her earlier decision. She could not help thinking that the Abbey should have produced it and felt that they could have done it more justice. She made an attempt to meet O'Casey, but he refused to see her – the rejection still clearly rankling him – however, this was a decision he regretted many years later.[24]

He continued to work and between 1939 and 1955 O'Casey published six volumes of a semi-fictional autobiography. By this time he had produced what was considered to be the best of his later plays, including *Red Roses for Me* (1943); *Purple Dust* (1945); *Cock-a-Doodle Dandy* (1949) and *The Bishop's Bonfire* (1955).[25] In 1958 *The Drums of Father Ned* was commissioned by the Dublin International Theatre Festival, but was withdrawn because of clerical opposition. In some of these plays, O'Casey demonstrated an intense dislike for Éamon de Valera and what he felt were the insular policies and bigotry that were encouraged in Ireland.[26]

At home with his family, O'Casey was a devoted father; he allowed his children to have a free-thinking spirit and believed in life before literature. However, tragedy struck in 1956 when Niall developed leukaemia. O'Casey saw his son for the last time on Christmas Day of that year and in their last moments together, O'Casey kissed him and heard his son murmur, 'it's hellish'. Niall died not long afterwards.

As he got older, O'Casey's health and sight began to deteriorate. Eileen was a great support; she read to him and acted as his ambassador, attending functions and other events. While theirs was a good marriage, it was celibate. However, Eileen, in her mid-fifties and still a strikingly good-looking woman, had strong sexual desires and, by her own admission, fulfilled these needs outside her marriage.

On 17 September 1964 O'Casey began bleeding profusely from the nose and was taken to a doctor's surgery nearby, where the bleeding stopped. He was taken home and Eileen cooked him an omelette, a dish he liked. O'Casey began talking about the children, explaining how she should advise them on certain matters, and she felt he knew the end was close. At 2 a.m. the following morning he suffered a clot, which caused him agonising pain. They drove him to hospital, but he died peacefully on the way. His body was taken to the Torquay Crematorium where, after a ten-minute Anglican service, he was cremated. His ashes were then taken away and spread in the same area, Golders Green, where Niall's had been distributed some years earlier.[27]

O'Casey never really forgave Ireland, though it was said that 'Ireland was ready to forgive one of her finest playwrights and the most honest observer of the brave deeds he wrote about.'[28] His supporters said that he was misunderstood, while others said that he was understood, but his views were unacceptable. After his death, the Abbey Theatre paid the following tribute to him, taken from a speech by American president John F. Kennedy: 'The artist has a lover's quarrel with the world. In pursuing his perceptions of reality he must often sail against the currents of his time. This is not a popular role.'[29]

While O'Casey fell out with Lady Gregory and other members of the Abbey Theatre, he was not vindictive towards her. This was in stark contrast to another one of the signatories, George Moore.

Exterior of the Old Abbey Theatre, 1913.
(*Courtesy of the Abbey Theatre Archive*)

The Abbey Theatre
logo designed
by Elinor Mary
Monsell.
(*Courtesy of the Abbey
Theatre Archive*)

Portrait of Frank Fay by John Butler Yeats. (*Courtesy of the Abbey Theatre Archive*)

W. G. Fay as The Beggarman in the 1905 Abbey Theatre production of *A Pot of Broth* by William Butler Yeats. (*Courtesy of the Abbey Theatre Archive*)

Portrait of Annie
Horniman by John Butler
Yeats. (*Courtesy of the Abbey
Theatre Archive*)

Lennox Robinson
(*Courtesy of the Abbey
Theatre Archive*)

John Edward Masefield
(*Courtesy of the Library of Congress,*
LC–DIG–ggbain–20817)

Lady Margaret Sackville
(*Courtesy of the Library of Congress,*
LC–DIG–ggbain–37284)

General Sir Ian Hamilton
(*Courtesy of the Library*
of Congress, LC–DIG–
ggbain–18025)

George Moore

Novelist 1852–1933

George Moore was born on 24 February 1852 in Moore Hall, Ballyglass, Co. Mayo.[1] He was the eldest of five children, the others being Maurice, Augustus, Nina and Julian. His parents were George Henry and Mary Moore (*née* Blake), and his father was a member of parliament for Co. Mayo. The Moore family were of English Protestant origin, but some time after settling in Ireland they changed their religion and became Roman Catholic. The family had a reputation as model landlords and never evicted tenants for profit as others had done.

It seems that their father was a nationalist and was sworn into the Fenian movement by James Stephens. George Henry Moore was also an excellent jockey and won the Irish Gold Whip and English Whip in the 1840s. During the Great Famine, one of his horses won the Chester Cup and he donated £1,000 of his winnings to support his tenants. In 1861, when George was nine years old, his father took him to a race meeting in England. Moore's horse, Croaghpatrick, won at Goodwood and Chester and this provided the finance for his son's education. George was sent to St Mary's College, a Catholic boarding school in Oscott near Birmingham, but he was very unhappy there, mainly because it was an extremely disciplined school. He was sent home in 1864 because of an illness and a priest, Fr James Browne, then tutored him at home. He liked reading and continued this pursuit outside school hours. In January 1865 Moore was sent back to St Mary's along with his brother Maurice. He was not inclined to study, his spelling was possibly the worst in the school and when he was returning home the following Christmas, the principal gave him a letter for his father explaining the situation. This caused a number of arguments between them and George returned to school with instructions to write a three-page letter to his father every week. He soon began making progress with his spelling. In July, when the other students were going home on holidays, Moore was forced to remain at school for additional study. He wrote to his father begging to be taken home. This was a memory he carried with him all his life.

In April 1870, while on parliamentary duty in London, George Henry Moore received news that his tenants had been issued with a notice warning them not to pay rent to landlords or their agents. The notice had been issued by Ribbonmen, a secret agrarian society who were against the landlord system. He left for Ireland immediately but arrived home feeling very ill and died of apoplexy just five days later.

George had an interest in art and, shortly after his father's funeral, he went to London where he met an artist named James Whistler. He also spent time in the studio of another artist, Jim Browne, who advised him to go to Paris if he wished to excel in painting.[2] He was twenty-one when he travelled to Paris to fulfil his ambition. He was soon moving around the artistic world of the French capital, rubbing shoulders with some of the top artists of the period. Perhaps it was because of such company that

Moore recognised his own inadequacy as a painter. However, he did discover his potential talent in literature and exchanged the brush for the pen. Writing really appealed to him and shortly afterwards two of his earliest publications in poetry appeared: *Flowers of Passion* (1878) and *Pagan Poems* (1881).[3]

Over the years Moore had relationships with a number of women. In 1876, while staying in Boulogne, he developed serious feelings for Mary de Ross Rose, a young heiress from Co. Limerick, and thought about marrying her but was unsure how to approach the subject. He even wrote to his mother asking her for information about Mary. When he discovered that she was only worth £800, he stopped pursuing her.[4]

His father's death had left him a wealthy landowner with over 12,000 acres surrounding Moore Hall. He had a luxury apartment in Montmartre where he kept a python he called Jack; he fed the snake once a month with a live guinea pig, dressing in a Japanese kimono for the occasion while a friend played the organ. In 1880 his life in Paris was interrupted by unrest at home because of agrarian agitation in rural Ireland. This was known as the land war and he had to return home to look after his interests. After reaching an agreement with the tenants, Moore travelled to London, where he secured work in journalism, but he returned to Mayo in 1883 and while there he wrote a novel, *A Drama in Muslin,* in which he attacked corruption among the Anglo-Irish in Dublin. The earlier threat of non-payment of rent by his father's tenants was certainly not to his liking either; in fact, he made some shocking remarks about them three years later in a collection of essays entitled *Parnell and His Island.* He wrote, 'Ireland is a bog, and the aborigines are a degenerate race, short, squat little men with low foreheads and wide jaws.'[5] While his words were intended as a revenge against the people involved in the rent issue, they only angered his tenants and did nothing to improve the situation.

He continued to pursue his writing career and experienced several failures before he produced his first really successful work, *Esther Waters*, in 1894, followed by a volume of short stories entitled *Celibates* (1895), and two novels, *Evelyn Innes* (1898) and *Sister Teresa* (1901). Other works about this time included his collection of short stories entitled *The Untilled Field*, which appeared in 1903, followed by his novel *The Lake* in 1905.[6]

While in London in 1891, Moore met Ada Leverson, an admirer of his work and the wife of Ernest Leverson, who was a self-styled capitalist and investor. Moore began visiting her and a relationship developed, but as she lived in fear of her husband discovering the affair, they were forced to meet in secret locations. They also corresponded and, despite her frequent requests that he burn the letters, he refused. It is not known for certain how the affair ended, but it may have been because she feared a scandal.

By 1893 he had developed feelings for a woman named Lena Milman, the daughter of the commandant of the Tower of London. Moore began taking her to galleries, balls and other such places and events, but she obviously didn't have any real feelings for him as she rejected his advances of intimacy. She became angry with him after he published *Modern Painting*, in which he wrote that women didn't often 'paint or write works of genius, because they couldn't transcend shame. They would never dare to make a full sexual confession.' She felt that this was a slur on her gender. Although he wanted to declare his love for her, the relationship failed and he returned to Paris. There, he met a very beautiful eighteen-year-old girl, and a passionate affair followed. By the time he returned to London, Lena had become close to the writer Thomas Hardy, whose work she greatly admired.

The identity of the girl in Paris is not known for certain, but there is a suspicion that it may have been Maud Burke, who was travelling around Europe with her aunt at the time. Maud was a gold-rush heiress from San Francisco. Moore met her at the London Savoy Hotel in May 1894 and she invited him to join her party for lunch. They began writing to each other, but it is not known how close they were because many of the letters are missing, yet those that have survived indicate a tender friendship. He once said that she was the only woman he knew that could hurt him, and she had often done so. She married Sir Bache Cunard in 1895, but remained close to Moore, and when in August of that year she went to Scotland on a shooting trip, Moore managed to secure an invitation. He had only one thing on his mind when he wrote to his brother saying, 'My young lady is trying to get away from her husband for a time – a week's adultery we agree would be charming.'[7] However, he didn't record any information about the trip, proving he could be discreet when necessary. Maud, now Lady Cunard, gave birth to a baby girl, Nancy, a year after she married. It was not known for certain if Moore was the father, but the two remained close all of their lives.[8]

Moore was convinced that a new theatre would be vital to any Irish Literary Renaissance and so made contact with other interested people. He had some experience in the theatre and had written a play, as well as developing a reputation as a critic while in London. Thus he found himself among the founding members of the Irish Literary Theatre.[9] Moore and Yeats collaborated in writing the play *Diarmuid and Grania*, but it was a very shaky partnership and caused much stress for both of them. Some people found Moore rather complex, including Lady Gregory. It was said that she understood 'everything except hunting, shooting, fishing and George Moore'.[10]

Moore said that his visit to Coole took place when he was writing *Diarmuid and Grania* with Yeats, and remembered passing away the miles on his way to Coole in happy meditation and contemplating the production of the play. He was aware that Douglas Hyde had visited Coole earlier and heard that he had been inspired to write *The Twisting of the Rope* while staying there. Perhaps it would be the same for him. He arrived at Coole just in time for breakfast and joined Lady Gregory at the table, but there was no sign of Yeats, who had arrived some days earlier. Lady Gregory was about to send a servant to enquire if Yeats would like to have breakfast in his room when the poet appeared. After breakfast, Lady Gregory told them to use the drawing room, where they would not be disturbed until teatime.[11] It was Moore who suggested that they should write the play together, but Lady Gregory was against the partnership and made no secret of this when talking to Yeats. She felt that Yeats had pure genius, while Moore had only talent. It was evident that Lady Gregory didn't trust Moore and was trying to minimise his influence over the poet. Yeats was contemplating going on an American tour with Moore, but Lady Gregory persuaded him not to go and was delighted when he decided against it. Moore was angry and was possibly aware of her part in the decision when he wrote, 'She is a very clever woman, I did not find out until lately how clever.'[12]

While it is not known for certain when Moore signed the tree, it was possibly during this period.

In 1899 Moore met Clara Christian, a former student of the Slade School of Fine Art. He liked her, but there was a problem as she had a lesbian lover named Ethel Walker, with whom she had arranged a trip on the Continent. Moore decided that he would interrupt the tour and enlisted the help of his cousin Edward Martyn of Tulira Castle. They followed the two women and met in a so-called accidental encounter. Moore and Clara began gravitating towards each other and they were soon spending a lot of time together, which left Ethel extremely unhappy. Martyn was also annoyed and returned home.

When Moore became involved in the Irish Literary Revival, he persuaded Clara to move to Dublin with him and introduced her to Douglas Hyde, who was not at all pleased that he had brought an English woman as a mistress. Although friends prompted him about marriage, Moore didn't propose to Clara and by 1904 the liaison had ended. She later married Charles McCarthy, a Dublin city architect. Despite all of his relationships, Moore never married.[13]

His presence in the Abbey Theatre was not always welcome, particularly to Maud Gonne, as he was not shy when it came to voicing his opinion on performances during rehearsals for *Diarmuid and Grania*. Gonne had taken part in a number of plays and did not agree with his opinions. She mentioned this in her letters to Yeats, making comments about Moore and his lack of understanding of the play, and wrote in one letter:

George Moore was at our second rehearsal when some of them

didn't quite know their parts ... he had many suggestions to offer which would have entirely changed the character of the play and which I think would have spoiled it, for instance he wanted Kathleen to get up when she talked about her beautiful green fields and walk to the door and come back again, in fact he wanted her to be wandering round the cottage all the time and make [the] most of her remarks from the front of the stage instead of from the corner of the fire. I don't agree with Moore at all about this, for I think one must keep up the idea of the poor old weary woman who would certainly sit down and rock herself over the fire and not get up and walk about until the idea of meeting her friends comes to her.[14]

Moore was initially intrigued and enthusiastic about the Irish literary society. He even defended Yeats' play *Countess Cathleen* when there was a doubt about it being staged because a cleric deemed it theologically unorthodox – a situation that arose when Edward Martyn showed the contents of the play to the cleric, who promptly denounced it as heresy. Moore was furious and wrote a letter to Martyn castigating him for his actions. The letter caused so much anger that Martyn announced he was going to resign from the society. However, Yeats persuaded him to withdraw his resignation.[15] Moore's later work *Principia Ethica* attacked religious and patriotic absolutes.[16]

As time went by, Moore became disillusioned with some members of the literary movement; this can be seen from an article he wrote for *The English Review* about his experiences in Dublin between 1901 and 1911. In the article he ridiculed Lady Gregory and Yeats, referring to Yeats' love for Maud Gonne as 'the common mistake of a boy'.[17] They weren't the only people to come under attack, as he was particularly insulting to the memory of John Millington Synge when he wrote, 'Synge's death seems to have done him a great deal of good; he was not cold in his grave when his plays began to sell like hot cakes.'[18]

Moore visited Dublin in June 1916, where he met his brother Maurice. That same year, writer Susan Mitchell published a vengeful essay against Moore because of his earlier book *Parnell and His Island*. Mitchell said that there was no art in *Parnell and His Island*, but there was sufficient truth in it to make it a horrible exhibition of Moore's soul. She also wrote that some men kiss and tell, while Moore tells but doesn't kiss – the nasty comments that he had written about others were coming back to haunt him. There was obviously a lot of resentment also between the brothers as, speaking to Mitchell about George, Maurice said that there was nothing nasty in him except his mind and also indicated that all of his love stories were lies.

In February 1923 a unit of the IRA arrived at Moore Hall and, having looted much of the contents, burned it to the ground. During the War of Independence Maurice Moore (in his brother's absence) had given permission to the IRA to use the hall as a billeting station, but he supported the Free State government during the subsequent Civil War and allowed the hall to be used by their troops. It was rumoured among the locals that the orders to burn Moore Hall came directly from Éamon de Valera. George Moore had no idea that the house was being used by any military as he was constantly away and had not spoken to his brother for a few years. He had no interest in politics and indicated that he would never visit Ireland again because of the burning of his house.

In November 1925 Sir Bache Cunard died. Moore and Lady Cunard travelled to Paris together soon after. On their return, she spent much of her time urging the British government to present Moore with the Order of Merit and enlisted the help of Edmond Grosse, an old friend of Moore, who was influential within government circles. However, rather than help, Grosse thwarted the plans, ensuring that such an award would never be presented. This was because Moore was a fierce critic of Thomas Hardy. While Grosse had earlier done his utmost to ensure a Nobel Prize for Hardy, some of Moore's negative comments had detrimentally affected Hardy's chance of securing the award.

Moore moved into a nursing home in 1928, having become ill. There, Nancy Cunard paid him a visit as she had suspicions about his relationship with her mother. She asked him directly if he was her father. He replied by saying that only her mother could answer that question. When Nancy told him she intended to approach her mother about this, he became upset and pleaded with her not to say anything. Moore said that, while he would like to think so, he didn't believe that he was her father. Although not fully recovered, and forced to wear a colostomy bag, Moore returned to his home in Ebury Street in April of that year.

Moore continued writing and in 1932 began *A Communication to My Friends*, but by January 1933 he was extremely ill and unable to complete the work. He died on 21 January. He had requested cremation and asked for his ashes to be taken to Lough Carra in Co. Mayo. His wishes were carried out and the urn was taken to an island on Lough Carra and covered by a cairn of stones.[19]

Douglas Hyde

President of Ireland and
Writer 1860–1949

Douglas Hyde was born on 17 January 1860, the third son of Reverend Arthur Hyde, the rector of Tibohine, Frenchpark, Co. Roscommon. His mother was Elizabeth, daughter of the Venerable John Oldfield, archdeacon of Elphin. There were three other siblings: Arthur, Oldfield and Annette. When he was thirteen years old, Douglas was sent to a boarding school in Dublin, but he caught the measles and was sent home after a few weeks. He never returned to the school.

While at home he became interested in the Irish language and travelled around nearby districts to meet the last generation of Irish speakers living in these areas. He began collecting their stories before the language died out. His writing at the time contained strong nationalist and anti-English feelings, which was probably due to the influence of his friend John Lavin, who was a Fenian.[1] Hyde was taught Irish by James Hart, who was known as the 'keeper of the bogs'. Over the following years he cycled around Connacht collecting stories, folklore and songs, which he later compiled into a series of articles entitled 'The Love Songs of Connacht' and published in *The Nation*.[2]

His father had ideas that he should follow a career in the

Church of Ireland, and in 1880 Hyde entered Trinity College Dublin. That same year he joined the Gaelic Union, which was a militant breakaway group of the Society for the Preservation of the Irish Language. The following year, 1881, he won the Bedell Scholarship, which was awarded to encourage preaching in the Irish language in the Church of Ireland. In 1884 he graduated in modern literature and divinity, being awarded a gold medal for his efforts. He then decided to study law and graduated in this also, though he didn't follow this career. Instead, he decided to establish himself as a writer and literary scholar.[3]

He had shown tremendous literary talent from the beginning, winning the Vice-Chancellor's Prize for English verse while at Trinity in 1885. The following year he won the same prize for prose and topped this success in 1887 by winning both awards.[4] Also in 1885, he had 'The unpublished songs of Ireland' printed in the *Dublin University Review*. A year later his 'A plea for the Irish Language' appeared in the same publication. He also contributed, along with a number of others, including Yeats, to *Poems and Ballads of Young Ireland*, which appeared in 1888. His *Leabhar Sgeulaigheachta* made its appearance the following year. This was based on a collection of stories he gathered while in the west of Ireland. In 1890 *Beside the Fireside,* another collection of stories, appeared in print. These works were translated into French and helped establish Hyde internationally as a folklorist and native scholar. One of his most important academic works during this period, *A Literary History of Ireland*, was published in 1899.[5]

In 1891 Hyde travelled to Canada as an interim professor of modern languages and lectured in the University of New

Brunswick. He returned to Ireland a year later as his heart was set on promoting the Irish language at home.[6] Hyde was fascinated with the language and gained valuable knowledge transcribing the poems and stories he had collected. He was extremely worried that the Irish language would become a victim of modern Ireland and die out forever. Determined to do something about this, he set out on a crusade to try to restore the language.

In 1892 he presented a lecture to the National Literary Society. During his talk he warned that all Irish place-names and those of its people were in danger of being lost. This would cause the extinction of the Irish language if something wasn't done soon to prevent such a tragedy. He felt that this would be the greatest blow to Irish culture. He also said that traditions and stories of past Irish heroes would be forgotten, and concluded by stating, 'In order to de-Anglicise ourselves we must at once arrest the decay of the language.'[7] His idea was to revive the language completely and have it spoken outside academic circles.

Something would have to be done urgently and this led to a meeting taking place in 9 Lower O'Connell Street on 31 July 1893. The meeting had a profound effect on the future of Ireland as it resulted in the formation of the Gaelic League. It was later said that Hyde was among the most distinguished creators of modern Ireland. His concerns can be seen in the following extract from a paper he later wrote on the subject:

Of the many linguistic miracles which the world has to show, few are more extraordinary than the suffering of the great Irish language which was spoken by, or at least known to, everybody of the Milesian race down to about the year 1750, or even 1800.

At the time of the Great Famine in 1847–8, it was the ordinary language of about four millions of people in Ireland. The famine knocked the heart out of everything. After that it just wilted away until little more than three quarters of a million, and the bulk of these aged people, knew anything about it … Between 1861 and 1891 the language died out with such rapidity, that the whole island contained in 1891, according to the census, less Irish speakers than the small province of Connacht had done thirty years before.[8]

The aim of the Gaelic League was to revive not just the Irish language, but also Irish music, dancing, poetry, literature and history, and to help to educate people in Irish culture, giving them a new sense of pride in their native heritage. One of the main achievements of the league was the introduction of the Irish language into schools. The league spread across Ireland quickly and eventually some 600 branches were established countrywide.[9] Hyde was a powerful force behind the movement and promoted and taught the language when and wherever possible.

One of the people he met was Maud Gonne and he tried to teach her Irish, but gave up after a short time, saying that she was too busy spreading revolutionary ideas to take lessons. Like other men, Hyde was taken with her beauty and enjoyed her company. An observer said that all males were stunned by her beauty and grace, but added that they soon got over it. Hyde and Gonne later served together on the board of directors in the Abbey Theatre.[10]

Hyde was a close friend of Frances Crofton, whom he had known since 1882, and seriously considered proposing marriage to her. However, Frances once told him that she had refused a marriage proposal from an army officer, saying that she would never marry, so Hyde changed his mind and dropped the idea. They had an open, honest and platonic relationship. She was musical and artistic and tried in vain to develop a singing voice in Hyde.

In 1892 he met a woman named Lucy Cometina Kurtz, who was friendly with his sister Annette. She was the daughter of a research chemist from Württemberg in Germany and a graduate of Trinity College. Hyde was immediately attracted to her, and in May 1893 Lucy arrived at his family home in Frenchpark for a two-week visit. She came back in June of that year and again in July, and he recorded in his diary, 'things took their course, between hope and despair, certainty and uncertainty, doubt and assurance, anxiety and confidence, but each day the net was closing around my neck until we decided firmly and finally that we were going to get married, and we were publicly engaged'.[11] The couple married on 10 October 1893 in Liverpool and their month-long honeymoon was spent between Paris, the French Riviera and London.

Having returned to Ireland, Hyde resumed his Gaelic League activities and, as president of the league, he was busy touring the country setting up branches and appointing teachers.[12] He was described at this time as a courteous Anglo-Irishman, who dressed in tweeds and had an inner vitality that was conveyed by his piercing eyes.

In the autumn of 1897 he met Lady Gregory while visiting Edward Martyn in Tulira Castle. She watched him as he wheeled his bicycle up the driveway, having combed the countryside in search of stories about Anthony Raftery, the noted blind poet. Because of his enthusiasm and love of stories and the Irish language, she became friends with him immediately and invited him to Coole. Lady Gregory introduced him to the tenants and he began gathering the local folklore stories. Hyde was impressed with life around Kiltartan and became a frequent visitor to Coole – he could arrive anytime during the summer or winter. He also befriended Robert Gregory and they would often hunt for pheasant and woodcock.

On 26 August 1900 a headstone was unveiled to Anthony Raftery at a Gaelic League meeting, of which Lady Gregory was patron, and the speakers included Hyde, W. B. Yeats and Edward Martyn. Hyde's wife, Lucy, accompanied him on this occasion and was described as fashionable but rather distant. Lady Gregory welcomed her departure from Coole as she did Jack Yeats' wife. Lady Gregory later wrote that she would gladly have Hyde and Yeats stay six months at Coole, but a few weeks with their wives would have her hiding in the woods.

Hyde was back in Coole for Christmas 1900, when Lady Gregory sought his advice on her own work and he helped with some translations. She also organised Irish lectures to be presented in Gort Courthouse with Hyde and W. B. Yeats as the speakers. Hyde's play, *The Twisting of the Rope*, was staged on 21 October 1901 for the final season of the Irish Literary Theatre and was said to be a fashionable event for nationalist Dublin. Hyde was under pressure to produce more plays while staying at Coole, where Lady Gregory and Yeats would use scenarios to influence him. One of these plays was *The Poorhouse*, which was the story of an estranged husband meeting his wife in a workhouse. Lady Gregory was certainly impressed by Hyde and considered him the 'apostle of the Irish language'.[13]

As a scholar of the Irish Literary Revival, he was invaluable to Yeats and Lady Gregory. The value he placed on Irish traditions was extreme and he once said he would advocate for the abolition of trousers for Irishmen as they were not in his opinion of Celtic origin.[14] His pioneering work in collecting and editing Irish poetry and stories endeared him to those who loved the Irish language and they knew him by his pen name *An Craoibhín Aoibhinn* (meaning Delightful Little Branch). His involvement in the Gaelic League also brought with it the goodwill and respect of the liberal Protestant population. His reputation as a scholar was widespread and he continued to make many friends among the upper levels of society and academia. Sean O'Casey once said that Hyde was rushing around and shouting in the gates of Dublin Castle, 'It's a Gael I am without shame to myself or danger to you.'[15]

Although they fought for the same cause, there were differences of opinion between Hyde and Patrick Pearse, who was also a member of the Gaelic League. Pearse was becoming more militant, saying that people must take action to save the language, while Hyde preferred the 'softly-softly' approach. One incident that certainly indicates these differences occurred in 1905, in a court case where the use of Irish signs on carts was challenged. At the time it was a legal requirement for owners to have their names on their carts, so the league took advantage of this and requested that the owners have their names displayed in Irish, which was illegal. Although the authorities were reluctant to confront anyone using the Irish names, Pearse still decided to challenge them and went down the legal route. He did this while Hyde was visiting the United States as he knew Hyde would not be in favour of such action. Many years later, Hyde wrote of his irritation:

I left the strictest orders that the question should not be opened in the law courts. I wanted the placing of the Irish forms on the carts to become so common that it could not be interfered with, and the government was not interfering. To my great annoyance this plan of mine was knocked on the head by Pearse, who being a barrister appealed to the higher courts against a fine and argued the case before the Lord Chief Justice Peter the Pecker (Lord O'Brien) and another (Mr Justice Andrews) who complimented him on his knowledge of Irish and his conduct of the case – and promptly decided against him, as any fool with half an eye must have foreseen that they would do. Thus it was made illegal not only to have the name in Irish letters but to have it in any form except the correct English form. I heard Pearse was quite pleased with the compliment the judges paid him, but that was poor compensation for bolting the barn door against Irish names for ever.[16]

In 1906 Hyde was appointed to the royal commission on university education and in 1908 he became a professor of Modern Irish at University College Dublin, a position he held until his retirement in 1932. He continued to publish, attracting both scholarly and popular audiences. He also began taking a modest part in public life.[17] In 1913, during the Dublin Lock-Out, Hyde was not in favour of James Larkin's policies regarding the strikes, which ended in so much suffering for the workers. He felt that Larkin had not fully considered the effect these would have on the workers, which eventually led to victory for the employers.[18]

Hyde continued advocating for the Irish language, saying that the revival of the national language was of paramount importance to the Irish soul. While he was firmly behind the restoration of an Irish identity, he was against physical force. In June 1913 he delivered an important address to the league warning of the dangers of becoming involved in politics. In a raised voice, he stated that it would be detrimental to the movement should this be allowed to happen and warned that involvement in politics would drive out their best members. This eventually became an issue when men like Pearse began making inflammatory speeches on an independent Ireland. Pearse was one of the most gifted and influential Gaelic League members and therefore had a strong following.

The establishment of the Irish Volunteers in November 1913 was a concern for Hyde because so many league members joined. Eoin MacNeill, who was a founder member of the league, was in command of the Volunteers and Hyde believed that he was advocating for an armed rebellion that would seriously undermine Hyde's position within the league. There was a split in the Volunteer movement following the outbreak of war in 1914, after John Redmond, leader of the Irish Party, pledged the Volunteers' support for the British in the war. Hyde was quick to exploit the split, saying that this was the only outcome when politics was involved. However, he did agree that members of the organisation had the personal right to take part in politics outside the Gaelic League.[19]

There were strong anti-Hyde feelings among members of the IRB, which came to a head in 1915 when Hyde was forced to resign as president of the Gaelic League. This was very difficult for him after twenty-two years of dedicated service to the cause of the Irish language; even Pearse was against this move by the

IRB and said that he loved and honoured Douglas Hyde above all leading Irishmen. Pearse's words rang true later when Hyde was described as 'an Irishman and a scholar of whom the Irish nation is justly proud – a man whose name is synonymous with everything patriotic, whole-souled and learned'.[20]

In 1925 Hyde was co-opted by the Free State government as a senator and was also appointed chairman of the Irish Folklore Institute, serving in that position from 1930 until 1934. Although he officially retired in 1932, he continued to work in a wide range of Irish affairs.[21] In 1937 there was a lot of discussion in the newspapers as to who would become the first president of Ireland after the constitution was adopted. When *The Irish Times* suggested Hyde for the position he was not overly impressed and said that this would end any chance he might have had. However, his fears were unfounded and in June 1938 he was inaugurated as the first president of Ireland, with the support of all the political parties.

It is interesting that after some months in office he complained about life in Áras an Uachtaráin because everything was being controlled in rigid civil service fashion. He said that he couldn't take fruit from the greenhouse without first being granted permission by the Board of Works and also complained that he was prevented from even poking the fire because someone would always insist on doing this for him.[22]

On 31 August 1939 President Douglas Hyde received the Freedom of Galway with the overwhelming support of the authorities and the people of the city. He was the first person to be honoured in such a manner in Galway.[23] He suffered a stroke the following year, but continued to carry out his duties from a wheelchair, working closely with An Taoiseach, Éamon de Valera, during the war years. He completed his term of office in 1945.

By this time he was experiencing a lot of illness, but he lived for another four years, dying on 12 July 1949 at his home in the Phoenix Park. His state funeral service took place to St Patrick's Cathedral, Dublin, after which his remains were taken to Frenchpark Churchyard in Co. Roscommon for burial.

Hyde treated everyone equally and was inspired by the people he met in his youth. Although he was sometimes accused of being a bit elusive, he was a passionate partisan and, at the same time, a peacemaker. His reputation as a writer, scholar and, indeed, a cultural patriot continued to grow after his death.[24]

Violet Florence Martin

'MARTIN ROSS'

Novelist 1862–1915

Violet Martin was born on 11 June 1862 in Ross House, Co. Galway. She was the youngest of ten children born to James and Anna Martin (*née* Fox). The Martins were descended from one of the old tribal families of Galway. As a child, Violet gained an understanding of the Irish language and the way of life of the people.[1] She later wrote accounts of everyday life on and around the Ross estate. Looking at her background one can see events that inspired her to write comical stories of Ireland and its people during those times.

Violet Martin was proud of her ancestry and didn't see anything wrong with the landlord system, her family having a good relationship with the tenants. Violet said that when her father died, a widow asked if she could see his body. When she was admitted to the room, there was a tremendous and sustained wail that went through the house, 'like the voice of the grave itself'. The following is Violet's description of their connection with the people:

> The old ways of life are unquestioned at Ross and my father went and
> came among his people in an intimacy as native as the soft air they

breathed. On the crowded estate the old routine of potato planting and cutting was pursued in tranquillity; the people intermarried and subdivided their holdings; few could read and many could not speak English. All were known to the Master, and he was known and understood by them ... subdivisions of the land were permitted and the arrears of rent were given time, or taken in boatloads of turf or worked off by day-labour, and eviction was unheard of. It was give and take, with the personal element always warm in it; as a system it was quite uneconomic, but the hand of affection held it together, and the tradition of centuries was at its back.[2]

Violet later used some of these experiences in the stories she wrote with Edith Somerville, and they were also used in stories of the darker side of Irish life. Ross House was deserted during the land war of 1880, all of the family having already moved away, but she was still affected by the situation and disappointed that the people disliked her class. She knew of one Galway landlord who felt so betrayed by his tenants that he requested that none of them be allowed touch his coffin after his death. She was horrified when she heard that the ears had been cut off a donkey belonging to the Blake family at Renvyle during the land agitation taking place at that time.[3]

Following the death of her father in 1872, the house was leased out on a fifteen-year contract as the family were unable to manage the place. Violet left for Dublin with her mother and her older brother, Robert. She attended Alexandra College, where she developed a strong devotion to the works of Shakespeare, Milton and many other great writers and had a gift for memorising and reciting extracts from their work. Robert Martin found employment as a comic songwriter and also produced some works for the theatre as a means of earning a living.[4]

Violet developed a close friendship with her cousin, playwright William Gorman Wills. As a boy he had been a regular visitor to her home at Ross and although he was much older than her – thirty-four years, in fact – they appear to have had a friendly as well as a good working relationship between 1885 and 1890. She accompanied him on an extended visit to London in 1885, where they attended a number of plays and shows together and also spent time walking in Kew Gardens. Wills had a great admiration for Violet and once told her so, saying that he didn't think he had ever met any lady half as intellectual. She also met Bram Stoker of *Dracula* fame while in London, as he was working as acting manager on a play by Wills.[5] However, though she enjoyed her time in London, her destiny lay in Ireland working with Edith Somerville.[6]

Edith was a second cousin to Violet and was born in 1858 on the Greek island of Corfu. Her father was an army officer and when he retired a year later, the family moved to Castletownshend in Co. Cork where, in 1886, the two women met for the first time and were immediately drawn to each other in friendship. Edith had another cousin named Violet, so she decided to call her new friend 'Martin' to avoid any confusion. By this time, Robert Martin was a well-regarded journalist in London and Violet chose to follow her brother's example and began writing. She decided to use a pseudonym, so she took Martin and added the name of the house in which she was born, thus becoming Martin Ross.[7]

She soon formed a writing partnership with Edith. It is

almost impossible to write about the life of Violet Martin without including Edith Somerville as they were a complete partnership in writing. They also had similar spiritual beliefs and attended church twice on Sundays. While in Dublin, Violet won prizes for Sunday school attendance. The pair not only exploited the rural Irish life when writing, but also included the charming nature of the scenic and picturesque Irish countryside. Their genteel background allowed them to write as commentators or observers of rural life and they did so in a humorous manner. [8]

Within a year of meeting they were working on their first novel, *An Irish Cousin*, which contained descriptions of the idle lifestyle of the landed gentry. A second book, *Naboth's Vineyard*, followed.[9] Both these books highlighted the violent Irish landscape of the land war.[10]

In June 1888 Violet returned to Ross with her mother and sister to try to make the estate financially viable again. This would have been a difficult task by any standard, but it was worse at Ross because the estate had suffered from years of neglect. Violet described the walk towards the house on the day of their arrival:

> The trees had been cut down and rabbits played on the front lawn … Geraldine (her sister) walked in front of us through the wide open gates, between the tall pillars with her face white and her black clothes. Thady O'Connor, the old steward, met her at the gate, and not in any way a 'Royal Enclosure' could be surpassed the way he took off his hat and came silently forward to her, while everyone else came back in dead silence too.[11]

The gardens and house had fallen into a deplorable condition and Violet immediately began to carry out restoration work herself by painting the interior of the house and even making repairs. Having cut down and cleared the wild vegetation that covered the gardens, which was an exhausting task, she replanted them.[12] She recorded that her hands were shaking from working on the avenue, cutting the overgrown edges, and said this would be her daily occupation forever because by the time she got to the end, she had to start all over again as the avenue was over a mile long and both sides had to be done. The family simply couldn't afford to employ the amount of people required to run the estate. Whenever Edith Somerville arrived for a visit, she had to contribute to the housekeeping fund.

They also faced problems previous generations had never known – the changed attitudes because of the rise of nationalism. Nevertheless, some local people did welcome them home and supplied the family with eggs, cabbage and even a chicken, all to be washed down with a bottle of port. Times had certainly changed as an account had to be kept of every penny spent and much of the work had to be carried out by the family themselves. Violet spent some time visiting other landed gentry families around the county and on one occasion she gave an account of the journey to the Morris family in Spiddal, saying that nothing could describe the length of the eleven Irish miles and the loneliness of the road. She said it was like being in mid-ocean with a slight mist that 'tended to increase the unboundedness of the stretches of moor and bog' on a landscape devoid of people.[13]

Regardless of the hard physical work, Violet maintained her collaboration with Edith Somerville, but it must have been a difficult writing partnership because of the actual distance between them. Violet working in Galway and Edith in Cork meant passing manuscripts through the post. This involved having to do corrections after family members had read through their work, and then returning the manuscripts again through the postal service. Nevertheless, they managed well despite the obstacles and became accustomed to working in this manner.[14]

In 1897 they hired a Scottish literary agent named James Pinker, who had a successful reputation and whose clients included Joseph Conrad, H. G. Wells, Oscar Wilde and Arnold Bennett. Pinker was a powerful figure in the business and knew the strengths and weaknesses of publishers.[15] A year later Violet was injured in a hunting accident, having fallen from her horse; this left her an invalid for some time. Although she attended doctors and visited spa towns hoping to gain some relief from the pain, she never fully recovered. Still, this didn't hinder her writing career or indeed her ability to meet deadlines.

That same year, 1898, Somerville and Ross began writing a series of light-hearted stories, and one of the series, entitled *Some Experiences of an Irish R.M.*, proved very successful. The publisher was Longmans and the stories reached a wide audience, having a knock-on effect financially for both of them. The stories centre on a bemused English magistrate, Major Sinclair Yeates, who finds himself dispensing justice amongst the peasantry in west Cork. The authors' own experiences of rural life in Ireland created an authentic feel to the series. (Many years later this became a popular television series and brought both writers to the notice of the general public long after their deaths.)

Violet was described as being small and slight in stature with a delicate feminine look. She had a good sense of humour and was prone to fits of almost unstoppable laughter, even in times when it was deemed inappropriate to laugh. She was outgoing and enjoyed meeting people – she was particularly amused when meeting someone who had presumed she was a man because of the pen-name. She was a relative of Lady Gregory and it was through this connection that she met W. B. Yeats.

Yeats and Violet took an instant liking to each other; perhaps this was because they were alike in some respects. Yeats helped her by doing a critical analysis of works such as *The Real Charlotte* (1894), which won her support in literary circles and among the general public.[16] The book achieved great success in its portrayal of the ascendancy society in the twilight of the Victorian age. Somerville and Ross were also writing travel articles for magazines at this time, including 'Through Connemara in a Governor's Cart' (1892), 'In the Vine Country' (1893), 'Beggars on Horseback' (1895), 'All on the Irish Shore' (1903) and 'Some Irish Yesterdays'.[17]

During a visit to Coole in 1901, Violet met Yeats again and they had a discussion about her work. While he liked Violet, he didn't agree with the comedy aspects of her writing and said that it was humour simply for the sake of humour. Both Yeats and Lady Gregory believed that Somerville and Ross should concentrate on novels exploring life in middle-class society in a more serious manner. Violet successfully defended their writing, pointing out that she enjoyed the comedy and that Pinker also favoured their comedy stories. Violet wasn't above criticising the work of others herself and attacked Synge's play *The Well of the Saints* for his use of dialect as she felt it was not authentic. Nor did she like Yeats and George Moore's production of *Diarmuid and Grania.* Both Somerville and Ross felt that Lady Gregory's use of dialect was not really convincing either and they declined an invitation from Lady Gregory to produce a play for the Irish Literary Theatre. A play would not have proved difficult for them as they had gained so much experience writing novels and had also been collecting Irish phrases, songs, jokes, letters and other items of interest since 1886, which later filled four notebooks that formed their *Collection of Irish Anecdotes.*[18]

Following the death of her mother in 1906, Violet moved to Castletownshend, avoiding the seasonal harvesting at home which would have prevented her from writing.

Both Somerville and Ross had an interest in the women's suffrage movement. In 1908 they travelled to London to attend a large rally in Hyde Park. Christabel Pankhurst was one of the leading organisers and she spoke profoundly on women's rights. They were so overwhelmed by the rally and the speakers that they joined the movement immediately. Upon returning to Ireland, they began campaigning for the cause.[19] They were totally committed to women's suffrage and were elected as president (Somerville) and vice-president (Ross) of the Munster Women's Franchise League. They were also involved in the Conservative and Unionist Women's Suffrage Association, the primary aim of which was to link together smaller suffrage societies that were spread across Ireland to facilitate effective propaganda and educate members on voting rights for women. Being successful writers, both were serious assets to the movement as they helped promote general welfare for women throughout the country.[20]

By 1912 Violet was also taking a serious interest in politics and becoming actively involved in the fight against Home Rule.

Early that year she corresponded with Harold Begbie of *The Daily Chronicle*, who was also arguing against it. The 1911 Act of Parliament had restricted the right of the House of Lords to veto a bill for more than two years, thus allowing the passage of Home Rule if it was passed by the House of Commons. Her concerns were over a change in attitudes of the Irish leadership towards the landlord classes and in April 1912 she attended an anti-Home Rule meeting in Cork organised by unionists. She later wrote that she travelled from Cork to Belfast to witness the signing of a covenant against Home Rule. Somerville had similar worries over Home Rule, but it seems she later mellowed towards the idea; however, Violet never changed her mind on the issue and remained firmly against its introduction.

Nevertheless, she was well aware of the importance of the Irish language and the significance of the Gaelic League, so, regardless of her political tendencies, she returned to studying Irish. She knew Douglas Hyde as he supported both writers and had encouraged Somerville to collect folklore stories from local people around Cork a number of years earlier. Despite her busy schedule, in 1912 Violet made time to visit Edward Martyn and went to Coole to spend some time with Lady Gregory. Her host had just returned from an American tour and they spent time walking and talking in the gardens of Coole. By then Violet was having health problems but continued to work.[21] It was possibly during this period that she signed the Autograph Tree.

With the outbreak of the Great War in 1914, the British government began to encourage the leaders of the suffrage movement to become involved in the war effort. The war changed the political spectrum of the suffrage movement as the women concentrated on supporting the troops at the Front; it also removed the immediate issue of voting rights for women. The government welcomed the women's involvement and recognised that the war could not be fought successfully without their support and their vital role in the munitions and other industries, jobs formerly dominated by men.[22] The war also heralded one of the last published works by the two writers, *With Thanks for the Kind Enquiries,* a pamphlet written for the Conservative and Unionist Women's Suffrage Association. It was an account of the aid that was sent to the Front by the Irish women's suffrage movement.

Violet's health had not been good for some time and it continued to deteriorate. In December 1915 she collapsed and was taken to Glen Vera Nursing Home in Cork, where the doctors believed that she was suffering from a brain tumour. Some people said this had been brought about by the fall from the horse all those years earlier. She didn't recover and died on 21 December. She was buried in the cemetery of St Barrahane in Castletownshend.[23]

Edith Somerville was devastated by the death of her friend, cousin and co-author. Writing to her brother, she said, 'It is no use to cry and to weep ... You might as well be dancing and singing ... Whether I sit on a safety valve or whether I cried my grief to the four winds it would make no difference. Half – the best half – of my life and soul is torn away and there is no words and no tears that can cure my trouble!' She quoted this from *The Real Charlotte.*[24]

Somerville continued to write after Violet's death and, as she had great faith in spiritualism, she believed that Violet still collaborated from beyond the grave through automatic writing during séances. Among the novels she produced during those years were *Mount Music* (1919), *An Enthusiast* (1921), *The Big House at Inver* (1925), *French Leave* (1928), *Sarah's Youth* (1932) and *An Incorruptible Irishman*, which was published later that same year. Because of her belief in Violet's presence in the writing, the books appeared in both their names.

Edith Somerville died on 8 October 1949 at her home in Castlestownshend.[25] Many tributes were paid to the working partnership of Somerville and Ross, but their popularity and reputation dwindled over the years. It seems strange that Somerville's initials do not appear on the Autograph Tree considering that Violet Martin's do.

Lady Margaret Sackville

Poet and Author 1881–1963

Lady Margaret Sackville was born on 24 December 1881 at 60 Grosvenor Street, Mayfair in London and was the youngest child of Reginald Windsor West and Constance Mary Elizabeth Baillie-Cochrane (Countess De La Warr). They had four other children, two boys and two girls. Constance was a second cousin of Queen Victoria and Margaret's father had the family name changed to Sackville-West by royal licence. Reginald was the 2nd Baron of Buckhurst and also held the title of 7th Earl of De La Warr. Furthermore, he had been rector of Withyam in Sussex and chaplain to Queen Victoria before inheriting his title.

Lady Margaret spent most of her youth in Sussex, sometimes interrupted by holidays in Scotland. She was just six years old when she composed her first poem and this began a lifelong love of poetry. Her father died when she was fourteen and two years later her poetry came to the notice of the poet and writer Wilfrid Scawen Blunt. He admired her work and they remained friends all of their lives. She focused much of her attention on entertaining children in her writing and poetry, and in 1901 she published a volume of children's poems. She was described as having a good sense of humour and was of a kind disposition.[1]

In the summer of 1905 Lady Margaret visited Coole with

W. B. Yeats and Countess Cromartie. Both women were admirers
of Yeats' work and it was possibly through this connection that
they were invited to Coole. Jack Yeats was also visiting Coole at
the time and he completed a watercolour sketch of a picnic scene
beside the lake, depicting Robert Gregory relaxed in the company
of Lady Margaret. She was beautiful, talented and well connected
in upper-class society and Lady Gregory may have thought she
might make a suitable wife for her son; however, this was not to
be. It was during this stay that Lady Margaret added her name to
the Autograph Tree. It seems that Lady Gregory later mentioned
to Blunt that she didn't have much interest in Lady Margaret as
she would surely marry and her ideals were likely to subsequently
disappear.[2]

Between 1906 and 1907 Lady Margaret took part in some
of Blunt's plays and he was delighted with her performances.
She also began to publish her poetry in various periodicals,
which included *The English Review, Country Life, The Nation, The
Englishwoman, The Spectator* and *The Pall Mall Gazette*. She wrote
mainly poetry books, which eventually accumulated into twenty-
one volumes. In 1909 she published *Fairy Tales for the Old and
Young*. A year later she expressed her opinion on women in poetry
and felt that this was the only way a woman could express herself
without opposition. She took the opportunity of conveying these
sentiments while writing the introduction for a book entitled *A
Book of Verse by Living Women*, which she had been requested to
edit. In 1911 she published *Bertrud and Other Dramatic Poems*,
a book of verse that displayed her dramatic side. Lady Margaret
became an officer in the newly founded Poetry Recital Society
and proved a great asset to the organisation. During this period

of her life she does not seem to have had much interest in men; however, this changed in 1912 when she met James Ramsay MacDonald.[3]

A prominent politician and labour leader, MacDonald was born on a farm in Lossiemouth, Scotland in 1866, which made him fifteen years her senior. He left school at thirteen years of age to work on the farm to help support his family. He travelled to London six years later, where he found employment as an office clerk and also worked as an accountant and journalist. Despite leaving school at such an early age, MacDonald had somehow managed to educate himself: he liked science, history and economics, and also became interested in socialism. MacDonald joined the Fabian Society and became one of its speakers.[4]

Meeting Lady Margaret had a huge impact on his life over the following years. He fell in love with her, but it was a romance that proved difficult for both of them as they were from two totally different social and educational backgrounds. He was the son of a farmer; she was the daughter of an earl. She was Catholic; he was Presbyterian. Nevertheless, he proposed to her on at least three occasions, but she refused all his offers of marriage. MacDonald had already been married, but his wife, who was also named Margaret, had died in 1911 from blood poisoning. Despite her refusal of marriage, Lady Margaret continued to see him and they also corresponded through letters. While many contemporaries, including a mutual friend, Lady Ottoline Morrell, stated that Lady Margaret and MacDonald were just friends, evidence to the contrary later came to light. In 1915, shortly after MacDonald had proposed to her for the second time, Lady Margaret received a letter from him in which he wrote about their love being wholehearted and immutable. He said that it was the most natural thing in the world that they should enter its holiest place. He addressed her as 'my own dearie' in many of his letters, of which about 150 have survived, and some of these indicate that they had a fully fledged love affair during those years. Another letter from MacDonald stated, 'Dearest beloved, it is such a beautiful morning that you ought to be here and we should be walking in the garden. And if we were walking in the garden, what more should we do where the bushes hid us?'[5]

MacDonald sometimes complained that she did not write as often as he did, or with the same fervour, and he was delighted on the occasions when she did write expressing her passion. Following one love letter, MacDonald responded by saying, 'That was a very loving letter I had from you yesterday. I feel its kisses. It brought you with it and I slept with my head on your breast last night.' Later he wrote, 'Do you dream that I come to you? Do I come to you when you are not dreaming? Do I kiss you and lie on your breast?' She also sent him flowers, which he described as 'fragile like kisses'. MacDonald was the father of six children; Lady Margaret never ignored them and sometimes sent them toys. MacDonald seems to have been a very understanding man; even after her refusals of marriage he wrote, 'It was so refreshing to see you again and so hard to part with you ... I am sure it is right that we should not marry but what heartaches you give me! You are my own loved one and I want you always.'[6] On another occasion he wrote about how much he would grieve if her love for him brought her into conflict with anyone. All of these extracts certainly dispel the notion that they were simply good friends!

It seems that it was formal barriers that prevented Lady Margaret from accepting his marriage proposals, though there was also the question of religion and she was possibly worried about how her aristocratic family and friends might view such a union.[7] Despite these concerns, she continued to write and sometimes expressed herself by sending him poetry. Much of her time was spent between Edinburgh and Midlothian in Scotland, and this resulted in them spending time together. She felt as much at home in Scotland as she did in England.

However, there were differences of opinion between them on certain issues. While she sympathised with his work against social injustice, she deplored his attacks on the landed gentry. As she was a pacifist, the outbreak of the Great War in 1914 caused her much distress and she joined the Union of Democratic Control, an unpopular anti-war movement. However, other members of her family held different views and in 1915 her brother, Lieutenant Gilbert Sackville, was killed in action. She could never fully understand why women supported the war effort, and in 1916 she published a collection of poems, *The Pageant of War*, where she denounced women who condoned the war as betrayers of their sons. Needless to say this collection was met with much hostility, but she would not change her opinions on the war and its brutal consequences.

In 1919 her collection of *Selected Poems* was published and Blunt had an input in this work.[8]

In 1924 the Labour Party, under the leadership of Ramsay MacDonald, formed the new British government. When summoned by the king to be installed as prime minister, MacDonald didn't wear the cloth cap, which had been worn by previous labour leaders; instead, he wore the proper frock coat and carried a ceremonial sword, which was seen almost as treachery to the labour movement. Many viewed it as a sell-out to an ancient and upper-class tradition.[9] Was his decision to adopt this aristocratic dress-style influenced by Lady Margaret?

Following his election, MacDonald invited her to stay with him in the official residence at Chequers in Buckinghamshire. Over the following years the affair stagnated and eventually ended. MacDonald would love again, but never with the same intensity that he experienced with his beautiful Lady Margaret Sackville.[10]

In 1925 she published *Three Fairy Plays* and became the first president of the Scottish PEN society. She was also a fellow of the Royal Society of Literature. In October 1930 she spoke before the society when presenting her work *Some Aspects of Modern Scottish Literature*. By 1936 Lady Margaret was living in Cheltenham and was the main reviewer for a local newspaper. Through her involvement in the local literary circle, she became the most prominent poet in Cheltenham. She was also a founder and first president of the North Gloucestershire Centre of Poetry. During the Second World War, she became involved in fundraising for the Duke of Gloucester's Red Cross and some of her activities included giving talks and reading poetry, her own as well as poems from the Great War poets.

She produced three illustrated poetry books during the 1940s and her achievements in literature were recognised in 1949, when she was awarded the Schroeder Foundation Medal. She continued to publish throughout the 1950s and her final work, a volume of essays on the Whitehouse Terrace salon, was released in 1963. She never married and does not seem to have had any relationships other than that with MacDonald.

On 18 April 1963 Lady Margaret Sackville died of a heart condition in Rokeby Nursing Home, Cheltenham. A bronze bust was commissioned in Edinburgh, which displayed a woman of great beauty.[11] Lady Margaret remained true to her feelings for MacDonald for almost thirty years after his death and kept their love affair and the letters a closely guarded secret. Some people must have known, but if they did, they were discreet, as this was not something that became the subject of idle gossip. The question still remains: why did the affair end? Was it perhaps because they felt that a union such as this could cause a scandal? The love letters only came to light after Lady Margaret's death and the fact that she kept them could indicate how much she truly loved MacDonald.[12] All of her letters were handed over to the Historic Manuscript Collection in Cheltenham, but the collection is incomplete as there are some letters missing. Nevertheless, it is from this collection that so much is now known of her liaisons with Ramsay MacDonald.[13]

Countess of Cromartie

Author 1878–1962

Sibell Lilian Sutherland-Leveson-Gower (Countess of Cromartie) was born on 14 August 1878. Her father was Francis Mackenzie Sutherland-Leveson-Gower, the 2nd Earl of Cromartie, and her mother was the Honourable Lilian Janet Macdonald. The couple had another daughter, Lady Constance Sutherland-Leveson-Gower.[1] The Earldom of Cromartie is a title that was created for members of the Mackenzie family and dates from 1703. The family had supported the Jacobite Rebellion of 1745 and lost their land, and two of them were captured and sentenced to death, having pleaded guilty to high treason before the House of Lords. However, both men were pardoned and thus escaped the hangman and, in 1784, an act of parliament restored the family estates. The title 'Cromartie' subsequently passed down through the family to Sibell's father. On his death in 1893 the title was suspended, but was re-established again in 1895, which ensured that Sibell became the 3rd Countess of Cromartie.[2]

Sibell married Lieutenant Colonel Edward Walter Blunt, a professional soldier, on 16 December 1899 in St Margaret's Church at Westminster in London.[3] There were eight bridesmaids supporting her with two little girls acting as train-bearers, and the guest list included many of the leading titled people of the period. Her uncle, the Duke of Sutherland, gave the countess away, and the newly married couple walked down an aisle lined on both sides with military officers representing the Royal Field Artillery and Royal Horse Artillery, with swords raised above the heads of the bride and groom to form an arch. The Duke and Duchess of Connaught presented the groom with a silver cigar box for the occasion, while the Marquis of Lorne gave the bride a gold watch bracelet with pearls.[4] They had four children: Lady Janet Frances, born in 1900; Roderick Grant Francis (1904); Walter Osra (1906) and Isobel (1911).[5] While most sources record her husband's surname as Blunt-Mackenzie, he only assumed the additional surname of Mackenzie in 1905 and the countess later discontinued the use of the surname Blunt. Her eldest son, later the 4th Earl of Cromartie, served as a major in the Seaforth Highlanders, fought in the Second World War, was captured by the Germans in 1940 and remained a prisoner of war until the war ended in 1945.[6]

The countess was a wealthy woman with several claims to distinction, being one of the largest female landowners in Scotland, Ireland and England. She was well known in the literary world as a writer of romance and stories of historical interest and Highland life. One of her books, *The End of the Song and Other Stories* (1904), enjoyed much success among lovers of Highland lore. The countess was also well connected in the high-society circles of the day; in fact it was Queen Victoria who reinstated the earldom title of Cromartie to her. It was said that the countess 'like so many modern women' had a deep interest in psychic matters and her one-act drama *The Finding of the Sword*, produced in 1907, had a strong supernatural presence.[7]

The countess visited Coole in the summer of 1905 with Lady Margaret Sackville. Lady Gregory had introduced her to W. B. Yeats during a previous visit to London and she invited him to tea the following evening in Suffolk House, the home of the Duchess of Sutherland, who was an aunt of the countess.[8] The name Stafford House meant nothing to Yeats and he went in his old blue coat. It was a magnificent town house, which was a favourite gathering place for artists and literary people, and the duchess was described as being very beautiful and a wonderful hostess. To his utter amazement, Yeats found himself in what he felt was a 'palace' and was shown to the Countess of Cromartie's room at the end of a long corridor. The Duchess of Sutherland came into the room a short time later; she said that there was a children's party going on in the other end of the house and invited them to join her. The countess, Yeats and the duchess then made their way to the party where there were some fifty to sixty children all playing together. A tall, very beautiful woman was standing amid the children. The duchess turned to Yeats and said, 'May I present you to the Queen?' It was Queen Alexandra. Having been introduced, they spoke for about five minutes during which time she told Yeats that she admired his poetry. He then returned with the countess for tea. The entire evening was a surprise for Yeats and he later commented that he had never seen so many beautiful people together. He also thought of what the 'United Irishmen' would think of the company he was keeping and looked forward to the effect it would have on 'Mrs MacBride', Maud Gonne.

The countess occasionally attended Yeats' poetry evenings in London. One man described her as a young witch, who looked very wicked and like a sorceress. She was a member of the Celtic Association and also had a strong interest in spiritualism, which was something she had in common with Yeats.[9] She became president of the Spiritualist Society of Great Britain, travelled widely in the Middle East and claimed to have a Phoenician spirit guide.[10]

Her writing career spanned many years and some of her books include *The Web of the Past* (1905), *Sons of the Milesians* (1906), *The Days of Fire* (1908), *Out of the Dark* (1910), *Sword-of-the-Crowns* (1910), *The Golden Guard* (1912), *The Decoy* (1914), *Whosoever Shall Receive* (1924), *The Temple of the Winds* (1925), *Heremon the Beautiful* (1930) and *Zeo the Scythian* (1935).[11]

She made her home at Kildary in the county of Ross and Cromarty in Scotland, located in a former maritime county in the Scottish Highlands. Ross and Cromarty is a historic region stretching from the North Sea to Minch. During the sixteenth century, these areas were occupied by different Scottish clans, including the ancestors of the countess.[12] In 1935 she handed over all her estates in Ross-shire to her son, Roderick, who was by then Lord Tarbat.[13] The Countess of Cromartie died on 20 May 1962.[14]

John Masefield

Poet and Novelist 1878–1967

John Masefield was born on 1 June 1878 in Herefordshire, England, the son of George and Caroline Masefield (*née* Parker) and the third of six children. His mother died in 1885 following the birth of her last baby and after her death, George, who was already suffering from mental illness, became more and more deranged, creating an unstable environment for the children. John was sent to Warwick School in 1888 and, when his father died in 1890, the children were sent to an uncle and aunt to be looked after.

The following year, the thirteen-year-old Masefield was appointed to HMS *Conway* in Liverpool, where he began training as an officer with the merchant navy. While the course was tough and there was the added dread of bullying, he was extremely happy working on-board. One of his first long voyages was to Chile in 1894 and the journey took him around the Cape of Good Hope, formerly known as the Cape of Storms.

Later he was dismissed from the navy; however, he returned to the sea and then, on a voyage to New York, jumped ship when the vessel docked and secured work in a public house for a short time before working in a carpet factory. Masefield spent much of his free time reading; he was particularly interested in poetry and soon realised that this was his true calling in life. He returned to England in July 1897, with few possessions beyond several pounds and a revolver. It seems Masefield said that if he didn't find work, he would use the gun on himself. However, he found a job as a clerk and also began writing, producing works such as *Salt-Water Ballads* and *Ballads and Poems*. His writing had seafaring themes. He began to attract the attention of the public, but his real introduction to the literary world came in 1900, when he met W. B. Yeats in London. This was an important encounter for Masefield as it led to him becoming a full-time writer.[1]

He met Yeats at the Rhymers' Club and they became friends. As a result, Masefield was soon part of a literary circle where he met many other poets and writers. The club had been established in 1891 by Yeats for people involved in the arts, including George Russell and Douglas Hyde. In 1903 Masefield was introduced to John Millington Synge after he had returned from Paris and they became good friends.

It seems that Masefield would sometimes study people and their habits and believed that men were on their best behaviour when talking to women. He felt that Synge confirmed this theory when he observed how at ease and clear the man was when talking to females. Synge was a good subject to observe as he was generally quiet and reserved. Speaking of his newfound friends from the Emerald Isle, Masefield said, 'I had known a good many Irish people; but they had all been vivacious and picturesque, rapid in intellectual argument, and vague about life.'[2] With Lady Gregory being part of the London literary circle, it was inevitable that they would meet and like so many others, he received and accepted an official invitation to Coole.

Masefield loved the English countryside and had a great knowledge of its people. He had many practical experiences of everyday life behind him at this stage. Life at sea was not easy in those days, but he had made the best of his experiences and carried many memories of this period into his birth as a poet and writer. One can see this from the following description by his biographer, L. A. G. Strong, of the qualities and impressions that moulded him into a man of the people:

> The sea and seafaring folk had been stamped upon the impression-able years of his adolescence. He had learned to fend for himself, and to observe people who worked hard for their living by earning his own amongst them; and, at the right time, the right reading had come his way in a book store, and the future Laureate had drunk of a pure English spring of inspiration, in a country which isolated him, and so increased his power. Strongest of all, his youth gave him a life-long and passionate sympathy with the under-dog, the underprivileged, the victim, the man or woman or child (or animal) who is hard done by.[3]

Masefield was described as a tall, rather thin man with blue eyes. He was well known for his courtesy and friendliness and later in his career he took much pleasure in helping young writers.

While in London, he met an Irishwoman named Constance de la Cherois Crommelin. She was of French Huguenot ancestry and the proprietor of a girl's school in London, and was extremely wealthy in comparison to Masefield. She was also eleven years his senior. Age difference or disparity of wealth made no difference to either of them, however, as soon a relationship developed. The couple were married in London on 23 July 1903 and had two children: a daughter, Judith (book illustrator), and a son, Lewis (novelist).

Masefield was known to have many relationships with women, but all are believed to have been platonic. One was with an actress named Elizabeth Robins, to whom he wrote every day. Another woman in his life was Florence Lamont, who supported him in his theatrical work. He was deeply interested in the theatre for many years and even set up a stage at his home in Boars Hill near Oxford, but he did not achieve the same success in the theatre as he did with his poetry and books.[4] Nevertheless, Masefield fared no worse than many other poets who turned playwright. In fact, he worked out somewhat better.

In 1909 his most successful play, *The Tragedy of Nan*, went into production. In 1911 the Home University Library published his book *Shakespeare*. Masefield had wondered for a long time about the works of Shakespeare and had discussed this with Synge, a man whom he felt burned with the same energy as Shakespeare. Yeats admired the work, saying that Masefield's *Shakespeare* blazed with energy. It is believed that this book was crucial in Masefield's life and was one of the few volumes written about Shakespeare up to that time, which was surprising to people in the world of theatre.[5] Also in 1911, his poem 'The Everlasting Mercy' appeared in print, and the following year *The Window in the Bye Street* was published.

In 1913 Masefield published his acclaimed *Dauber*, influenced by his time at sea. In 1914, when the Great War broke out, Masefield joined the Red Cross, and in 1915 sailed with the British troops to Gallipoli, where his newfound position as a humanitarian exposed him to the horrors of the conflict. The assault on Gallipoli by the Allies began at dawn on 25 April 1915 under the command of Sir Ian Hamilton.[6] Following an intense bombardment, the troops began landing at a number of locations along the sea front. The war in Gallipoli continued until the Allies pulled out later that year, by which time both sides had suffered appalling casualties.[7] Masefield sailed home with the troops and carried with him the terrible memories of the suffering the soldiers had endured so far from home. After his return to England, his horrific experiences led him to publish *Gallipoli*, which has been described as one of the finest accounts of modern warfare, giving graphic insights into the horrors experienced by common soldiers. Masefield then travelled to the United States, representing the government, to give accounts of the British war efforts, and in 1917 he was awarded honorary doctorates from both Harvard and Yale universities, which were the first of many honours bestowed on him. He was also offered a knighthood, but refused this accolade and did so on several occasions throughout his life.[8]

In 1919 Masefield produced his most popular poem, 'Reynard the Fox', which is about a fox hunt but represents how the animal would view the event. 'Reynard the Fox' is a typical example of Masefield's good nature and of his concern for wildlife. He later revealed his reason for writing the poem and how the idea came to him: one day, while walking through a wooded area, he was a bit shocked when saw a fox hole blocked up. He then placed himself in the position of the fox and pondered what it would be like to be hunted across miles of countryside only to discover, on reaching your place of safety, that there was no refuge. It was described as the finest English narrative poem of the century and also one of the most outstanding in the English language.

His book *Lost Endeavour* also achieved complete success and has been described as a single sustained blaze of imagination about a boy who is kidnapped while out on an errand for his schoolmaster, taken overseas and sold as a slave. As the story progresses, it turns into a treasure hunt, but for a treasure of an unusual kind.

Masefield's other children's books were also described as excellent and included *The Midnight Folk* and its sequel *The Box of Delights*, which were said to be among the most robust volumes ever written for children. They have a touch of magic to them. *The Midnight Folk* is about a boy whose governess is a witch and she is finally defeated with the help of a group of animals, including a rat. In the sequel, she returns to prevent the celebration of Christmas, but is again defeated. His work proved most attractive to children. It has been said that the real test of a good children's book is that adults can also enjoy the story and Masefield sailed through this test triumphantly, satisfying all imaginations and tastes.

While he experienced wonderful credits for most of his work, his poem 'The Everlasting Mercy' caused consternation in some quarters because he described belching at meals and placing feet on the table. Although there were questions about its quality as a poem, its originality and power were beyond doubt. L. A. G. Strong, said that anyone who could make the British public argue about poetry, 'however stupidly, has accomplished the feat of a lifetime'.[9] Masefield had certainly achieved this: not only those interested in poetry, but also those who didn't have an understanding of his poems were discussing this work. These disputes by the populace contributed to the foundations to his fame.[10]

In 1930 Masefield became poet laureate, a position he took very sincerely and more seriously than his predecessors.[11] There was always a great deal of debate about the function and responsibility of someone in this position. The popular view at the time was that whoever was appointed had to celebrate in verse any event of national importance. However, many people felt that, because of the quality of his work, Masefield should simply go on writing the type of poetry that earned him the title. He ultimately felt obliged to justify the honour by producing the sort of work that he believed was expected of him. However, he justified himself many times over when he wrote *The Nine Days Wonder*, subtitled *The Operation Dynamo*, which had more of an impact than all of his official poems combined. This book of just fifty-seven pages of prose and poems is a short account of the last nine days of the campaign in Belgium. With regard to *The Nine Days Wonder*, it was said that if he had written nothing else in his life, this small book would have made his appointment a memorable one.

Masefield was a copious writer and one of the most uneven of his time; nevertheless, it was believed that unevenness in writing where there was a prolific output was the sign of a genius. His position as poet laureate also stimulated him to produce a number of other works and, while he was somewhat shy, Masefield was an effective speaker in public once he grabbed the attention of the audience. He was a sensitive man who was burning with an abundance of creative energy, and both of these qualities must have been of great benefit in his prestigious role. However, he was happiest among simple people and comfortable in their surroundings.

There was a mystical feeling to some of his work and a spirituality that was recognised by Strong when he wrote:

> For Masefield the visible universe everywhere glimmers with eternal light. It has been his great quality as a poet, the quality which entitles us, in spite of all his unevenness, his banalities, his failure to sustain a high tension, to use the word great in talking of him[self], that he has managed to dramatise his feelings for spiritual reality in movement. The movement of the events he describes, the movement of his verse, the sudden impetuous quickening which so often surprise and delight the reader, embody a mysticism which less sensitive, less robust nerves would have left nebulous and unexpressed.[12]

Among his best novels were *The Bird of Dawning*, which appeared in 1933, followed by *Dead Ned* in 1938. Masefield was awarded the Order of Merit in 1935 and two years later he was elected president of the Society of Authors. He worked tirelessly for this organisation from the moment of his appointment. From 1944 to 1949 he served as president of the National Book League. While his subjects covered periods taken from throughout the centuries, he is best known for his children's books. Masefield continued to write even in old age, by which time his *Collected Poems* had sold over 200,000 copies. This must have pleased him greatly, not just from a financial viewpoint, but also because he always wished to be associated with the people. He was also an avid writer of letters, one source estimating that he wrote over 250,000 letters in his lifetime.

His wife, Constance, died in 1960, but he lived on until 1967. His daughter, Judith, took care of him in his old age, until he died on 12 May of that year at his home, Burcote Brook near Abingdon. His death was caused by gangrene, which developed in his foot. He refused to have it amputated and the outcome was fatal. His body was cremated and his ashes interred in Poet's Corner at Westminster Abbey, London.[13]

Masefield was a poet of the people. Of his contribution to the world of poetry it was written:

Masefield throughout his life posed the great questions, and, as a poet should, mimed the answers. The score, then, for John Masefield, his contribution to the life and literature of his time, is one supreme long narrative poem, wholly English, which no one but he could have written: two or three other long poems, original in matter and manner, which brought violent gusts of energy to the polite, faintly countrified air of poetry in their days: a handful of short pieces which have passed into current thought: a just, spare, and impassioned commentary upon England's greatest writer: two chronicles of high achievement which match their theme: and other books, poems and plays lit with flashes of intense but intermittent light. He has never written meanly, coldly, or carelessly. He has always sided with the weak against the strong. Sensitive, gentle, and brave, he has found his mainspring in love of life and compassion for all that live it … Masefield has given to every task the best he could command; when all the bells of his talent chimed with the occasion, the result has been noble.[14]

Robert Ross

Journalist and Gallery Manager
1869–1918

Robert Ross was born in Tours, France on 25 May 1869. His father, John Ross, of Irish descent, was the attorney general for Upper Canada and had married twice, with second wife Augusta Elizabeth Baldwin being the mother of Robert. She was the daughter of Robert Baldwin, the former prime minister of Upper Canada. John Ross had seven children between both marriages and Robert was the youngest. John died while Robert was still very young and his mother took the entire family to live in London, where Robert was educated by a private tutor because of an illness.[1] His health had obviously improved as a teenager and he was able to attend university. While in Oxford, in 1886, Ross met thirty-two-year-old Oscar Wilde, who was on a visit there.

Wilde was married to Constance Mary Lloyd and they had two children, Cyril and Vyvyan, at the time. However, Wilde had a loathing for his wife because he felt that her body was out of shape after she had given birth to his two sons. By this time, Ross was aware of his own homosexuality and it seems he made no secret of it, or at least not to Wilde. In fact, he made it clear that he was attracted to him; they became close and had their first sexual encounter in October of that year. Within a short time,

Ross had moved into the Wilde household as a paying guest and Wilde carried on this affair with his teenage lover without his wife suspecting. Nevertheless, he had no intention of leaving Constance, as he had to keep up appearances and didn't wish to be separated from his children either. This situation went on for some three months, after which it is believed the sexual relationship ended, but Ross remained close to Wilde throughout his life and became his most trusted and reliable friend.[2]

In 1888 Ross enrolled in King's College, Cambridge, where among his studies, he took history.[3] Physical attacks on known or indeed suspected homosexuals were common at that time. Ross's long hair attracted the attention of some of his peers, and he was attacked and thrown into a fountain by some of the undergraduates. He developed pneumonia and almost died following this incident, but the people who instigated the attack were never charged with the assault.[4]

At the end of his first year in Cambridge, he travelled to Edinburgh to begin training as a journalist with *The Scots Observer*. Ross changed his religion in 1894, converting to the Roman Catholic Church. He had two other serious homosexual relationships, one with William More Adey, which lasted some fifteen years, during which time they shared a house together. The second was with Freddie Stanley Smith and was a shorter relationship, with the affair ending in 1917 when Smith was assigned to the diplomatic service in Stockholm.[5]

Ross was in the company of Oscar Wilde when Wilde was arrested for suspected homosexual activities in 1895, allegedly with Lord Alfred Douglas. While the case against Wilde had nothing to do with Ross, the fact that he was with the defendant during the arrest caused much concern for his relatives. Ross was involved in some clubs and forced to resign from them because of the situation. It was clear to both men that a trial was imminent; Wilde could have evaded it, but chose to remain in the country, which meant that he would face the charges in public.

Ross had earlier made Constance aware of the impending arrest, which upset her terribly; she burst into tears and told him that she hoped her husband would leave the country before the warrant could be issued.[6] Ross continued to support Wilde throughout the ordeal, but the outcome of the court case was a prison sentence for Wilde and he served two years. Following his release in 1897, he travelled to France.

When he died in Paris on 30 November 1900, Wilde left Ross as the executor of his will and estate, which was, in effect, bankrupt.[7] Over the following years, Ross assumed the responsibility of clearing Wilde's debts so that his estate could be released from receivership. He had finished the payments by 1906 and secured the copyright for Wilde's children, who had taken a new surname, Holland, because of the scandal.[8] Ross later told a close friend, Christopher Millard, that the reason he helped the children was because he had been the first person to lead their father astray.[9]

In 1901 Ross was appointed as director and administrator of the Carfax Art Gallery in Ryder Street, London. Under his eight-year term, the gallery gained a reputation for exhibiting the work of unknown artists. In 1908 he published *The Collected Works of Oscar Wilde* (fourteen volumes) and from 1908 to 1912 he worked as an art critic with *The Morning Post*. He took this position very seriously and, in addition to his other functions, he did his utmost to introduce the general public to the world of art, encouraging people to have an opinion on the subject. Ross was not shy when it came to expressing his opinions and was a great supporter of French impressionism and a strong critic of post-impressionists. He was very outspoken as an art critic and would express his views regardless of whether they were supportive or critical, which was evident from the fact that in 1910 he dismissed the work of Cézanne as a failure during the artist's exhibition that year.[10] He also published book reviews in *The Times*. Ross was a friend of George Moore and reviewed some of his work.[11] It was possibly through this connection that Ross was invited to Coole and became immortalised on the tree.

Ross was also a member of the Contemporary Art Society, and in 1912 he was elected to the executive committee of the National Arts Collection Fund. That same year he was appointed as the London director of the new Johannesburg Art Gallery. Moreover, he worked for the Board of Inland Revenue, which included estimating the value of paintings and drawings in various collections.

While he was absorbed in work, his private life was catching up with him and in 1913 he became embroiled in several court litigations with Lord Alfred Douglas.[12] The problem had been caused by the publication of *De Profundis*, a letter written by Oscar Wilde to Douglas and entrusted to Ross. While Ross had omitted all references to Douglas in his publication, the edited text hinted at a relationship between Douglas and Wilde. Douglas had since married and converted to Catholicism and was adamant that such a relationship had never existed. He threatened legal action any time the issue was raised in books or articles. A year earlier, in 1912, he had taken Arthur Ransom to court over a publication that connected him to Wilde, and during the court proceedings the contentious letter in *De Profundis* was read. Douglas was furious and stormed out of court. Because of this he set out on a campaign of revenge against Ross. This continued until 1915, when Ross decided to take legal action himself and sued Douglas for libel, but the court case caused more harm to Ross's reputation – due to the revelations about his sexuality – than it did to Douglas, and Ross was lucky to escape prosecution. The anxiety caused from the public attacks by Douglas contributed to the health problems that Ross later experienced.[13]

Some of his friends united and decided to raise finance in support of Ross because of the harm caused to his reputation during the court appearances. But Ross insisted that any money raised should be donated to the Slade School of Fine Art in London and was to be used as a Robert Ross memorial prize. During the Great War of 1914–18, his home in London became a place of respite for battle-weary soldiers on leave from the Front. Two of the soldiers who took advantage of this sanctuary were the renowned poets Siegfried Sassoon and Wilfred Owen. None of these men were involved with Ross beyond finding refuge in his apartment at 40 Half Moon Street in Mayfair.

In 1917 Ross acted as the London buyer for the Felton bequest of the Melbourne Art Gallery and also served as a trustee for the Tate Gallery. He died suddenly on 5 October 1918 at his home in Mayfair. His wish – to be cremated – was honoured by his family and friends. However, it took many years for his second request to be carried out – to have his ashes placed in the tomb of Oscar Wilde in Père Lachaise Cemetery in Paris. This happened on 30 November 1950, the fiftieth anniversary of Wilde's death.[14]

Elinor Monsell

Engraver and Portrait Painter
1871–1954

Elinor Monsell was a noted Irish illustrator, engraver and portrait painter. According to most sources, she was born in Limerick in 1871.[1] However, another record indicates that her birth took place in 1879.[2] While it seems more likely that she was born in Limerick, *The Encyclopedia of Ireland* indicates the she may have been born in Co. Kerry. It mentions that following the death of her father, her brother, John Robert Monsell, was sent to Limerick, where he and Elinor were brought up by an uncle.[3]

John later moved to London where he worked as a magazine and book illustrator and became a children's author. Elinor also moved to London, having been awarded a scholarship, and began studying at the Slade School of Fine Art. It's believed that while still a student she learned the art of wood engraving from the Japanese print enthusiast and poet Laurence Binyon, who wrote the famous Great War poem 'For the Fallen'. In 1903 Monsell's work appeared in *The Venture*, an annual of art and literature, which was edited by Laurence Housman and W. Somerset Maugham.

Although she lived in England, she was involved in the Irish Literary Revival, being a close acquaintance of W. B. and Jack

Yeats, and Lady Gregory and her son, Robert. She had sketched with Robert Gregory and both were students of the Slade School. It seems that she met W. B. Yeats during a visit to Coole in 1899 and he liked her work, so, in 1904, Monsell was invited by Yeats to design the Abbey Theatre logo. Her creation was a pear-wood engraving of a romantic image of the ancient Queen Maeve of Connacht with an Irish wolfhound. It was designed for the opening of the theatre and was extremely well received.

She married Bernard Darwin on 31 July 1906 in St Luke's Church, Chelsea, London. Bernard was a grandson of the British naturalist Charles Darwin, and was born in Kent in 1876. The couple had three children: Ursula, Robert and Nicola Darwin. Ursula was known for her work as a potter and studied at the Royal College of Art under William Murray. She later worked with Michael Cardew at both Winchcombe Pottery and Wenford Bridge Pottery.

In 1906 Monsell created the cover for Stephen Gwynn's *The Fair Hills of Ireland*, which was published that year. In 1907 Yeats commissioned her to design the pressmark for the Dun Emer Press, co-founded in 1902 by Evelyn Gleeson and the Yeats sisters, Lily and Lolly. It was Evelyn Gleeson who came up with the idea for the company logo. She was influenced by the Gaelic revival and decided to name her home and the company 'Emer' after the wife of legendary Irish hero Cú Chulainn. Monsell completed the design, which portrayed the Irish mythical figure of Emer standing beside a tree. The company evolved into the Cuala Press and functioned under this name from 1908 up to the late 1940s, publishing a wide range of works by Irish authors, such as Yeats, Lady Gregory and John Millington Synge amongst others. Monsell also provided the original wood-engraved designs for Vale Press publications, founded by Charles Ricketts.

Her other work included paintings such as 'A Doorway', 'Child with Toy Bird' and 'The Annunciation', which were exhibited in 1913 at the Whitechapel Exhibition of Irish Art in London. She also painted a portrait of the poet and author Aubrey Thomas De Vere when he was eighty-seven years old. In addition, this gifted artist was an excellent illustrator and some of her drawings appeared in the second annual volume of *The Shanachie*, an 'Irish Miscellany Illustrated' collection, along with works by Jack B. Yeats and William Orpen. This accompanying text was the work of a number of Irish writers, including W. B. Yeats, Stephen Gwynn, Lady Gregory and George Bernard Shaw. Moreover, Monsell introduced her husband's cousin Gwen Raverat (*née* Darwin) (1885–1957) to the process of wood engraving. Raverat later became one of the leading figures in the British wood-engraving revival.

In 1924 Monsell had her illustrations published in *The Dublin Magazine*, an Irish literary journal founded and edited by the poet Seumas O'Sullivan. A monthly magazine, it featured fiction, poetry, drama and reviews, and most of the contributors were Irish writers, including Samuel Beckett, Austin Clarke, Patrick Kavanagh and Padraic Fallon. Monsell was competing against the top artists when one considers that the first issue was designed by Harry Clarke.

By this period, Bernard Darwin was writing books for children and Monsell worked closely with her husband creating the illustrations. The first of these was *The Tale of Mr Tootleoo*, published in London in 1925–26 by Nonesuch Press and described as a charming children's tale surrounding a character named Mr Tootleoo. A number of other books involving this character followed in a series. Another children's book she illustrated was *Every Idle Dream*, described as a wonderful work with charming illustrations.

Elinor Monsell Darwin died on 2 May 1954 and was buried in St Mary the Virgin Churchyard, Downe, Kent, close to Down House, the old home of the Darwin family. Her husband Bernard died on 18 October 1961 in Filsham House Nursing Home, St Leonards-on-Sea. It could be said that outside of her illustrative work, Monsell left a lasting legacy in the Abbey Theatre logo, as the new configuration of the logo still contains her three original elements: Queen Maeve, the Irish wolfhound and the Rising Sun.[4]

Dame Ethel Smyth

Composer, Writer and
Suffragist 1858–1944

Dame Ethel Smyth was born on 22 April 1858 in 5 Lower Seymour Street, London, the fourth of eight children born to Major-General John Smyth and his wife Emma Struth. In her early years, Ethel was educated mainly at home, and later at a school in Putney. From childhood, she loved the outdoor life and sports, particularly tennis, and was also a keen hunter, so she was considered a bit of a tomboy. While music was not a prominent part of her early childhood, she developed an interest in it, having been influenced by a governess who had been a student at Leipzig Conservatory.[1]

Her father was commander of the Artillery Depot at Woolwich and later served in a similar post with the Royal Artillery at Aldershot. General Smyth was an uncompromising man and rigid in his views, so he ruled his home with strict Victorian codes of conduct. In contrast, his wife was witty and elegant and had an artistic temperament.

Most of Ethel's childhood was spent at their country home in Frimley near Aldershot. From an early age she proved strong-willed and somewhat rebellious.[2] General Smyth could resort to physically beating the children when he felt it was required and Ethel once received a thrashing from him for stealing some barley sugar. Such was the punishment that the marks were still noticeable two weeks later. Ethel was understandably always closer to her mother, whom she adored. She remembered her mother appearing at their bedside to kiss the children goodnight. She wrote of her mother looking like a dazzling apparition before leaving for an evening party. Ethel often lay sleepless and weeping at the thought of her mother one day growing old and less beautiful.

Despite the influence of her governess, Ethel later said it was her mother who first introduced her to music, being one of the most naturally musical people she had ever known. Emma was said to be a wonderful singer, but she loved to hear Ethel sing. She seldom performed for her mother and regretted this later in life.[3] In 1875 she began taking professional music lessons under the tuition of Alexander Ewing, a Royal Artillery officer known mainly for his composition of the hymn-tune 'Jerusalem the Golden'. He was an excellent music teacher and introduced his highly motivated student to opera and orchestration. His wife, a children's author, also encouraged Ethel, but her father severed the connection with Ewing because he distrusted his intentions towards Ethel. Nevertheless, his actions didn't deter Ethel and she became more determined to follow a musical career, even though her father was totally against the idea and once said that he would sooner see her beneath the sod. Over the following two years she wore him down and he finally agreed with her plans to become a musician. In fact, such was her persistence that she even convinced him to provide an allowance to support her while she was studying at the Leipzig Conservatorium.[4]

In July 1877 she travelled to Leipzig to study music, but was not impressed by the teachers there and, a year later, decided to study music privately under Heinrich von Herzogenberg. When she became acquainted with his wife, Lisl, a love affair developed between the two women and was the first of many such relationships that Ethel Smyth had during her lifetime. The Herzogenbergs were close friends of Brahms and were highly respected members of the German musical society. It was through this connection that Smyth was introduced to leading musical figures in Leipzig. Over time she developed other important friendships that brought her to the attention of prominent musical people on a national scale, including some of the most eminent conductors and performers. These people were essential to her career as a composer. She began travelling around Europe, but always returned to England during the summer months.

During a winter visit to Florence in 1882–83, Smyth met the American writer and philosopher Henry Brewster, whose wife, Julia, was a sister of Lisl Herzogenberg. Brewster was attracted to Smyth and she felt the same about him; she returned to Florence the following year, but was careful not to allow a love affair to develop between them. When Lisl became aware of the situation, she broke off her relationship with Smyth, which caused the latter great anguish for a number of years, and they were still not reconciled when Lisl died in 1892. Julia followed her in death in 1895 and it was only then that Smyth and Brewster became lovers, but they remained in separate homes and never married. Smyth continued to pursue relationships with women during this period and Brewster was not at all jealous of her liaisons.[5] He did propose marriage to her, but she declined for fear of losing her independence. While her relationship with Brewster continued until his death in 1908, she was always more comfortable with women. She once wrote to him saying, 'I wonder why it is so much easier for me to love my own sex more passionately than yours. I can't make it out for I am a very healthy-minded person.'[6]

Smyth was described as a woman of formidable character who pursued her interests with amazing passion. Once she set her mind on something, it was followed through to its conclusion with the utmost vigour and commitment. Although Smyth had a manner that sometimes annoyed people, this didn't seem to affect their views when it came to her music and the critics took her seriously as a composer.[7]

Smyth had made an impact as a composer in Leipzig by 1889, and she returned to England to build up her reputation at home. Her performances in Crystal Palace of *Serenade* and the *Overture of Antony and Cleopatra* created much excitement and were influenced by some of the great composers: Beethoven, Brahms and Dvořák. One of the people she befriended while travelling in Europe was Eugénie, the former French empress. This was a very beneficial friendship for Smyth, as it included financial support as well as opening many important doors for her. Smyth also had an intimate relationship with Mary Ponsonby, one of Queen Victoria's ladies of the bedchamber, which presented her with an opportunity to perform before the Prince of Wales, who was the patron of the Royal Choral Society. Smyth continued to build up a network of influential women throughout her life.[8]

All her contacts were vital because she struggled financially for most of her career and depended on support from several people, including her older sister, Mary. Another important connection for Smyth was Pauline Trevelyan, a devout Catholic, and it was through her that Smyth discovered religion. This led her to creating the *Mass in D*, which proved a landmark in her career. Empress Eugénie paid for the publication of this work, having personally attended the performance. Through the empress, Smyth was introduced to Queen Victoria, and thus she gained an extremely powerful and influential ally. Referring to the *Mass*, a critic from *The Times* wrote that this work definitely placed her among the most eminent composers of her time.

George Bernard Shaw was a great friend of Smyth and a supporter of her music from the very early stages. In 1893, seeing her rise, he declared that this was the beginning of what he had often prophesied as the conquest of popular music by women. It stood the test of time, as many years later Shaw wrote to her saying, 'Thank you for bullying me into going to hear that *Mass*. The originality and beauty of the voices parts are as striking today as they were thirty years ago, and the rest will stand up in the biggest company. Magnificent!' He signed off 'Your dear big brother'.[9]

She was an active woman, pursued interests in hiking and mountain climbing, and was renowned for wearing tweed suits and masculine-like hats. She had a great love of dogs, particularly English sheepdogs, which she kept as pets throughout her life. Smyth was described as being sincere, generous and shrewd, but could also be abrupt.

She was encouraged by the renowned German conductor Hermann Levi to compose an opera, but ran into a number of problems. Eventually, on 24 May 1898, *Fantasio*, her first opera, made its début in Weimar, Germany and was warmly received by the public. Another opera, *Der Wald,* based on a tragic love story, premiered in Berlin in 1901, but the attendance was disappointing. She believed that sexual discrimination and the Boer War were to blame, but there were also internal problems within the theatre.

In 1903 she travelled to New York and Boston to have the opera performed at venues in both cities. Her third opera, *The Wreckers* (1904) – perhaps her finest work – was set on the Cornish coast during the eighteenth century and was a tragic story of two lovers who were trying to prevent the practice of luring ships into places of danger using false beacons. While the opera was staged in Germany and Prague, it was 1910 before it opened in Covent Garden, with Thomas Beecham conducting. The reason it took so long was due to a lack of financial support in England as the management of the opera house felt that the risk was too great for the investment. It was an American friend, Mary Dodge, who provided the finance for Smyth to stage the performance. She was by now recognised in England and in 1910 the University of Durham awarded her an honorary doctorate in music.

In 1911 Smyth took a career break and devoted two years to supporting the women's suffrage movement.[10] It seems that she had little or no interest in politics or indeed votes for women until she met Emmeline Pankhurst, the leader of the women's suffrage movement, with whom she fell passionately in love. They immediately formed a close friendship and it was then that Smyth began to take a more serious interest in the aims of the movement.

In 1912 the Suffragettes began carrying out more militant forms of protest and attacked one of the official residences in

Downing Street with stones, after which both women were arrested. Smyth served two months in prison for her involvement and recorded that while the prison term was unpleasant, it wasn't a problem because Emmeline Pankhurst was locked up next to her. They were placed in adjoining cells and it seems that the matron was kind and understanding and allowed them to see each other more often than was normally permissible. She allowed Smyth to visit Pankhurst's cell for tea, so they could spend time together. The matron would sometimes lock the cell and leave them alone for a considerable length of time, so they possibly saw more of each other in prison than they had while living in freedom.

Smyth used her musical talent to produce the suffrage battle hymn 'The March of the Women', and the women would sing this as they walked around the exercise yard.[11] Fighting the female cause was not new to her, as she had always stood up against sexual discrimination. Her experiences in the suffrage movement led her to write the feminist polemic *Female Pipings of Eden*, in which she expressed a belief that her career as a composer had been hampered because of her gender.

Having been released from prison, Smyth travelled to Egypt so she could concentrate on composing again away from the troubles of the suffrage movement. It was also a chance to re-concentrate her efforts as a composer as her connection with Pankhurst and the suffrage movement strengthened her resolve to fight for women's liberation in music.[12]

Soon after her return from Egypt, she began exploring the idea of producing an opera based on Synge's play *Riders to the Sea*. This led her to visit Ireland, where she became immersed in the traditions and customs of the country. The fact the she was a close friend of George Bernard Shaw is possibly what ensured an invitation to Coole. However, she abandoned the idea of this opera after a time.[13]

The outbreak of the Great War in 1914 had a serious effect on her connections in Germany and she was forced to cancel some planned performances there. She worked as a radiographer in Paris during the war. It was around this time that she began to show early symptoms of deafness, and her hearing continued to deteriorate over the following years.

In 1919 she published a volume of her memoirs, *Impressions that Remained,* which was a great success. She also began writing articles and found willing publishers for her work. In 1922 she was made a Dame Commander of the Order of the British Empire. The University of Oxford presented her with an honorary degree in 1926 and this was followed by a similar honour in 1928 from the University of St Andrews.

Although struggling with deafness, she continued to compose, but her last sizable work, *The Prison* (1929), didn't receive the credits she had envisaged. She loved to travel and explored Egypt and Greece, which resulted in *A Three-Legged Tour in Greece* (1927) and *Beecham and Pharaoh* (1935). Between 1921 and 1940, she also published eight more volumes of her memoirs.

As old age loomed, Smyth was bitterly disappointed because she felt that her work as a composer had not really been recognised in the manner she had expected. Despite her personal opinions, though, her music was well received in operatic circles and by the public. Her seventy-fifth birthday was celebrated with a festival of her music, some of which was broadcast over the airwaves.

Dame Ethel Smyth died of pneumonia on 8 May 1944 at home at Coign in Woking.[14] The following is an extract from her obituary, which gives a good description of her in old age:

> Dame Ethel was a small figure of volcanic temperament, with strong features, piercing grey eyes, a shrill voice and a mass of grey hair, which she wore parted in the middle and piled, not too tidily, on top of her head. ... Ethel Smyth was a friend of Queen Victoria, of the Empress Eugenie, of Brahms, the Schumanns, Grieg, Saint-Saëns and Tchaikovsky. Once she dined with Kaiser Wilhelm II, and had the amusement of hearing him lay down the law on art to the unhappy Court painter ... Ethel kept all her vigour and vitality to a great age, and when well over 80 could be seen gaily cycling in the country around Woking, where she lived, with her hat on one side and her ear-trumpet bumping on her shoulder. She played golf with zest and [had] a handicap of 24.[15]

Derek Hyde wrote that in her lifetime she also became very well known for her writing. It is true that her lively and rather unconventional style, as well as her honesty and witty observations on human behaviour, brought her to a wider public audience than her music had. Regarding her music, he wrote that she was the first professional woman composer in England and that her main aim was to have her performance and music received on equal terms with those of male composers. She dedicated her life to this cause and used whatever means available to get her music recognised, 'usually the time-honoured ones of wealth (other people's), influence (Queen Victoria's for example) and sheer hard work'.[16] Smyth was a woman of great determination and worked hard to achieve success in a world dominated by male composers.

Theodore Spicer-Simson

Sculptor and Medallist 1871–1959

Theodore Spicer-Simson was a world-famous sculptor and medallist whose work is still much sought after today, as his creations are very collectable and considered by some people as works of art. He created busts in bronze and other materials, but his most outstanding work was a series of medallion images of leading world figures and literary giants made during the first half of the twentieth century.

Born in Le Havre, France on 25 June 1871, Theodore was the eldest son of Frederick and Dora Simson (*née* Spicer). The family moved to Tasmania around 1874 and remained there until 1879. Upon returning to Europe, Spicer-Simson spent his educational years attending boarding schools in London, Germany and France. Once finished college, he enrolled in the École des Beaux-Arts in Paris, as his ambition was to study art and sculpture. There he met Margaret Schmidt, to whom he was extremely attracted. When she left for the United States, he followed her shortly thereafter, and a relationship developed which grew into a love affair. They married on 1 July 1896 in Washington DC. It seems that by this time he was already attracting attention as a skilled artist of portraits and busts.

In 1898–99 the Spanish-American War broke out and this

is believed to have influenced the couple's decision to return to Paris.[1] They set up home in the Montparnasse section of the city, an area that was much favoured by artists and literary figures of the day. While living there Spicer-Simson met people such as Leo and Ella Mielziner, Henri Monod, James Stephens and many others. It was in Paris that he also met the noted sculptor Jean Dampt and began working with him.

In 1903 he produced his first medallions, and his skill and creativity in this work set him apart from other artists in this field. His talent and expertise quickly developed and he built up a strong reputation as a medallist across Europe and the United States. Many prominent people on both sides of the Atlantic posed for Spicer-Simson, such as three United States presidents, including William Howard Taft who sat for him in 1911.[2] He later remembered President Taft as being a very understanding type of person. One day while he was sitting at the president's desk in the White House, Taft walked into the room. It was protocol to stand when the president entered, but being so engrossed in his drawings, Spicer-Simson forgot to stand. When he apologised the following day, President Taft understood and acknowledged that he was simply concentrating on his work.[3]

In 1914 he produced a cast of President Woodrow Wilson's right hand, which was supposed to be used as a propaganda image along with a war-time slogan calling to 'Uphold the President's Hand', but this never appeared. President Franklin Delano Roosevelt also sat for Spicer-Simson.[4] Some of his other works included metallic images of Winston Churchill, the automobile giant Henry Ford, and authors H. G. Wells, John Galsworthy, Sherwood Anderson and Joseph Conrad. He also completed medallions for poets A. E. Housman, Elinor Wylie, Robert Frost and 'Abdu'l-Bahá, the Persian religious reformer. In addition, he created a metallic image of Ignacy Jan Paderewski, who was chosen as the first president of Poland. Between 1911 and 1915 he received an award for outstanding work he had carried out in Brussels and was also honoured at the Grand International Exhibition. Also in 1915 he won awards for his medals at the Panama–Pacific International Exposition held in San Francisco.

In 1921 Spicer-Simson began working on a unique project to produce medallic portraits of some of the most important literary figures in both Ireland and England called 'Men of Letters of the British Isles'. The project also included a series of critical essays on each of the chosen authors to be compiled by Stuart Sherman, as it was planned as a joint venture between Sherman and Spicer-Simson. Among the authors invited to sit for a portrait were George Bernard Shaw and W. B. Yeats, and this led to Spicer-Simson being invited to Coole. It seems that there was also a plan to capture the image of Lady Gregory on a medallion.[5] He arrived at Coole in May of the following year to carry out the work with the threat of civil war hanging over the country. While Yeats was sitting for Spicer-Simson, Lady Gregory arrived and mentioned an incident that had happened the previous night involving the gamekeeper's sons. Knowing that she was fearful of the IRA anti-Treatyites in the area, Yeats arranged to have Free State soldiers stay at the house with her, which brought a degree of security to the hostess and her guests. Spicer-Simson continued with his work and completed a medallion for both of them before leaving.[6]

During a visit to the United States in 1925, Spicer-Simson

became reacquainted with an old friend named David Fairchild and was invited to his home in Miami. He loved Miami and had a house built in Coconut Grove, which was let out for rent while he was living in Bourron, France. Spicer-Simson and his wife remained in France during the Second World War and he was arrested by the Germans in 1940 because he was a holder of British citizenship. Being an American citizen, his wife Margaret was not arrested because America was not directly involved in the war at that time. In April 1941 Spicer-Simson was released, having spent some months in a prison camp, and returned to his home in Bourron. In the autumn of 1946 he and his wife travelled to their home in Miami, where the climate suited both of them, and they decided to remain in the United States.

Additional honours that Spicer-Simson received for his exceptional work included fellowship of the Numismatic Association, National Sculpture Association and National Academy of Design. He was the recipient of the J. Stanford Saltus Medal from the American Numismatic Society and was made associataire du Salon des Beaux-Arts.

Theodore Spicer-Simson died at his adopted home in Coconut Grove after a long illness on 1 February 1959.[7] In 1960 his widow, Margaret, presented his medallions and personal papers on loan to the University of Miami Library and the library purchased the collection in 1971, so they are now held in the Special Collections Department of the University of Miami Library.[8]

General
Sir Ian Hamilton
Soldier 1853–1947

Sir Ian Standish Monteith Hamilton, born on 16 January 1853 on the island of Corfu, was the eldest son of Christian Monteith Hamilton, a lieutenant colonel with the Gordon Highlanders. His mother, Maria Corinna, was the daughter of John Prendergast Vereker, 3rd Viscount Gort; she died of consumption when Hamilton was only three. His paternal grandparents in Argyll looked after him and his aunt Camilla supervised his early education.

When he was ten years old, Hamilton was sent to a private school at Cheam and became the victim of bullies, receiving both physical and verbal abuse. The headmaster was sometimes as cruel as the bullies, so these were unhappy years for Hamilton and he was glad to leave the school behind in 1867, when he was sent to Wellington College. He showed little promise as a scholar, so he decided to follow a career in the army and obtained a commission. He was given the opportunity to study abroad and decided to do so under General I. S. Drammers in Dresden, Germany, gaining valuable experience. When he returned to England in 1871, he entered the Royal Military College at

Sandhurst. A year later he joined the 12th Suffolk Regiment, then stationed at Athlone, Ireland. Eighteen months later, he transferred to his father's old regiment, the 92nd Gordon Highlanders in India.

He took his army career very seriously and worked hard at his profession. He was described as being intelligent and in possession of a formidable gift of expression that few British officers could match; furthermore, he was a good sportsman, witty and alert, and seemed indifferent to personal danger. Hamilton was not afraid of taking on tough assignments or making hard decisions. He was also a keen hunter of big game and would pursue this activity whenever the opportunity arose. Outside of hunting and military activities, he loved painting, music and poetry.

Hamilton became a musketry instructor and was seen as a modern soldier. He was convinced that infantry training needed to be changed and believed that the infantry tactics used at that time would not stand up to the latest weapons of war. Although he was correct, he encountered prejudice from those who clung to the old, traditional methods of warfare. Nevertheless, he continued along his own course of training and his superiors began to take notice when reports came back that his regiment's musketry efficiency was proving to be one of the best in the British Army.

His baptism of fire came during the Second Anglo-Afghan War in 1879. This military conflict was fought between the British Raj and the Emirate of Afghanistan and led to the British invading Afghanistan. Hamilton's regiment accompanied Sir Frederick Roberts in the march to Kabul. Hamilton was struck by malaria in July of that year, but he still took part in the rescue of survivors when the Afghans overran a British outpost.

He became separated from his regiment while in pursuit of the enemy and found himself alone and engaged in a gun battle with the Afghans. He somehow managed to hold them back until his men arrived. It was a milestone in his military career, as he was decorated for courage and mentioned in the dispatches twice.

In 1881 he found himself in South Africa after the Boers in the Transvaal revolted against British rule (First Boer War). Three of his companies formed part of a small British force that was defeated at Majuba Hill. During this battle, Hamilton's left wrist was shattered and he was also wounded in the back of the head, which left him unconscious. The Boers found him and, after he regained consciousness, released him, believing he was going to die. Somehow he survived. Having been invalided home, Hamilton was given a hero's welcome and was invited to dine with Queen Victoria. It seems that he was recommended for the Victoria Cross, an honour that failed to materialise because some felt he was too young.

In October 1884 Hamilton went to Egypt and joined the Gordon Highlanders' relief expedition. During this mission he saw action at the battle of Kirbekan and, while the expedition failed, Hamilton again proved himself an excellent soldier. Once more he was decorated and mentioned in dispatches. In 1886 he resumed a former duty as aide-de-camp to Sir Frederick Roberts, who was now the commander-in-chief of the British forces in India. That same year Hamilton met and fell in love with Jean Miller Muir, and they were married in February 1887.

In 1890 he was appointed assistant adjutant-general of musketry and was allowed to develop new battlefield tactics, which improved the firing efficiency of his men to such a degree that his system was extended to other British regiments. Hamilton was rewarded the following year when he was promoted as the youngest colonel in the army. In 1899 the Second Boer War broke out and Hamilton took part in some of the fiercest fighting, again displaying tremendous courage throughout the campaign. He was recommended for the Victoria Cross a second time, but army policy prevented him from receiving the award because of his rank.

In 1904 he was delighted to be offered an opportunity to serve as a British military attaché with the Japanese army in the Russo-Japanese War. Britain was obliged to support Japan because of an alliance signed between the two countries in 1902. Hamilton made a good impression on the Japanese generals and they held him in high esteem. He returned to England in April 1905 and was appointed to the British headquarters at Salisbury Plain. Hamilton and his wife moved into Tidworth House, where they became noted for entertaining guests with lavish events.[1]

Hamilton was a relative of Lady Gregory. He also had a great love of painting, music and poetry. Perhaps it was this cultural side that encouraged him to take time out from his busy military lifestyle to visit her at Coole, earning him the privilege of having his name recorded on the Autograph Tree. All visitors to Coole were aware that Lady Gregory paid special attention to her regular guest, Yeats, and during one visit Hamilton recorded a short, but revealing, account of the extent to which she would go to ensure that Yeats' needs and comfort were looked after. One can see from the following account that there was also a degree of sarcasm in his tone:

Along the passage for some distance on either side of Yeats' door were laid thick rugs to prevent the slightest sound reaching the holy of holies – Yeats's bed. Down the passage every now and then would tiptoe a maid with a tray bearing beef tea or arrowroot, though once I declare I distinctly smelt eggs and bacon. All suggestions that I could cheer him up a good deal if I went into his room and had a chat were met with horror.[2]

In 1915 Hamilton was given command of the Gallipoli landings during the Great War, and the sixty-two-year-old set off with no real plan or experienced staff to call on for advice.[3] Hostilities began in this theatre of war because Turkey controlled all shipping through the Dardanelles, so, in March 1915, the British deployed a naval force to try to open up the Dardanelles in order to send supplies to their Russian allies. However, they were forced to call off the attack because of heavy gunfire and underwater mines, and realised that the only way to secure the area was an assault on the Gallipoli Peninsula.

This began with a bombardment at dawn on 25 April 1915. Hamilton ordered the attack and shortly afterwards the Allies began landing at various points along the peninsula. The British found themselves under heavy Turkish fire that caused enormous casualties. Once the landings had been achieved, the Allies pushed for more ground and bitter fighting continued over the following months. Despite the arrival of reinforcements, they failed to defeat the Turks. By the end of September 1915 the British had virtually abandoned the Gallipoli offensive, with the Allies reporting over 265,000 dead during one of the bloodiest campaigns of the war. Hamilton suffered the humiliation of being relieved of his command the following month.[4] Despite this failure, he was described as a gallant general.

Hamilton later stated that naval operations in the Dardanelles were planned without consulting him and that any element of surprise at Gallipoli had been lost as a result of these naval exploits, so he had been forced to reorganise the troops and place the regiments in the correct order before landing, which should have been done before they left England. Another problem arose because he believed that he could not commit all of his troops at Gallipoli as he was told that some were required for action in other areas of conflict around the Mediterranean.[5] Although he was judged harshly because of the Gallipoli campaign, he never actively tried to defend himself, hoping that history would vindicate him.

In 1918 Hamilton was appointed lieutenant of the Tower of London. Following his retirement in 1920, he became involved in the British Legion and was a much sought-after speaker for military societies. Between 1932 and 1935 he held the position of lord rector of Edinburgh University in Scotland. Hamilton and his wife had no natural family, but adopted two children, a boy and a girl. Not much is known of their adopted daughter, but the boy grew up to become a commissioned officer in the Scots Guards. He was killed in action fighting against the Germans in North Africa in 1941. Jean died that same year; General Sir Ian Hamilton died on 12 October 1947 and was buried with his wife in Doune, Perthshire.[6]

General
Sir Neville Lyttelton

Soldier 1845–1931

General Sir Neville Gerald Lyttelton was born on 28 October 1845 at Hagley in Worcestershire, the son of George William Lyttelton and Mary Glynne. Mary's sister was married to William Gladstone, who was godfather for Lyttelton. The Lyttelton family were devout Anglicans and were brought up in the strict teachings of that Church. Neville was the third of eight boys.

His early education began in a private school at Geddington in Northamptonshire and he entered Eton College in 1858, where he excelled and was appointed as president of the students union. He had his sights set on a military career and in January 1865 was commissioned as an ensign into the Rifle Brigade, having passed his army exams. A year later, he found himself in Canada, helping to put down a surprise Fenian uprising – an effort by the IRB to force Britain to withdraw from Ireland by attacking British posts in Canada. The rising ended in failure for the Fenians.

In October 1877 Lyttelton was promoted to captain and another promotion followed in 1882 when he assumed the rank of major. During that same year, Lyttelton served in the Egyptian campaign as aide-de-camp to Sir John Miller Adye and was mentioned in dispatches following the battle of Tell El Kebir. In 1883 he served as military secretary to the governor of Gibraltar and also served in various posts in Ireland, England and India. He acted as private secretary to H. C. E. Childers, secretary of state for war in the Gladstone government.

On 1 October 1883 he married his second cousin, Katharine Sarah Stuart-Wortley, and in 1885 was appointed as military secretary to Donald Mackay, governor of Bombay. Over the following years he served in Ireland and India again, and in the Sudan under Kitchener. In 1899 he was placed in command of the 2nd Brigade at Aldershot, England, and when the Boer War broke out that year, he was sent to South Africa and placed in command of the 4th Brigade in Natal under General Sir Redvers Buller.[1] Lyttelton was in action throughout the campaign. One notable battle was at Colenso, where he fought against the Boers and the famous Irish Brigade under Major John MacBride.[2] Lyttelton's military skills as a commander were recognised in actions at Spion Kop, Vaal Krantz, and during the relief of Ladysmith. The war in South Africa enhanced his reputation greatly and he was one of the few senior British officers to emerge from the conflict with such acknowledgement. Following the cessation of hostilities, Lyttelton was appointed commander-in-chief in South Africa, a position he held until January 1904. During his time he tried to reconcile the British and Boers and held discussions with the enemy commander, General Louis Botha.

In 1904 the War Office was reorganised and Lyttelton was appointed as chief of general staff. He was assigned to the new Army Council and became involved in the military reforms taking place at that time. It seems that Edward VII suggested his appointment. In 1912 he was appointed as governor of the Royal Hospital in Chelsea, London, and during the Great War he was appointed to support the conflict in Mesopotamia. He continued his duties at the Royal Hospital until he died on 6 July 1931. He was survived by his wife and three daughters, Lucy Blanche, Hilda Margaret and Mary.[3]

There are questions around his visit to Coole which have been asked by a number of people over the years. How and why was he there? He was not a man involved in the arts, theatre or poetry, but it is possible that he visited Coole in the company of Sir Ian Hamilton as both were military men and served in the same military campaigns. Or might it have been during one of his postings in Ireland? One can only surmise that if he was there with Hamilton, he was invited to record his name on the tree out of courtesy. Of course this is mere speculation and the answer is waiting to be uncovered. Nevertheless, Sir Neville Lyttelton is the last signatory of the Autograph Tree recorded in this publication.

Coole

Memories to Carry Forward
(Autumn Gathering)

Coole Park is today a nature reserve consisting of approximately 1,000 acres. The complex is designated as a special protection region for birds. The grounds are open to the public all year round and a visitor's centre is open between April and September, operated by the Irish National Parks & Wildlife Service. It is located a few miles west of Gort, Co. Galway.

The Coole Park Visitor Centre includes one of the original stables from the park and still contains elaborate stalls for five horses. The overhead loft in the stables was used for storing hay and maintenance tools. The remains of the coach and harness rooms are located across the old cobbled stable yard where a variety of coaches were stationed. The grain was stored in the coach house loft and above was a dovecote. Keeping pigeons and doves is believed to be a tradition dating from medieval times or perhaps earlier. This became popular with some gentry families during the eighteenth century and Coole was no exception. There was a practical purpose to having a dovecote on the estate, as pigeons could provide fresh meat and eggs during winter months when meat and other food commodities were scarce.

The Visitor Centre contains an audio-visual presentation

entitled 'Lady Gregory of Coole'. A literary history of Coole Park and a multi-media exhibition, 'Coole Park through the eyes of "Me and Nu", Granddaughters of Lady Gregory', can also be viewed. The presentations last approximately thirty minutes each and admission is free. Guided tours are available for groups when booked in advance and books, maps, trail booklets, postcards and heritage cards are also on sale.

Coole invites people to experience for themselves the magic and serenity of the landscape that Yeats captured in his poetry. One can explore the natural history of the park in an ideal setting as there are nature trails through the woods taking you along the river and turlough (a type of lake found mostly in limestone areas), across bare limestone with a view of Coole Lake.

There are two trails to follow. 'The Family Trail' is an easy 1.75km walk that takes visitors past the deer pen and the site of the house and into the walled garden to view the famous Autograph Tree. One can also follow 'The Seven Woods Trail' of 4.5km, which connects the different wood areas made famous by Yeats and which so enchanted Lady Gregory and her guests. Depending on the season, you might see bluebells and violets, jays, red squirrels, stoats, various butterflies and dragonflies during a walk. Swans and other wetland birds are also an attraction.

There is an array of wildlife exposed in these wonderful forest walks, which Lady Gregory described when writing in 1931: 'These woods have been well loved, well tended by some who came before me, and my affection has been no less than theirs. The generations of trees have been my care, my comforters. Their companionship has often brought me peace.'[1] On another occasion she recorded, 'The beauty, the romance of our Seven

Woods, the mysteries of the ebbing and flowing lake are dear to me, have been well loved, and are now in hands that will care and tend them it is likely for ever.'[2] Her husband, Sir William Gregory, also took an active interest in the woodlands and, during the spring and autumn of 1853, devoted himself with enthusiasm to the construction of a nut wood at Coole: 'I ransacked the nursery grounds of Bristol, Liverpool, and Exeter, and planted all the specimens that were invented and got up by ingenious nurserymen for the benefit of Conifer maniacs, as we were then called.'[3]

There are a number of interesting features to be seen as one follows along The Seven Woods Trail. The following are just examples. At Stop 2 there is a limekiln that was used for converting limestone rock into lime, which was then used for fertiliser and whitewash for houses. Stop 13 tests the ability of the observer as they seek out the kidney-shaped mound which indicates the location of an ancient cooking site, known in Irish archaeological terms as a Fulacht Fiadh. Stop 16 invites one to relax on a limestone seat which was constructed in 1908 and faces east towards the Slieve Aughty Mountains. It was here that many of Lady Gregory's literary friends rested during their walks. There are many more exciting features to discover along the trail as there are some twenty stops for those with enquiring minds.

The Family Trail is also very interesting, with its own set of stops. These take in the Coole river, the horse pump and the turlough. There is also a Ha Ha, a stone-lined trench in the ground, constructed so as not to impede the view from the manor house while at the same time preventing livestock from approaching the residence. There is also a deer pen; these animals were introduced to Coole in 1971. As already mentioned, the walled garden is included on this trail and among its features is a bust of Maecenas, the distinguished Roman statesman and literary patron. Lady Gregory truly loved this garden and spent many peaceful hours sitting under the shade of the catalpa tree located just inside the gate, which was planted as a sapling, having been transported across a desert wrapped in a hemp sack on a camel's back. Speaking of the garden, Lady Gregory wrote, 'I have gone far out in the world, east and west in my time, and so the peace within these enclosing walls is fitting for the evening of my days.'[4]

***

In 1992 Lady Gregory's two granddaughters, Anne and Catherine, arrived at Coole Park for the first time since the death of their grandmother some sixty years earlier. Their brother, Richard, had died in 1981. Driving along the tree-lined avenue, these ladies found it difficult to hold back tears as childhood memories came flooding back. They were delighted with the forest walks and the visitors centre, and were happy to renew their connection with this very special place.[5] Their memories brought them back to a time when they played games in the woodlands. In the evenings, their grandmother would read stories to them, such as *Huckleberry Finn* and *Tom Sawyer*, but one of their favourites was *The Last of the Mohicans*. Another great favourite was *Swiss Family Robinson,* and they would try to act out the excitement of the story the following day.

While the lake at Coole was a wonderful place for the

children, they preferred the woods, especially the nut wood. The paths were almost covered with violets and primroses, and masses of deep thick moss grew around the trees. Christmas was a wonderful time for the children at Coole and every year John Quinn sent them a large case of apples. He also sent the largest box of sweets that they had ever seen. They looked forward to these treats and would put their arms around the large sweet boxes to see if they were as big as they remembered from the previous year. The dining room at Coole looked like 'fairyland' to the children, with the enormous Christmas tree topped by a silver star almost reaching the ceiling. The flickering candlelight appeared to make the pictures on the walls move, giving the place a magical appearance. Although they looked strange to the children, they loved when the Wren boys made their way to the house and performed in song and dance.

Tree climbing was also exciting for Anne and Catherine, and they had a great choice at Coole. One of their favourite trees to climb was a large thuya outside the flower garden as its branches were formed almost like a ladder. The gooseberry bushes were always raided and they continued eating the berries until there were none left. Coole and their grandmother had been everything to the children. Looking back many years later, Anne wrote that the joy of living at Coole with their grandmother was 'Knowing that whatever we said or did – however silly other people thought we were – Grandma not only understood everything we meant to say, she also very often made us even cleverer than we had thought we were ourselves.'[6]

***

In 1995 the 'Lady Gregory of Coole Park Autumn Gathering Group' was set up by the late Sheila O'Donnellan. Other founders included Lois Tobin, Sighle Meehan, Mary McDonagh and Marie Cadden. One of the main objectives of the Gathering was to provide a literary weekend, during which people could share and be exposed to an array of rich literature. There are lectures, tours and other cultural events arranged throughout the weekend, which is normally held in September.[7]

The Autumn Gathering was born out of a need to acknowledge the achievements and contribution of Lady Gregory to Irish literature and culture.[8] Sheila O'Donnellan always recognised Lady Gregory, not just for the richness in culture that she nurtured in Ireland, but also for her independence as a woman. Speaking of Lady Gregory, Sheila once said, 'She was such a modern woman in the sense that despite her conservative and Unionist background, she was her own woman and identified with the emerging culture of Nationalism of the time.'[9]

Sheila O'Donnellan deserves enormous credit for her devotion to the memory of Lady Gregory and the organising of the annual Gathering. She was a great enthusiast of Irish literature. She lectured and made an audiotape telling the story of Lady Gregory and Coole. Her work in this capacity ensured that there was a greater awareness of Irish literature.

The Gathering always attracts an array of talented guest speakers who continually expose people to the richness of Irish culture. In the early years, Anne and Catherine were regular attendees as guests and this connection continued until their deaths. The late Michael Yeats, son of the poet, also attended on occasion.[10]

The launch of the Autumn Gathering and many of its events take place in the Lady Gregory Hotel in Gort and Thoor Ballylee. The Gathering has recently celebrated its 25th Anniversary under the chairmanship of Ronnie O'Gorman, a man who has been involved with the Gatherings from the beginning.

The Kiltartan Gregory Museum, opened in August 1996, is located in the former schoolhouse at Kiltartan Cross and contains many interesting items relating to Coole and Lady Gregory. One of the items given to the museum was a silver cup that was presented to Lady Gregory in 1913 by the Philadelphia Players for her contribution to Irish theatre.[11]

The future of Irish literature and culture is assured with such organisations as the Friends of Coole Park and the Autumn and Spring Gatherings. Although we have moved into the twenty-first century, Lady Gregory and Coole continue to have an extraordinary influence over Irish literature and culture, the walled garden providing a wonderful sanctuary where the living memories of great artists, writers and poets are captured on the bark of the Autograph Tree.

Autograph Tree Lists

The Coole Park lists of signatures differ in some cases from the one compiled by Colin Smythe for his book *A Guide to Coole Park, County Galway*. He records General Sir Neville Lyttelton, who is not included in the Coole Park list. George Moore is not mentioned on the Colin Smythe list, but is included in the Coole Park record. Both lists are included below. There are sixteen names numbered as these have been clearly identified. It seems that the remainder were not numbered because of the deterioration that occurred over time, and these names cannot be clearly identified any longer. However, these people are known to have signed their initials on the Autograph Tree.

Coole Park List	Colin Smythe List
(1) Theodore Spicer-Simson	(1) Theodore Spicer-Simson
(2) George Bernard Shaw	(2) George Bernard Shaw
(3) John Masefield	(3) Augustus John
(4) Countess of Cromartie	(4) Douglas Hyde
(5) Augustus John	(5) Lady Augusta Gregory
(6) Elinor Monsell	(6) Robert Gregory
(7) Douglas Hyde	(7) Violet Martin
(8) Lady Augusta Gregory	(8) George William Russell

(9) Robert Gregory	(9) William Butler Yeats
(10) William Butler Yeats	(10) Sean O'Casey
(11) Sean O'Casey	(11) Elinor Monsell
(12) John Millington Synge	(12) John Millington Synge
(13) Violet Martin	(13) John Masefield
(14) George William Russell	(14) Jack Butler Yeats
(15) Jack Butler Yeats	(15) Dame Ethel Smyth
George Moore (Not on Smythe list)	(16) Countess of Cromartie
Sara Allgood	Sara Allgood
Lennox Robinson	Lennox Robinson
Lady Margaret Sackville	Lady Margaret Sackville
Frank Fay	Frank Fay
William Fay	William Fay
James Dickson Innes	James Dickson Innes
Robert Ross	Robert Ross
General Sir Ian Hamilton	General Sir Ian Hamilton
John Quinn	*General Sir Neville Lyttelton (Not on Coole list)*
Dame Ethel Smyth	John Quinn

Notes

Augusta Persse 'Lady Gregory'

1. 'Lady Isabella Augusta Gregory, 1852–1932', *Galway – Official Guide*, (Condor Publishing Co., 1986), p. 63.

2. 'The Importance of Lady Gregory', *Galway Advertiser*, 28 September 1995.

3. Hill, Judith, *Lady Gregory: An Irish Life* (Sutton Publishing Company Gloucester, 2005), pp. 2–4, 16–17, 20, 22–25, 27.

4. 'The Gregory Country that Inspired Yeats', *The Connacht Tribune*, 25 August 1967.

5. 'The Woman who wanted to leave more than a monument of champagne bottles', *Galway Advertiser*, 16 February 2006.

6. Hill (2005), pp. 27, 31, 33–35, 38.

7. 'The Woman who wanted to leave …', *Galway Advertiser*, 16 February 2006.

8. Hill (2005), pp. 38, 41–42, 46–49, 55, 81–83.

9. 'The Woman who wanted to leave …', *Galway Advertiser*, 16 February 2006.

10. Mac Liammóir, Mícheál and Boland, Eavan, *W.B. Yeats and his World* (Thames and Hudson, London, 1978), pp. 58–59, 62.

11. Ó Céirín, Kit and Cyril, *Women of Ireland: A Biographic Dictionary* (Tir Eolas, Galway, 1996), p. 94.

12. 'Her Ladyship's Cake', *Galway Advertiser*, 5 January 1995.

13. Smythe, Colin, *A Guide to Coole Park, Co. Galway: Home of Lady Gregory* (Colin Smythe Ltd, Buckinghamshire, 2003), p. 19.

14. Jordan, A. J., *Willie Yeats and the Gonne-MacBrides* (Anthony J. Jordan, Dublin, 1997), p. 120.

15. Ó Céirín (1996), p. 94.

16. Henry, William, *Forgotten Heroes: Galway Soldiers of the Great War 1914–1918* (Mercier Press, Cork, 2007), p. 133.

17. 'Lady Gregory and the Fate of Coole Park', *Galway Advertiser*, 26 January 1995.

18. Ó Céirín (1996), p. 94.

19. 'Her Ladyship's Cake', *Galway Advertiser*, 5 January 1995.

20. 'Lady Gregory and the Fate of Coole Park', *Galway Advertiser*, 26 January 1995.

21. O'Connor, Gary, *Sean O'Casey A Life* (Atheneum Macmillan Publishing Co., New York, 1988), p. 167.

Robert Gregory

1. Hill (2005), pp. 34–35, 38, 61, 69, 77, 80–83, 87, 103, 128, 130, 136.

2. *County Galway Cricket Club 1971–1996* (County Galway Cricket Club, 1996), p. 9.

3. Hill (2005), pp. 147, 153, 165.

4. 'The Lady who sold Coole Park', *Galway Advertiser*, 25 October 2012.

5. Hill (2005), p. 214.

6. 'The Lady who sold Coole Park', *Galway Advertiser*, 25 October 2012.

7. Gregory, A., *Me and Nu: Childhood at Coole* (Colin Smythe Ltd, Buckinghamshire, 2009), p. 8.

8. 'The Lady who sold Coole Park', *Galway Advertiser*, 25 October 2012.

9. Hill (2005), pp. 222, 269, 270, 274.

10. Gregory (2009), pp. 48, 98–99.

11. Hill (2005), pp. 222, 269, 270, 274.

12. 'The Lady who sold Coole Park', *Galway Advertiser*, 25 October 2012.

13. 'An Irishman Foresees His Death', *Galway Advertiser*, 5 October 2006.

14. Hill (2005), pp. 283, 285.

15. Gregory (2009), p. 97.

16. Henry (2007), p. 133.

17. Whittle, Paul, *World War I in Photographs* (Eagle Editions, London, 2003), pp. 106–107.

18. Hill (2005), pp. 291, 294–296.

19. Henry (2007), p. 133.

20. Gregory (2009), pp. 8, 107, 112–114.

21. 'Her Ladyship's Cake', *Galway Advertiser*, 5 January 1995.

22. Henry, William, *Blood for Blood: The Black and Tan War In Galway* (Mercier Press, Cork, 2012), pp. 225–226.

23. Gregory (2009), pp. 18, 20–24.

24. 'The Lady who sold Coole Park', *Galway Advertiser*, 25 October 2012.

25. Duane, O. B., *W.B. Yeats: Romantic Visionary* (Brockhampton Press, London, 2007), p. 59.

William Butler Yeats

1. Mac Liammóir and Boland (1978), pp. 5, 8, 12–13, 16–23.

2. Martin, Augustine, *W.B. Yeats* (Gill & Macmillan, Dublin, 2006), pp. 34, 38.

3. Ross, David, *The Irish Biographies: W.B. Yeats* (Geddes & Grosset, New Lanark, 2001), pp. 27–28.

4. Mac Liammóir and Boland (1978), pp. 25–26.

5. Ross, *Yeats* (2001), pp. 29, 31.

6. Mac Liammóir and Boland (1978), pp. 27–32.

7. Ward, Margaret, *Maud Gonne: Ireland's Joan of Arc* (Pandora Press, London, 1990), pp. 1–2, 24–25, 55–57, 75, 79.

8. Martin (2006), p. 54.

9. 'The Woman who wanted to leave ...', *Galway Advertiser*, 16 February 2006.

10. Mac Liammóir and Boland (1978), p. 58.

11. Ross, *Yeats* (2001), pp. 60–62, 181.

12. Ward (1990), pp. 56–57.

13. Martin (2006), pp. 60–61.

14. Fitz-Simon, C., *The Abbey Theatre: Ireland's National Theatre, The First 100 Years* (Thames & Hudson, London, 2003), p. 9.

15. Wallace, Martin, *Famous Irish Writers* (Appletree Press, Belfast, 1999), p. 43.

16. Ward (1990), pp. 56, 84–85, 88.

17. Mac Liammóir and Boland (1978), pp. 89, 91.

18. Ward (1990), pp. 94, 111.

19. Mac Liammóir and Boland (1978), p. 91.

20. Ross, *Yeats* (2001), pp. 111–112.

21. Martin (2006), pp. 80–81.

22. Mac Liammóir and Boland (1978), pp. 92, 94–95, 97, 99.

23. Yeats, M. B., *Cast a Cold Eye: Memories of a Poet's Son and Politician* (Blackwater Press, Dublin, 1998), pp. 1–2, 28, 30, 35.

24. Mac Liammóir and Boland (1978), pp. 100, 103–106, 109.

25. Ross, *Yeats* (2001), pp. 154–156.

26. Mac Liammóir and Boland (1978), p. 122.

27. Ward (1990), p. 94.

28. 'Hotel Meyrick – Major Thunder & His Guests', *Galway Independent*, 2 November 2011.

Jack Butler Yeats

1. 'Yeats, John Butler (Jack)', *Oxford Dictionary of National Biography*, Vol. 60 (2004), p. 764.

2. Kiely, David M., *John Millington Synge: A Biography* (St Martin's Press, New York, 1995), pp. 147, 149.

3. 'Yeats, John Butler', *Oxford Dictionary*, pp. 764–765.

4. Jordan (1997), pp. 15, 42.

5. 'Yeats, John Butler', *Oxford Dictionary*, p. 765.

6. Hill (2005), pp. 143, 147.

7. Kiely (1995), pp. 147–149.

8. 'Yeats, John Butler', *Oxford Dictionary*, pp. 765–766.

9. Kiely (1995), pp. 199, 277–287.

10. Matthews, Ann, *Renegades: Irish Republican Women 1900–1922* (Mercier Press, Cork, 2010), p. 72.

11. Stevens, Julie Anne, *The Irish Scene in Somerville and Ross* (Irish Academic Press, Dublin, 2007), pp. 6–7, 200.

12. Plunkett Dillon, Geraldine, *All in the Blood: A Memoir of the Plunkett Family, the 1916 Rising and the War of Independence* (A & A Farmar, Dublin, 2006), pp. 65–67.

13. 'Yeats, John Butler', *Oxford Dictionary*, p. 766.

14. Foster, R. F., *The Oxford Illustrated History of Ireland* (Oxford University Press, New York, 1989), pp. 240, 288–289, 309.

15. 'Yeats, John Butler', *Oxford Dictionary*, p. 766.

16. Hill (2005), p. 341.

17. Mac Liammóir and Boland (1978), p. 113.

18. 'Yeats, John Butler', *Oxford Dictionary*, p. 767.

19. Martin (2006), pp. 12–13.

20. McDonald, Ferdie, *Eyewitness Travel Guides: Ireland* (Dorling Kindersley, London, 1997), pp. 68, 166, 217, 226.

John Millington Synge

1. Kiely (1995), pp. 9–12.

2. 'Synge, (Edmund) John Millington', *Dictionary of Irish Biography*, Vol. 9 (2009), pp. 213–214.

3. Kiely (1995), pp. 12–13.

4. 'Synge, John Millington', *Dictionary of Irish Biography*, pp. 213–214.

5. Henry, William, *Supreme Sacrifice: The Story of Éamonn Ceannt, 1881–1916* (Mercier Press, Cork, 2005), p. 12.

6. 'Synge, John Millington', *Dictionary of Irish Biography*, p. 214.

7. Wallace (1999), p. 56.

8. Mac Liammóir and Boland (1978), pp. 72–73.

9. Wallace (1999), p. 56.

10. Kiely (1995), pp. 1, 3, 7–8.

11. Spellissy, Seán, *Window on Aran* (The Book Gallery, Ennis, 2003), pp. 18, 38, 112, 146.

12. Lecture: 'Dún Crocbhur, Inishmaan, Aran Islands', Professor Etienne Rynne, Summer, 1992.

13. Kiely (1995), pp. 29–30, 38.

14. Wallace (1999), p. 56.

15. Hill (2005), p. 171.

16. Jordan (1997), pp. 44, 92–93, 97.

17. O'Connor (1988), p. 48.

18. Hill (2005), pp. 190, 192, 195.

19. MacConghail, Muiris, *The Blaskets: People and Literature* (Country House, Dublin, 1994), pp. 132–133.

20. Hill (2005), pp. 190, 192, 195.

21. Kiely (1995), pp. 136–138, 157–162.

22. Hill (2005), p. 195.

23. Kiely (1995), pp. 136–138, 157–162.

24. Spellissy (2003), pp. 112–113.

25. O'Connor (1988), pp. 49–50.

26. Mac Liammóir and Boland (1978), p. 76.

27. Jordan (1997), pp. 92–93, 112.

28. Kiely (1995), pp. 204, 207, 209–210.

29. Skelton, Robin, *Four Plays and the Aran Islands* (Oxford University Press, London, 1969), p. 14.

30. 'Allgood, Sara', *Oxford Dictionary of National Biography*, Vol. 1 (2004), p. 853.

Sara Allgood

1. 'Allgood, Sara', *Oxford Dictionary*, p. 852.

2. Broderick, Marian, *Wild Irish Women; Extraordinary Lives from History* (O'Brien Press, Dublin, 2001), p. 279.

3. Hill (2005), p. 181.

4. Broderick (2001), pp. 279–280.

5. 'Allgood, Sara', *Oxford Dictionary*, p. 852.

6. Hill (2005), pp. 181–182, 188.

7. Broderick (2001), p. 280.

8. Hill (2005), pp. 158, 181, 188.

9. Broderick (2001), p. 280.

10. 'Allgood, Sara', *Oxford Dictionary*, pp. 852–853.

11. Robinson, L., *Ireland's Abbey Theatre: A History 1899–1951* (Sidgwick and Jackson, London, 1951), pp. 55–56, 98.

12. Hill (2005), pp. 218, 226.

13. 'Allgood, Sara', *Oxford Dictionary*, pp. 852–853.

14. Broderick (2001), p. 281.

15. 'Allgood, Sara', *Oxford Dictionary*, pp. 852–853.

16. O'Connor (1988), pp. 157, 159, 182, 192, 205, 279.

17. 'Allgood, Sara', *Oxford Dictionary*, p. 852.

18. O'Connor (1988), p. 279.

19. 'Allgood, Sara', *Oxford Dictionary*, pp. 852–853.

Frank Fay

1. 'Fay, Frank J.', *Dictionary of Irish Biography*, Vol. 3 (2009), p. 730.
2. Jordan (1997), p. 120.
3. Hill (2005), p. 181.
4. 'Fay, Frank J.', *Dictionary of Irish Biography*, p. 730.
5. Robinson (1951), pp. 25–26.
6. 'Fay, Frank J.', *Dictionary of Irish Biography*, p. 730.
7. Frazier, Adrian, *George Moore 1852–1933* (Yale University Press, London, 2000), pp. 303, 319.
8. O'Connor (1988), p. 48.
9. Morash, Christopher, *A History of Irish Theatre 1601–2000* (Cambridge University Press, Cambridge, 2004), pp. 121–122, 142–143.
10. 'Fay, Frank J.', *Dictionary of Irish Biography*, pp. 730–731.
11. *Ibid.*
12. Robinson (1951), p. 26.
13. Fitz-Simon (2003), p. 54.
14. Morash (2004), p. 122.
15. Robinson (1951), pp. 28–29.
16. 'Fay, Frank J.', *Dictionary of Irish Biography*, p. 730.
17. Fitz-Simon (2003), p. 54.
18. 'Fay, Frank J.', *Dictionary of Irish Biography*, p. 731.
19. Morash (2004), pp. 175–176, 188.
20. 'Fay, Frank J.', *Dictionary of Irish Biography*, p. 731.
21. Robinson (1951), p. 58.

William George Fay

1. 'Fay, William George', *Oxford Dictionary of National Biography*, Vol. 19 (2004), pp. 198–199.
2. Hill (2005), p. 181.
3. 'Fay, William George', *Oxford Dictionary*, pp. 198–199.
4. Robinson (1951), pp. 27, 29.
5. *Ibid.*, pp. 29–30.
6. *Ibid.*, p. 40.
7. *Ibid.*

8.   Hill (2005), p. 184.

9.   Robinson (1951), p. 40.

10.   'Fay, William George', *Oxford Dictionary*, p. 199.

11.   'Fay, Frank J.', *Dictionary of Irish Biography*, p. 731.

12.   'Fay, William George', *Oxford Dictionary*, p. 199.

13.   Robinson (1951), pp. 26, 52.

14.   Mac Liammóir and Boland (1978), p. 70.

15.   'Fay, William George', *Oxford Dictionary*, p. 199.

16.   Morash (2004), pp. 131–132.

17.   'Fay, William George', *Oxford Dictionary*, p. 199.

18.   Hill (2005), pp. 200, 202–203, 216–218.

19.   Frazier (2000), p. 337.

20.   Robinson (1951), pp. 56–57.

21.   Fitz-Simon (2003), p. 30.

22.   Robinson (1951), p. 57.

23.   'Fay, William George', *Oxford Dictionary*, p. 199.

George William Russell

1.   'Russell, George William *pseud Æ*', *Oxford Dictionary of National Biography*, Vol. 48 (2004), p. 256.

2.   Jordan (1997), p. 11.

3.   Mac Liammóir and Boland (1978), pp. 23–24.

4.   'Russell, George William', *Oxford Dictionary*, pp. 256–257.

5.   Hill (2005), pp. 114, 126.

6.   'Russell, George William', *Oxford Dictionary*, pp. 257–258.

7.   Hill (2005), p. 171.

8.   'Russell, George William', *Oxford Dictionary*, p. 258.

9.   Fargnoli, A. N. and Gillespie, M.P., *James Joyce A to Z: The Essential Reference to the Life and Work* (Facts and File Inc., New York, 1995), p. 194.

10.   Jordan (1997), p. 112.

11.   'Russell, George William', *Oxford Dictionary*, p. 258.

12.   Macardle, Dorothy, *The Irish Republic* (The Camelot Press, London, 1937), p. 97.

13.   'Russell, George William', *Oxford Dictionary*, p. 258.

14. O'Connor (1988), p. 73.

15. *Ibid.*

16. Carty, James, *Ireland from The Great Famine to The Treaty of 1921* (CJ Fallon, Dublin, 1966), pp. 190–194.

17. Macardle (1937), pp. 391–392.

18. 'Russell, George William', *Oxford Dictionary*, p. 259.

19. Jordan (1997), p. 189.

20. 'Russell, George William', *Oxford Dictionary*, p. 259.

John Quinn

1. 'Quinn, John', *Dictionary of Irish Biography*, Vol. 8 (2009), p. 362.

2. Hill (2005), pp. 167–168.

3. 'Quinn, John', *Dictionary of Irish Biography*, p. 362.

4. Ward (1990), pp. 85–86.

5. Jordan (1997), pp. 95, 105–116.

6. 'Quinn, John', *Dictionary of Irish Biography*, p. 363.

7. Jordan (1997), pp. 116, 124.

8. Hill (2005), pp. 247, 254, 256–258, 260–261.

9. 'Quinn, John', *Dictionary of Irish Biography*, p. 363.

10. Ward (1990), pp. 99, 108.

11. Jordan (1997), pp. 131, 142–144.

12. 'Quinn, John', *Dictionary of Irish Biography*, p. 363.

13. Fargnoli and Gillespie (1995), pp. 188, 211, 222.

14. Hill (2005), p. 340.

15. 'Quinn, John', *Dictionary of Irish Biography*, p. 364.

Augustus John

1. 'John, Augustus Edwin', *Oxford Dictionary of National Biography*, Vol. 30 (2004), p. 205.

2. John, Augustus, *Chiaroscuro: Fragments of Autobiography* (Jonathan Cape, London, 1954), pp. 4–7.

3. 'John, Augustus Edwin', *Oxford Dictionary*, p. 205.

4. John (1954), pp. 7, 17–19.

5. 'John, Augustus Edwin', *Oxford Dictionary*, p. 205.

6. John (1954), pp. 24, 30–31.
7. 'John, Augustus Edwin', *Oxford Dictionary*, pp. 205–206.
8. Rothenstein, John, *Augustus John* (Phaidon Press, London, 1945), pp. 9, 12–13.
9. John (1954), p. 64.
10. *Ibid.*, pp. 64–68.
11. *Ibid.*, pp. 69–71.
12. O'Connor (1988), p. 275.
13. 'John, Augustus Edwin', *Oxford Dictionary*, p. 207.
14. John (1954), p. 91.
15. 'John, Augustus Edwin', *Oxford Dictionary*, p. 207.
16. Interview with Bill Scanlan, Galway City Museum, 20 May 2006.
17. John (1954), p. 164.
18. 'John, Augustus Edwin', *Oxford Dictionary*, pp. 207–208.
19. Rothenstein (1945), pp. 5, 12.

James Dickson Innes
1. 'Innes, James Dickson', *Oxford Dictionary of National Biography*, Vol. 29 (2004), pp. 299–300.
2. John (1954), p. 153.
3. Rothenstein (1945), p. 18.
4. John (1954), p. 153.
5. 'Innes, James Dickson', *Oxford Dictionary*, p. 300.
6. John (1954), pp. 154–155.
7. Rothenstein (1945), p. 17.
8. 'Innes, James Dickson', *Oxford Dictionary*, p. 300.
9. John (1954), p. 73.
10. 'Innes, James Dickson', *Oxford Dictionary*, p. 300.
11. Rothenstein (1945), p. 17.

George Bernard Shaw
1. 'Shaw, George Bernard', *Dictionary of Irish Biography*, Vol. 8 (2009), p. 857.
2. Ross, David, *The Irish Biographies: George Bernard Shaw* (Geddes & Grosset, New Lanark, 2001), pp. 23, 25–35, 39–40.
3. 'Shaw, George Bernard', *Dictionary of Irish Biography*, pp. 857–858.

4. O'Connor (1988), p. 317.

5. Wallace (1999), p. 47.

6. Hill (2005), p. 232.

7. Ross, *Shaw* (2001), pp. 89–93.

8. Wallace (1999), p. 47.

9. Kiely (1995), pp. 57–58.

10. Hill (2005), p. 188.

11. O'Connor (1988), pp. 48, 56–57.

12. Hill (2005), pp. 232–233.

13. Wallace (1999), p. 48.

14. Hill (2005), pp. 234–235.

15. 'Getting to know George Bernard Shaw', *Galway Advertiser*, 25 September 2001.

16. Hill (2005), pp. 270–271, 281.

17. 'Getting to know George Bernard Shaw', *Galway Advertiser*, 25 September 2001.

18. Hill (2005), pp. 284, 294–295, 318.

19. Macardle (1937), pp. 193–194. Robert Emmet was an Irish nationalist patriot and rebel leader, who was executed following an abortive rebellion in 1803 against British rule in Ireland. The Manchester Martyrs were three members of the Irish Republican Brotherhood, unjustly executed for the murder of a police officer in Manchester in 1867.

20. Wallace (1999), p. 48.

21. O'Connor (1988), pp. 311, 317.

22. Coogan, Tim Pat, *De Valera: Long Fellow, Long Shadow* (Hutchinson, London, 1993), pp. 559–560.

23. Ross, *Shaw* (2001), pp. 176, 180, 184.

24. 'Shaw, George Bernard', *Dictionary of Irish Biography*, p. 861.

25. 'Getting to know George Bernard Shaw', *Galway Advertiser*, 25 September 2001.

Lennox Robinson

1. 'Robinson, (Esme Stuart) Lennox', *Oxford Dictionary of National Biography*, Vol. 47 (2004), p. 380.

2. Hill (2005), pp. 240–241.

3. Mac Liammóir and Boland (1978), pp. 79–80.

4. Jordan (1997), p. 117.

5. Mac Liammóir and Boland (1978), pp. 79–81.

6. 'Robinson, Lennox', *Oxford Dictionary*, p. 380.

7. Hill (2005), pp. 253, 312.

8. 'Robinson, Lennox', *Oxford Dictionary*, p. 181.

9. O'Connor (1988), p. 146.

10. Henry, William, *Robinson, Son of Robin* (Merv Griffin, Galway, 1999), p. 3.

11. 'Robinson, Lennox', *Oxford Dictionary*, p. 382.

12. O'Connor (1988), pp. 167, 182, 191, 193, 225, 375.

13. *Ibid.*, pp. 167, 182, 191, 193.

14. Gregory (2009), pp. 105–106.

15. 'Robinson, Lennox', *Oxford Dictionary*, p. 381.

16. O'Connor (1988), p. 349.

17. 'Robinson, Lennox', *Oxford Dictionary*, pp. 381–382.

Sean O'Casey

1. Wallace (1999), p. 67.

2. 'O'Casey, Sean', *Oxford Dictionary of National Biography*, Vol. 41 (2004), p. 410.

3. O'Connor (1988), pp. 13–16.

4. Hodges, M., *Ireland: From the Uprising to Civil War* (B. T. Batsford Ltd, London, 1987), pp. 46–47.

5. 'O'Casey, Sean', *Oxford Dictionary*, p. 410.

6. O'Connor (1988), pp. 19, 23–25, 28, 39.

7. Hodges (1987), p. 47.

8. 'O'Casey, Sean', *Oxford Dictionary*, p. 410.

9. Hodges (1987), p. 47.

10. 'O'Casey, Sean', *Oxford Dictionary*, pp. 410–411.

11. Hodges (1987), p. 45.

12. Jordan (1997), pp. 179–180.

13. Ward (1990), pp. 151–153.

14. *Ibid.*

15. 'An unlikely friendship', *Galway Advertiser*, 26 August 2010.
16. O'Connor (1988), pp. 167–168, 187.
17. Hill (2005), pp. 16, 89.
18. *Ibid.*, pp. 16, 89, 330–331.
19. Gregory (2009), pp. 62–63.
20. 'O'Casey, Sean', *Oxford Dictionary*, p. 411.
21. O'Connor (1988), pp. 215–216, 234–238.
22. 'O'Casey, Sean', *Oxford Dictionary*, p. 411.
23. Hodges (1987), pp. 47–48.
24. Hill (2005), pp. 348–349, 353.
25. Wallace (1999), p. 68.
26. 'O'Casey, Sean', *Oxford Dictionary*, p. 412.
27. O'Connor (1988), pp. 371, 364–365, 371, 373–375.
28. Hodges (1987), p. 48.
29. *Ibid.*

George Moore

1. Wallace (1999), p. 41.
2. Frazier (2000), pp. 1–6, 8, 10–11, 14–17, 22–25.
3. Wallace (1999), p. 41.
4. Frazier (2000), pp. 40–42.
5. Kiely (1995), pp. 41–42.
6. Wallace (1999), pp. 41–42.
7. Frazier (2000), pp. 222–223, 228–230, 239–241, 258–259.
8. *Ibid.*, pp. 258–259.
9. Hill (2005), p. 137.
10. Mac Liammóir and Boland (1978), pp. 58, 64–65.
11. Kelly, Cornelius, *The Grand Tour of Galway* (Cailleach Books, Cork, 2002), pp. 129–130.
12. Hill (2005), pp. 141–143.
13. Frazier (2000), pp. 277–278, 299–300, 335–336.
14. Jordan (1997), pp. 74, 80, 82.
15. Mac Liammóir and Boland (1978), pp. 62–63.
16. O'Connor (1988), p. 310.

17. Jordan (1997), p. 132.

18. 'Putting right the wrong done at Coole', *Galway Advertiser*, 2 October 2003.

19. Frazier (2000), pp. 141–142, 396–397, 433–434, 450–452, 259, 464–466.

Douglas Hyde

1. Daly, Dominic, *The Young Douglas Hyde: The Dawn of the Irish Revolution and Renaissance 1874–1893* (Irish University Press, Dublin, 1974), pp. 14, 21.

2. 'Fantasy and reality at Coole Park', *Galway Advertiser*, 21 April 2005.

3. 'Hyde, Douglas', *Oxford Dictionary of National Biography*, Vol. 29 (2004), pp. 117–118.

4. Daly (1974), pp. 12, 15.

5. 'Hyde, Douglas', *Oxford Dictionary*, pp. 117–118.

6. Daly (1974), pp. 12, 15.

7. Carty (1966), pp. 13–15, 102–103.

8. *Ibid.*, pp. 13–14.

9. Henry (2005), p. 12.

10. Ward (1990), pp. 21, 74.

11. Daly (1974), pp. 162–163, 164–165.

12. *Ibid.*

13. Hill (2005), pp. 121–122, 135, 140, 153, 160, 167.

14. Kiely (1995), p. 37.

15. Edwards, Ruth Dudley, *Patrick Pearse: The Triumph of Failure* (Victor Gollancz Ltd, London, 1990), pp. 19–20.

16. *Ibid.*, pp. 79–80.

17. 'Hyde, Douglas', *Oxford Dictionary*, p. 118.

18. Edwards (1990), pp. 181–182.

19. Daly (1974), pp. 169–171.

20. Edwards (1990), pp. 230–231.

21. 'Hyde, Douglas', *Oxford Dictionary* , p. 118.

22. Yeats (1998), p. 33.

23. Henry, William, *Role of Honour: The Mayors of Galway City 1485–2001* (Galway City Council, Galway, 2002), p. 236.

24. 'Hyde, Douglas', *Oxford Dictionary*, pp. 118–119.

Violet Florence Martin – 'Martin Ross'

1. 'Martin, Violet Florence *pseud* Martin Ross', *Oxford Dictionary of National Biography*, Vol. 36 (2004), p. 988.
2. Somerville-Large, Peter, *The Irish Country House: A Social History* (Sinclair Stevenson, London, 1995), p. 295.
3. *Ibid.*, pp. 247, 257, 313, 317–318.
4. 'Martin, Violet Florence', *Oxford Dictionary*, pp. 988–989.
5. Stevens (2007), pp. 15, 43–45.
6. 'Martin, Violet Florence', *Oxford Dictionary*, pp. 988–989.
7. Wallace (1999), p. 49.
8. Stevens (2007), pp. 1–2, 54.
9. Wallace (1999), p. 49.
10. Stevens (2007), p. 15.
11. Somerville-Large (1995), pp. 321–322, 327, 348.
12. 'Martin, Violet Florence', *Oxford Dictionary*, p. 988.
13. Somerville-Large (1995), pp. 321–322, 327, 348.
14. 'Martin, Violet Florence', *Oxford Dictionary*, pp. 990.
15. Stevens (2007), p. 99.
16. 'Martin, Violet Florence', *Oxford Dictionary*, pp. 989–990.
17. Wallace (1999), p. 49.
18. Stevens (2007), pp. 2, 6, 99.
19. 'Martin, Violet Florence', *Oxford Dictionary*, pp. 989–990.
20. Cullen Owens, Rosemary, *Smashing Times: A History of the Irish Women's Suffrage Movement 1889–1912* (Attic Press, Dublin, 1984), p. 43.
21. Stevens (2007), pp. 163, 192–193.
22. 'Votes For Women', *Galway Independent*, 27 July 2011.
23. 'Martin, Violet Florence', *Oxford Dictionary*, pp. 989–990.
24. Stevens (2007), p. 224.
25. Wallace (1999), p. 50.

Lady Margaret Sackville

1. 'Sackville, Lady Margaret', *Oxford Dictionary of National Biography*, Vol. 48 (2004), p. 539.
2. Hill (2005), p. 192.

3. 'Sackville, Lady Margaret', *Oxford Dictionary*, p. 539.

4. 'MacDonald, James Ramsay', *The World Book Encyclopaedia*, 'M', Vol. 13 (Chicago, World Book Inc., 1986), p. 5.

5. 'Secret love affair of Labour Prime Minister and Lady Margaret is revealed 80 years on', *The Telegraph*, 2 November 2006.

6. 'My dear provocation', *The Guardian*, 3 November 2006.

7. 'Secret love affair ...', *The Telegraph*, 2 November 2006.

8. 'Sackville, Lady Margaret', *Oxford Dictionary*, pp. 539–540.

9. Hanley, Cliff, *History of Scotland* (Lomand Books, Greenwich, 1999), pp. 183–185.

10. 'Secret love affair ...', *The Telegraph*, 2 November 2006.

11. 'Sackville, Lady Margaret', *Oxford Dictionary*, p. 540.

12. 'My dear provocation', *The Guardian*, 3 November 2006.

13. 'Secret love affair ...', *The Telegraph*, 2 November 2006.

Countess of Cromartie

1. 'Sibell Lilian Mackenzie, suo jure Countess of Cromartie', https://www.geni.com/people/Sibell-Lilian-Mackenzie-suo-jure-Countess-of-Cromartie/6000000003221246866. Accessed 13 March 2019.

2. Lecture Notes: 'Earldoms of Ireland and Scotland' (GMIT, Summer, 1994).

3. 'Col Edward Walter *Blunt* Blunt-Mackenzie', https://www.findagrave.com/memorial/94248371/edward-walter-blunt_mackenzie. Accessed 10 May 2013.

4. 'The Countess of Cromartie's Wedding', *The Manchester Guardian*, 18 December 1899.

5. 'Sibell Lilian Mackenzie, suo jure Countess of Cromartie', https://www.geni.com/people/Sibell-Lilian-Mackenzie-suo-jure-Countess-of-Cromartie/6000000003221246866. Accessed 13 March 2019.

6. Lecture Notes: 'Earldoms of Ireland and Scotland' (GMIT, Summer, 1994).

7. 'The Countess of Cromartie', *Every Woman's Encyclopaedia*, 1910.

8. Hill (2005), p. 192.

9. *The Collected Letters of W.B. Yeats*, Electronic Edition, NUIG, 2019.

10. 'Two Sisters, Sibell and Constance Mackenzie', https://www.castleleod. org.uk/stories/sibel-mackenzie/. Accessed 14 March 2019.

11. 'Countess of Cromartie', http:www.abebooks.co.uk/books-search/author/ cromartie-the-countess-of/page-1. Accessed 10 May 2013.

12. 'Sibell Lilian Mackenzie, suo jure Countess of Cromartie', https:// www.geni.com/people/Sibell-Lilian-Mackenzie-suo-jure-Countess-of-Cromartie/6000000003221246866. Accessed 13 March 2019.

13. 'Countess Hands Over Estate', *The Manchester Guardian*, 10 August 1935.

14. 'Sibell Lilian Mackenzie, suo jure Countess of Cromartie', https:// www.geni.com/people/Sibell-Lilian-Mackenzie-suo-jure-Countess-of-Cromartie/6000000003221246866. Accessed 13 March 2019.

John Masefield

1. 'Masefield, John Edward', *Oxford Dictionary of National Biography* Vol. 37 (2004), pp. 141–143.

2. Kiely (1995), pp. 122, 126–127, 213, 224, 271.

3. Strong, L. A. G., *John Masefield: Writers and their Works* (Longmans, Green & Company, Essex, 1964), p. 7.

4. 'Masefield, John Edward', *Oxford Dictionary*, pp. 142–143.

5. Strong (1964), pp. 8–9, 25–26.

6. 'Masefield, John Edward', *Oxford Dictionary*, pp. 142–143.

7. William Henry, *Galway and the Great War* (Mercier Press, Cork, 2006), pp. 194, 196, 198.

8. 'Masefield, John Edward', *Oxford Dictionary*, p. 142.

9. Strong (1964), pp. 7–10, 13, 17–18, 21, 30.

10. *Ibid.*, pp. 18–19.

11. 'Masefield, John Edward', *Oxford Dictionary*, p. 143.

12. Strong (1964), pp. 5, 7–8, 30–31, 33.

13. 'Masefield, John Edward', *Oxford Dictionary*, p. 143.

14. Strong (1964), pp. 34–35.

Robert Ross

1. 'Ross, Robert Baldwin', *Oxford Dictionary of National Biography*, Vol. 47 (2004), p. 840.

2. Pritchard, David, *The Irish Biographies: Oscar Wilde*, (Geddes & Grosset, Scotland, 2001), pp. 76, 80–81, 88.

3. 'Ross, Robert Baldwin', *Oxford Dictionary*, p. 840.

4. Pritchard (2001), p. 90.

5. 'Ross, Robert Baldwin', *Oxford Dictionary*, pp. 840–841.

6. Melville, Joy, *Mother of Oscar: The Life of Jane Francesca Wilde* (John Murray, London, 1994), pp. 197, 257.

7. 'Ross, Robert Baldwin', *Oxford Dictionary*, p. 840.

8. Pritchard (2001), p. 178.

9. Melville (1994), p. 197.

10. 'Ross, Robert Baldwin', *Oxford Dictionary*, pp. 840–841.

11. Frazier (2000), pp. 23, 370, 385.

12. 'Ross, Robert Baldwin', *Oxford Dictionary*, pp. 840–841.

13. Pritchard (2001), pp. 178–179.

14. 'Ross, Robert Baldwin', *Oxford Dictionary*, p. 841.

Elinor Monsell

1 'Monsell, Elinor Mary', Drawn to the Page: Irish Artists & Illustration 1830–1930, https://dttp.tcd.ie/artist/35. Accessed 6 June 2019.

2 Potter, Matthew, *William Monsell of Tervoe, 1812–1894* (Irish Academic Press, Dublin, 2009), p. 193.

3 Lalor, Brian, *The Encyclopedia of Ireland* (Gill & Macmillan, Dublin, 2003). p. 735.

4 Lecture Document: University of Limerick 1990, 'Monsell, Elinor Mary (1871–1954)'.

Dame Ethel Smyth

1. 'Smyth, Dame Ethel Mary', *Oxford Dictionary of National Biography*, Vol. 51 (2004), p. 432.

2. Hyde, Derek, *New-Found Voices: Women in Nineteenth-Century English Music* (Ashgate Publishing, Aldergate, 1998), p. 156.

3. 'Ethel Smyth', https://spartacus-educational.com/Jsmythe.htm. Accessed 30 April 2013.

4. Hyde (1998), p. 157.

5.   'Smyth, Dame Ethel Mary', *Oxford Dictionary*, pp. 432–433.

6.   Hyde (1998), p. 158.

7.   'Ethel Smyth: from prison to the Proms', *The Telegraph*, 31 July 2008.

8.   'Smyth, Dame Ethel Mary', *Oxford Dictionary*, p. 433.

9.   Hyde (1998), pp. 154–155, 159–160.

10. 'Smyth, Dame Ethel Mary', *Oxford Dictionary*, pp. 432–433, 435.

11. 'Ethel Smyth', https://spartacus-educational.com/Jsmythe.htm.

12. 'Smyth, Dame Ethel Mary', *Oxford Dictionary*, p. 433.

13. Hyde (1998), p. 175.

14. 'Smyth, Dame Ethel Mary', *Oxford Dictionary*, pp. 434–435.

15. 'Obituary – Dame Ethel Smyth', *The Advocate*, 11 May 1944.

16. Hyde (1998), pp. 153, 155.

Theodore Spicer-Simson

1.   The war was an armed conflict between Spain and the United States that began in the aftermath of the explosion of *USS Maine* in Havana, Cuba. This led to the United States intervention in the Cuban revolt against Spanish rule.

2.   'Theodore Frederick Spicer-Simson', https://www.geni.com/people/ Theodore-Spicer-Simson/5331820719080111754. Accessed 6 June 2012.

3.   'Medal Medallion Mystery Solved', http://master-in-america.blogspot. com/2011/05/.

4.   'Theodore Spicer-Simson – Biographical Sketch', Private Notes, Dublin, 1982.

5.   Lecture Notes: 'Earldoms of Ireland and Scotland' (GMIT, Summer, 1994).

6.   Hill (2005), pp. 327–328.

7.   Lecture Notes: 'Earldoms of Ireland and Scotland' (GMIT, Summer, 1994).

8.   'Theodore Frederick Spicer-Simson', https://www.geni.com/people/ Theodore-Spicer-Simson/5331820719080111754. Accessed 6 June 2012.

General Sir Ian Hamilton

1.   'Hamilton, Sir Ian Standish Monteith (1853–1947)', *Oxford Dictionary of National Biography*, Electronic Edition (2004). Accessed 30 May 2013.

2.   Hill (2005), p. 222.

3. Joseph (Jr), A. M., *The American Heritage History of World War I* (American Heritage Publishing Company Inc., New York, 1964), pp. 85–86.

4. Henry (2006), pp. 194, 196, 198.

5. Hammerton, J. A. and Wilson, H. W., *The Great War: The Standard History of the All-Europe Conflict*, Vol. 4 (The Amalgamated Press, London, 1915), pp. 409–410.

6. 'Hamilton, Sir Ian Standish' *Oxford Dictionary of National Biography*, Electronic Edition (2004). Accessed 30 May 2013.

General Sir Neville Lyttelton

1. 'Lyttelton, Sir Neville Gerald (1845–1931)', *Oxford Dictionary of National Biography*, Electronic Edition (2004). Accessed 30 May 2013.

2. McCracken, Donal, *MacBride's Brigade: Irish Commandos in the Anglo-Boer War* (Four Courts Press, Dublin, 1999), pp. 56–57.

3. 'Lyttelton, Sir Neville Gerald (1845–1931)', *Oxford Dictionary of National Biography*, Electronic Edition (2004). Accessed 30 May 2013.

Coole – Memories to Carry Forward

1. Pamphlet: *Coole Park & Gardens Guide*, 2009.

2. Booklet: *The Seven Woods Trail and The Family Trail, Coole* (2003), p. 2.

3. *Ibid.*, p. 21.

4. *Ibid.*, pp. 2, 5, 16, 20–21, 29.

5. 'Lady Gregory's "missing" grandson', *Galway Advertiser*, 2 October 2008.

6. Gregory (2009), pp. 12, 37, 73, 75, 117, 123, 128.

7. 'In Celebration', *Galway Life*, July 1999, p. 54.

8. 'Commemorating the life of Lady Gregory', *Galway Advertiser*, 25 September 2003.

9. 'Ghosts', *Galway Advertiser*, 23 September 1999.

10. 'Lady Gregory's granddaughter dies – unique link with Galway's literary past', *Galway Advertiser*, 9 March 2000.

11. 'An April gathering at Coole', *Galway Advertiser*, 13 April 2000.

BIBLIOGRAPHY

Books

Albright, D., *W.B. Yeats: The Poems* (Everyman's Library, London, 1992)

Burke, B., *Burke's Genealogical and Heraldic History of the Landed Gentry of Ireland*, 4th Edition, edited by L. G. Pine (Burke's Peerage, London, 1958)

Broderick, M., *Wild Irish Women; Extraordinary Lives from History* (O'Brien Press, Dublin, 2001)

Carty, J., *Ireland from The Great Famine to The Treaty of 1921* (CJ Fallon, Dublin, 1966)

Cullen Owens, R., *Smashing Times: A History of the Irish Women's Suffrage Movement 1889–1912* (Attic Press, Dublin, 1984)

Coogan, T. P., *De Valera: Long Fellow, Long Shadow* (Hutchinson, London, 1993)

Daly, D., *The Young Douglas Hyde: The Dawn of the Irish Revolution and Renaissance 1874–1893* (Irish University Press, Dublin, 1974)

Duane, O. B., *W.B. Yeats: Romantic Visionary* (Brockhampton Press, London, 2007)

Edwards, R. D., *Patrick Pearse: The Triumph of Failure* (Victor Gollancz Ltd, London, 1990)

Fargnoli, A. N. and Gillespie, M. P., *James Joyce A to Z: The Essential Reference to the Life and Work* (Facts on File Inc., New York 1995)

Fitz-Simon, C. *The Abbey Theatre: Ireland's National Theatre, The First 100 Years* (Thames & Hudson, New York, 2003)

Foster, R. F., *The Oxford Illustrated History of Ireland* (Oxford University Press, New York, 1989)

Frazier, A., *George Moore 1852–1933* (Yale University Press, London, 2000)

Gregory, A., *Me and Nu: Childhood at Coole* (Colin Smythe Ltd, Buckinghamshire, 2009)

Hammerton, J. A. and Wilson, H. W., *The Great War: The Standard History of the All-Europe Conflict*, Vol. 4 (The Amalgamated Press, London, 1915)

Hanley, C., *History of Scotland* (Lomond Books, Greenwich, 1999)

Henry, W., *Robinson, Son of Robin* (Merv Griffin, Galway, 1999)

— *Role of Honour: The Mayors of Galway City 1485–2001* (Galway City Council, Galway, 2002)

— *Supreme Sacrifice: The Story of Éamonn Ceannt 1881–1916* (Mercier Press, Cork, 2005)

— *Galway and the Great War* (Mercier Press, Cork, 2006)

— *Forgotten Heroes: Galway Soldiers of the Great War 1914–1918* (Mercier Press, Cork, 2007)

— *Blood for Blood: The Black and Tan War in Galway* (Mercier Press, Cork, 2012)

Hill, J., *Lady Gregory: An Irish Life* (Sutton Publishing Limited, Gloucestershire, 2005)

Hodges, M., *Ireland: From the Uprising to Civil War* (B.T. Batsford Ltd, London, 1987)

Hyde, D., *New-Found Voices: Women in Nineteenth-Century English Music* (Ashgate Publishing Limited, Aldershot, 1998)

John, A., *Chiaroscuro: Fragments of Autobiography* (Jonathan Cape, London, 1954)

Joseph (Jr), A. M., *The American Heritage History of World War I* (American Heritage Publishing Company Inc., New York, 1964)

Jordan, A. J., *Willie Yeats and the Gonne-MacBrides* (Anthony J. Jordan, Dublin, 1997)

Kelly, C., *The Grand Tour of Galway* (Cailleach Books, Cork, 2002)

Kiely, D. M., *John Millington Synge: A Biography* (St Martin's Press, New York, 1995)

Lalor, B., *The Encyclopedia of Ireland* (Gill & Macmillan, Dublin, 2003)

Macardle, D., *The Irish Republic* (The Camelot Press, London, 1937)

MacConghail, M., *The Blaskets: People and Literature* (Country House, Dublin, 1994)

Mac Liammóir, M. and Boland, E., *W.B. Yeats and his World* (Thames and Hudson, London, 1978)

Martin, A., *W. B. Yeats* (Gill & Macmillan, Dublin, 2006)

Matthews, Ann, *Renegades: Irish Republican Women 1900–1922* (Mercier Press, Cork, 2010)

McCracken, D., *MacBride's Brigade: Irish Commandos in the Anglo-Boer War* (Four Courts Press, Dublin, 1999)

McDonald, F., *Eyewitness Travel Guides: Ireland* (Dorling Kindersley, London, 1997)

Melville, J., *Mother of Oscar: The Life of Jane Francesca Wilde* (John Murray, London, 1994)

Morash, C., *A History of Irish Theatre 1601–2000* (Cambridge University Press, Cambridge, 2004)

Ó Céirín, K. and C., *Women of Ireland: A Biographic Dictionary* (Tir Eolas, Galway, 1996)

O'Connor, G., *Sean O'Casey: A Life* (Atheneum Macmillan Publishing Co., New York, 1988)

Plunkett Dillon, G., *All in the Blood: A Memoir of the Plunkett Family, the 1916 Rising and the War of Independence* (A & A Farmar, Dublin, 2006)

Potter, Matthew, *William Monsell of Tervoe, 1812–1894* (Irish Academic Press, Dublin, 2009)

Pritchard, D., *The Irish Biographies: Oscar Wilde* (Geddes & Grosset, Scotland, 2001)

Robinson, L., *Ireland's Abbey Theatre: A History 1899–1951* (Sidgwick and Jackson, London, 1951)

Ross, D., *The Irish Biographies: George Bernard Shaw* (Geddes & Grosset, New Lanark, 2001)

— *The Irish Biographies: W.B. Yeats* (Geddes & Grosset, New Lanark, 2001)

Rothenstein, J., *Augustus John* (Phaidon Press, London, 1945)

Skelton, R. *Four Plays and the Aran Islands* (Oxford University Press, London, 1969)

Smythe, C., *A Guide to Coole Park, Co. Galway: Home of Lady Gregory* (Colin Smythe Ltd, Buckinghamshire, 2003)

Somerville-Large, P., *The Irish Country House: A Social History* (Sinclair Stevenson, London, 1995)

Spellissy, S., *Window on Aran* (The Book Gallery, Ennis, 2003)

Stevens, J. A., *The Irish Scene in Somerville and Ross* (Irish Academic Press, Dublin, 2007)

Strong, L. A. G., *Writers and their Works: John Masefield* (Longmans, Green & Company, Essex, 1964)

Wallace, M., *Famous Irish Writers* (Appletree Press, Belfast, 1999)

Ward, M., *Maud Gonne: Ireland's Joan of Arc* (Pandora Press, London, 1990)

Whittle, P., *World War I in Photographs* (Eagle Editions, London, 2003)

Yeats, M. B., *Cast a Cold Eye: Memories of a Poet's Son and Politician* (Blackwater Press, Dublin, 1998)

Booklets – Pamphlets – Documents

Coole Park & Gardens Guide, pamphlet, 2009

County Galway Cricket Club 1971–1996 (County Galway Cricket Club, 1996)

Galway – Official Guide to City and County (Condor Publishing Co., 1986)

Lecture Document: University of Limerick 1990, 'Monsell, Elinor Mary (1871–1954)'

Lecture Notes: 'Earldoms of Ireland and Scotland' (GMIT, Summer, 1994)

The Collected Letters of W. B. Yeats, Electronic Edition, NUIG, 2019

'The Countess of Cromartie', *Every Woman's Encyclopaedia*, 1910

'Theodore Spicer-Simson – Biographical Sketch', Private Notes, Dublin, 1982

The Seven Woods Trail and The Family Trail, Coole, pamphlet, An Roinn Comhshaoil Oidhreachta Agus Rialtais Aitiuil, Department of the Environment, Heritage and Local Government, Dublin, 2003

Internet Articles (Electronic Editions)

'Blunt, Edward Walter', www.geni.com/people/Edward-Blunt/6000000003221 246873. Accessed 10 May 2013.

'Ethel Smyth', https://spartacus-educational.com/Jsmythe.htm. Accessed 30 April 2013.

'Col Edward Walter *Blunt* Blunt-Mackenzie', www.findagrave.com/memorial/ 94248371/edward-walter-blunt_mackenzie. Accessed 10 May 2013.

'Countess of Comartie', www.abebooks.co.uk/books-search/author/cromartie-the-countess-of/page-1. Accessed 10 May 2013.

'Monsell, Elinor Mary', Drawn to the Page: Irish Artists & Illustration 1830–1930, https://dttp.tcd.ie/artist/35. Accessed 6 June 2019.

'Sibell Lilian Mackenzie, suo jure Countess of Cromartie', www.geni.com/
people/Sibell-Lilian-Mackenzie-suo-jure-Countess-of-Cromartie/60000
00003221246866. Accessed 13 March 2019.

'Two Sisters, Sibell and Constance Mackenzie', www.castleleod.org.uk/stories/
sibel-mackenzie/. Accessed 14 March 2019.

'Theodore Frederick Spicer-Simson', www.geni.com/people/Theodore-Spicer-
Simson/5331820719080111754. Accessed 6 June 2012.

Interviews/Lectures

'Dún Crocbhur, Inishmaan, Aran Islands', Professor Etienne Rynne, 1992

Interview with Bill Scanlan, Galway City Museum, 20 May 2006

Magazine and Newspaper Articles

Galway Life

'In Celebration', July 1999

The Connacht Tribune

'The Gregory Country that Inspired Yeats', 25 August 1967

Galway Advertiser

'An April gathering at Coole', 13 April 2000

'An Irishman Foresees His Death', 5 October 2006

'An unlikely friendship', 26 August 2010

'Commemorating the life of Lady Gregory', 25 September 2003

'Fantasy and reality at Coole Park', 21 April 2005

'Getting to know George Bernard Shaw', 25 September 2001

'Ghosts', 23 September 1999

'Her Ladyship's Cake', 5 January 1995

'Lady Gregory and the Fate of Coole Park', 26 January 1995

'Lady Gregory's granddaughter dies – unique link with Galway's literary past',
9 March 2000

'Lady Gregory's "missing" grandson', 2 October 2008

'Putting right the wrong done at Coole', 2 October 2003

'The Importance of Lady Gregory', 28 September 1995

'The Lady who sold Coole Park', 25 October 2012

'The Woman who wanted to leave more than a monument of champagne
bottles', 16 February 2006

Galway Independent
'Hotel Meyrick – Major Thunder & His Guests', 2 November 2011
'Votes For Women', 27 July 2011

The Advocate
'Obituary – Dame Ethel Smyth', 11 May 1944

The Guardian
'My dear provocation', 3 November 2006

The Manchester Guardian
'The Countess of Cromartie's Wedding', 18 December 1899
'Countess Hands Over Estate', 10 August 1935

The Telegraph
'Ethel Smyth: from prison to the Proms', 31 July 2008
'Secret love affair of Labour Prime Minister and Lady Margaret is revealed 80
    years on', 2 November 2006

Oxford Dictionary of National Biography – Oxford University Press, 2004 (Editors: H.C.G. Matthew and Brian Harrison)
Vol. 1, Aaron–Amory, 'Allgood, Sara (1883–1950)', Susan C. Triesman
Vol. 19, Fane–Flatman, 'Fay, William George (1872–1947)', Robert Sharp
Vol. 29, Hutchins–Jennings, 'Hyde, Douglas (1860–1949)', Norman Vance
Vol. 29, Hutchins–Jennens, 'Innes, James Dickson (1887–1914)', Matthew Sturgis
Vol. 30, Jenner–Keayne, 'John, Augustus Edwin (1876–1961)', Michael Holroyd
Vol. 36, Macquarie–Martin, 'Martin, Violet Florence *pseud* Martin Ross (1862–1915)', Gifford Lewis
Vol. 37, Martindale–Meynell, 'Masefield, John Edward (1878–1967)', David Gervais
Vol. 41, Norbury–Osborn, 'O'Casey, Sean (1880–1964)', Richard Allen Cave
Vol. 47, Rippon–Rowe, 'Robinson, (Esme Stuart) Lennox (1886–1958)', Christopher Murray
Vol. 47, Rippon–Rowe, 'Ross, Robert Baldwin (1869–1918)', Maureen Borland.

Vol. 48, Rowell–Sarsfield, 'Russell, George William *pseud* Æ (1867–1935)', Peter R. Kuch

Vol. 48, Rowell–Sarsfield, 'Sackville, Lady Margaret (1881–1963)', Harriet Blodgett

Vol. 51, Smillie–Sprott, 'Smyth, Dame Ethel Mary (1858–1944)', Elizabeth Kertesz

Vol. 60, Wolmark–Zuylestein, 'Yeats, John Butler (Jack) (1871–1957)', Nicola Gordon Bowe

Electronic Edition, January 2011, George H. Cassar, 'Hamilton, Sir Ian Standish Monteith (1853–1947)', www.oxforddnb.com/view/article/33668. Accessed 30 May 2013.

Electronic Edition, May 2012, Roger T. Stearn, 'Lyttelton, Sir Neville Gerald (1845–1931)', www.oxforddnb.com/view/article/34657. Accessed 30 May 2013.

Dictionary of Irish Biography – Cambridge University Press, 2009 (Editors: James McGuire and James Quinn)

Vol. 3, D–F, 'Fay, Frank J. (Francis John) (1870–1931)', Patrick M. Geoghegan

Vol. 8, Patterson–Stagg, 'Quinn, John (1870–1924)', Lawrence William White

Vol. 8, Patterson–Stagg, 'Shaw, George Bernard (1856–1950)', Nicholas Grene

Vol. 9, Staines–Z, 'Synge, (Edmund) John Millington (1871–1909)', Declan Kiberd

The World Book Encyclopedia

'MacDonald, James Ramsay', 'M', Vol. 13 (Chicago, World Book Inc., 1986)

INDEX

A

Abbey Theatre 11, 12, 23, 29, 42, 47,
  63–67, 69, 71, 72, 74, 75, 78–82,
  86–91, 99, 101, 109, 110, 119,
  135, 137, 142–148, 152, 155, 157,
  158, 160, 167, 174, 220, 222
Adey, William More 214
Alderney Manor 117
Aldershot 223, 244
Allgood, George 70
Allgood, Margaret 70
Allgood, Molly 64–70, 72, 84
Allgood, Sara 12, 64, 69, 70–76, 84,
  87, 146
Anderson, Margaret 111, 112
Anderson, Sherwood 234
Aran Islands 41, 60–63, 66, 118
Archer, William 134
Arenig valley 126, 127

B

Baillie-Cochrane, Constance Mary
  Elizabeth 193
Baldwin, Augusta Elizabeth 213
Barnacle, Nora 121
Beckett, Samuel 221
Begbie, Harold 190
Ben Bulben 47
Benson, Frank 78
Binyon, Laurence 219
Birmingham, George 54
Blavatsky, Madame 39, 95
Blunt, Edward Walter 200, 201
Blunt, Wilfrid Scawen 19, 20, 193,
  194, 197
Blunt-Mackenzie, Isobel 201
Blunt-Mackenzie, Janet Frances 201
Blunt-Mackenzie, Walter Osra 201
Brewster, Henry 225, 226
Brewster, Julia 225
Browne, Fr James 162
Browne, Jim 162
Buller, Redvers 244
Burke, Maud 165, 170

C

Cadden, Marie 251
Cardew, Michael 220
Castletownshend 184, 189, 191
Cheltenham 198, 199
Childers, H. C. E. 244
Christian, Clara 167
Churchill, Winston 140, 234
Clarke, Austin 221
Clarke, Harry 221
Clarke, Tom 151
Coates, Dorothy 108, 109
Colum, Mary 71
Colum, Padraic 53
Connolly, James 100, 151
Conrad, Joseph 110, 187, 234
Corbett, Éamonn 145
Corfu 184, 237
Cork 57, 58, 106, 142, 144, 184, 187,
  190, 191
Crofton, Frances 174, 175

Cromartie, Countess of
  See Sutherland-Leveson-Gower,
  Sibell Lilian
Cumann na mBan 153
Cunard, Bache 165, 170
Cunard, Nancy 165, 170
Cusack, Cyril 75

D

Dampt, Jean 234
Darwin, Bernard 220–222
Darwin, Charles 59, 220
Darwin, Ursula 220
Davies, Washington 126
de Basterot, Count 21, 41
de la Cherois Crommelin, Constance
  206, 212
de Ross Rose, Mary 163
de Valera, Éamon 55, 57, 104, 140,
  159, 169, 181
De Vere, Aubrey Thomas 221
de Walden, Lord Howard 129
Devoy, John 108
Digges, Dudley 84
Dirrane, Pat 61, 62
Dodge, Mary 228
Donaghy, Lyle 55
Doolin 61, 117
Douglas, Alfred 214, 216, 217
Drumcliff 47
Dublin 10, 18, 35–41, 44, 48, 51,
  54, 56–59, 63–65, 67, 68, 70, 71,
  74, 77, 80, 82, 84, 86, 94–96, 98,
  99, 101, 102, 104, 105, 110, 115,
  118–120, 131, 133, 135, 136, 138,
  140, 143, 145, 146, 148, 149, 153,
  156–158, 163, 167–169, 171, 176,
  177, 181, 183, 185
Dublin Drama League 145

E

Edinburgh 197, 199, 214, 242

Elgar, Edward 79

F

Fairchild, David 236
Fallon, Gabriel 74, 82, 146
Fallon, Padraic 221
Farrell, Seán 18
Fay, Frank 12, 71, 73, 76, 77–83, 84,
  87–89, 92
Fay, Freda 82
Fay, Gerard 82
Fay, Martha 77
Fay, William 77
Fay, William George 12, 71, 73, 76,
  77, 79–81, 83, 84–93
Ford, Henry 234
Foster, Jeanne 112
French, Percy 53
Frost, Robert 235
Fryern Court 122

G

Gaelic League 10, 22, 60, 67, 107,
  150, 152, 173–177, 179, 190
Gaelic Union 172
Galsworthy, John 234
Galway 15, 18, 21, 25, 27, 28, 34,
  36, 41, 44, 47, 53, 62, 77, 89, 106,
  119, 121, 129, 145, 180, 182, 183,
  187, 246
Germany 60, 175, 228, 230, 233, 237
Gibbon, Monk 103
Gladstone, William 243
Glanmore Castle 58
Gleeson, Evelyn 54, 220
Glynne, Mary 243
Gogarty, Oliver St John 103, 118
Gonne, Maud 39–44, 47, 63, 70, 99,
  108, 110, 153, 167, 168, 174, 202
Gort 18, 20, 23, 28, 29, 35, 44, 62,
  119, 154, 176, 246, 252
Granville-Barker, Harley 136

Gregory, Anne 24, 29, 32–34, 137, 156, 249–251

Gregory, Lady Augusta 9–13, 15–26 27, 29, 31, 32, 34, 35, 41, 42, 44–46, 51, 53, 55, 62–67, 69, 71, 72, 80, 83–85, 88–91, 96–98, 104, 107, 108–110, 112, 118, 119, 129, 135–137, 142–147, 149, 150, 152, 154–156, 158, 160, 166, 168, 175–177, 188–190, 194, 202, 205, 220, 221, 235, 240, 247–249, 251, 252

Gregory, Catherine 24, 29, 137, 249–251

Gregory, Margaret 24, 29, 31–36, 119, 137

Gregory, Richard 24, 29, 33, 34, 119, 249

Gregory, Robert 11, 18, 19, 24, 25, 27–36, 51, 118, 119, 138, 155, 176, 194, 220

Gregory, William 16–20, 27, 248

Griffith, Arthur 63, 78, 99

Grosse, Edmond 170

Gurly, Lucinda Elizabeth 131

Gwynn, Stephen 220, 221

H

Hamilton, Christian Monteith 237

Hamilton, Ian Standish Monteith 12, 208, 237–242, 245

Hardy, Thomas 154, 165, 170

Hart, James 171

Head, E. J. 115

Heap, Jane 111, 112

Henson, Gerald 74

Henson, Mary 74

Hitchcock, Alfred 75, 76

Horniman, Annie 86, 88–90, 143, 144

Housman, A. E. 235

Housman, Laurence 219

Hughes, John 95

Hyde, Annette 171, 175

Hyde, Arthur 171

Hyde, Douglas 12, 22, 39, 79, 107, 166, 167, 171–181, 190, 205

Hyde, Elizabeth 171

Hyde-Lees, Georgiana 43–47

Hyde Park 134, 157, 189

I

Inishmaan 61, 62, 66

Innes, Alfred 124

Innes, Alice 124

Innes, Jack 124

Innes, James Dickson 12, 124–130

Innes, John 124

Irish Citizen Army 151, 154, 157

Irish National Dramatic Society 80, 84, 85

Irish National Theatre Society 71, 72, 82, 84, 85

Irish Republican Army (IRA) 35, 169, 235

Irish Republican Brotherhood (IRB) 151, 179, 180, 243

J

John, Augusta 113

John, Augustus Edwin 12, 29, 61, 110, 113–123, 124–129, 156

John, Casper 116

John, David 116

John, Edwin 113

John, Gwen 113, 115, 122

John, Henry 116

John, Poppet 117

John, Pyramus 117

John, Robin 116

John, Romilly 117

John, Thornton 113

John, Vivien 117

John, Winifred 113

Johnston, Charles 95
Joyce, James 100, 110–112, 121
Judge, William 96

K

Kavanagh, Patrick 103, 221
Kerrigan, Joseph 84
Killeeneen 106
Kiltartan 17, 25, 36, 45, 176, 252
King-Noel, Annabella 19, 20
Kurtz, Lucy Cometina 175, 176

L

Lamb, Euphemia 125, 127
Lamb, Henry 125
Lamont, Florence 207
Lane, Hugh 23, 135, 155
Larkin, James 100, 101, 151, 178
Lavin, John 171
Lee, George John Vandeleur 132, 133
Leipzig 223–226
Leverson, Ada 164
Leverson, Ernest 164
Levi, Hermann 227
Limerick 106, 163, 219
Liverpool 48, 55, 73, 116, 146, 175, 204, 248
Lloyd, Constance Mary 213–215
Lock-Out 100, 110, 151, 178
London 19–21, 28, 29, 31, 32, 35, 37, 39–41, 44, 48–51, 54–56, 74, 75, 91–93, 101, 104, 115–117, 121, 122, 124, 125, 128, 129, 133, 134, 136, 143, 156–158, 162–165, 175, 184, 189, 193, 195, 200, 202, 205–207, 212, 213, 215–217, 219–221, 223, 233, 242, 245
Lough Carra 170
Lyttelton, George William 243
Lyttelton, Hilda Margaret 245
Lyttelton, Lucy Blanche 245

Lyttelton, Mary 245
Lyttelton, Neville Gerald 12, 243–245, 253

M

MacBride, John 41–43, 108, 111, 154, 244
MacBride, Seán 42, 47
MacDonagh, Thomas 82
MacDonald, James Ramsay 195–199
Macdonald, Lilian Janet 200
Mackay, Donald 244
Mackenzie, Roderick Grant Francis 201, 203
MacNamara, Francis 61
MacNeill, Eoin 179
Maguire, Samuel J. 145
Mair, George Herbert 69
Manchester 73
Mannin, Ethel 46
Markievicz, Constance 154
Martin, Anna 182
Martin, James 182
Martin, Robert 183, 184
Martin, Violet 12, 53, 182–192
Martyn, Edward 11, 21, 41, 167, 168, 175, 176, 190
Masefield, Caroline 204
Masefield, George 204
Masefield, John 12, 53, 204–212
Masefield, Judith 207, 212
Masefield, Lewis 207
Mathers, MacGregor 39
Maugham, William Somerset 219
McCarthy, Charles 167
McDonagh, Mary 251
McGuinness, Marian 155
McKenna, Siobhán 146
McNamara, Francis 117, 118
McNeill, Dorothy 116, 117
McNulty, Matthew 133
Meehan, Sighle 251

Melbourne 74, 217
Middleton, George 150
Mielziner, Ella 234
Mielziner, Leo 234
Millard, Christopher 215
Milman, Lena 164
Mitchell, Susan 169
Monod, Henri 234
Monsell, Elinor 12, 219–222
Monsell, John Robert 219
Moore, Augustus 161
Moore, George 12, 41, 78, 79, 89, 98, 104, 160, 161–170, 188, 216, 253
Moore, George Henry 161, 162
Moore Hall 161, 163, 169
Moore, Julian 161
Moore, Mary 161
Moore, Maurice 161, 162, 169
Moore, Nina 161
Morgan, Sydney 87
Morrell, Lady Ottoline 195
Morris, May 109
Mount Arenig 126, 127
Mount Jerome Cemetery 57, 68, 105
Mount Vernon 29, 31
Muir, Jean Miller 239, 240, 242
Murphy, William Martin 101
Murray, William 220

N

Nettleship, Ida Margaret 116, 117
Nettleship, John 116
New York 42, 53–55, 92, 106, 107, 109, 111, 112, 204, 228
nic Shiubhlaigh, Máire 72
North, Violet 98, 104

O

O'Casey, Brecon 157
O'Casey, Michael 149
O'Casey, Niall 157, 159
O'Casey, Sean 12, 13, 25, 55, 67, 71, 74, 75, 101, 120, 135, 145–148, 149–160, 177
O'Casey, Shivaun 157
O'Casey, Susan 149
O'Connor, Frank 103
O'Connor, Thady 185
O'Dempsey, Brigit 87
O'Dempsey, Thomas 87
O'Donnellan, Sheila 251
O'Donovan, Fred 87
O'Farrell, Ayamonn 67
O'Leary, Ellen 40
O'Leary, John 38–40
O'Malley, William 66
O'Sullivan, Seumas 221
Oldfield, John 171
Ormonde Dramatic Society 84
Orpen, William 115, 116, 118, 221
Owen, Wilfred 217
Oxford 28, 29, 207, 213, 230

P

Paderewski, Ignacy Jean 235
Pankhurst, Christabel 189
Pankhurst, Emmeline 228, 229
Paris 29, 30, 42, 60, 108, 117, 121, 125, 162, 163, 165, 170, 175, 205, 215, 218, 230, 233, 234
Payne, Ben Iden 88
Payne-Townshend, Charlotte 134, 135, 140, 141
Pearse, Patrick 137, 177–180
Persse, Arabella 15, 25
Persse, Dudley 15
Persse, Frances 15
Persse, Frank 15
Persse, Gertrude 15
Pinker, James 187, 188
Plunkett, Horace 98, 104
Plunkett, Joseph 82
Poel, William 73
Pollexfen, George 39

Pollexfen, Susan Mary 37, 48, 50
Pollexfen, William 48–50, 52
Ponsonby, Mary 226
Porter, Kingsley 104
Pound, Ezra 110
Pryse, James 96
Pyle, Hilary 52

Q

Quinlin, Mary 106
Quinn, James William 106
Quinn, John 12, 19, 23, 42, 52,
    106–112, 250

R

Raftery, Anthony 107, 175, 176
Raverat, Gwen 221
Reynolds, Eileen Carey 75, 156, 157,
    159
Roberts, Frederick 238, 239
Robins, Elizabeth 207
Robinson, Andrew 142
Robinson, Emily Anne 142
Robinson, Lennox 12, 74, 77, 80, 83,
    87, 141–148, 155, 158
Ross, John 213
Ross, Robert 12, 213–218
Rothenstein, John 122
Roxborough House 15, 16, 24, 27,
    31
Ruddock, Margaret 46
Russell, Brian 98
Russell, Bryan 98
Russell, Diarmuid 98
Russell, George William 12, 38, 46,
    51, 65, 80, 84, 85, 94–105, 108,
    205
Russell, Marianne 94
Russell, Mary 94
Russell, Thomas 94
Ryan, Frederick 84

S

Sackville, Gilbert 197
Sackville, Lady Margaret 12, 192,
    193–199, 202
Sampson, John 116
Samson, John 128
Sassoon, Siegfried 217
Schmidt, Margaret 233, 236
Sergeant, John 116
Shakespeare, Olivia 41
Shannon, Mary 118
Shaw, Agnes 131, 133
Shaw, George Bernard 12, 13, 33, 61,
    72, 74, 119, 120, 131–141, 143,
    156, 221, 227, 230, 235
Shaw, George Carr 131
Shaw, Lucinda 131
Shaw, Richard 132
Sheehy-Skeffington, Francis 157
Sheehy-Skeffington, Hanna 153
Sheppard, Oliver 95
Sheridan, Mary 15
Shine, Ruth 51
Simson, Dora 233
Simson, Frederick 233
Sinclair, Arthur 69, 87
Slade School of Fine Art 29, 115,
    116, 124, 167, 217, 219, 220
Sligo 37, 39, 41, 47, 48, 50, 57
Smith, Freddie Stanley 214
Smyth, Dame Ethel 12, 223–232
Smyth, John 223, 224
Smyth, Mary 227
Society for the Preservation of the
    Irish Language 172
Somerville, Edith 53, 183–192
South Africa 41, 139, 239, 240, 244
Spicer-Simson, Theodore 12,
    233–236
Steer, Philip Wilson 124, 125
Stephens, James 161, 234

Stratford 73
Struth, Emma 223, 224
Stuart-Wortley, Katharine Sarah 244, 245
Summers, Gerald 31, 32
Summers, Nora 31, 32
Sutherland-Leveson-Gower, Constance 200
Sutherland-Leveson-Gower, Francis Mackenzie 200
Sutherland-Leveson-Gower, Sibell Lilian 12, 194, 200–203
Symons, Arthur 41
Synge, Annie 58
Synge, Edward 58, 59
Synge, John Hatch 58
Synge, John Millington 12, 53, 58–69, 71, 73, 81, 87, 90, 91, 99, 108–110, 145, 169, 188, 205, 207, 220, 229
Synge, Kathleen 58
Synge, Robert 58, 68
Synge, Samuel 58

T

Taft, William Howard 234
Tenby 113, 114, 116
Thoor Ballylee 44, 46, 252
Tobin, Lois 251
Trafalgar Square 122, 156
Travers-Smith, Dorothy 147
Trevelyan, Pauline 227
Trinity College 60, 104, 147, 172, 175
Tulira 11, 21, 41, 167, 175
Twain, Mark 52
Tynan, Katharine 39

U

University College Dublin 178

V

Vereker, John Prendergast 237
Vereker, Maria Corinna 237
von Herzogenberg, Heinrich 225
von Herzogenberg, Lisl 225

W

Walker, Ethel 167
Weekes, Charles 96
Wells, H. G. 187, 234
West, Reginald Windsor 193
Whistler, James 162
White, Mary Cottenham 50, 51, 53, 56, 155, 176
Wicklow 58, 59, 63, 65, 132
Wilde, Cyril 213, 215
Wilde, Oscar 187, 213–218
Wilde, Vyvyan 213, 215
Wills, William Gorman 184
Wylie, Elinor 235

Y

Yeats, Anne 44, 45
Yeats, Elizabeth 'Lolly' 37, 54, 220
Yeats, Jack Butler 12, 28, 31, 37, 48–57, 107, 155, 176, 194, 220, 221
Yeats, John Butler 37, 48, 50, 108
Yeats, Michael 44–46, 251
Yeats, Susan 'Lily' 37, 50, 54, 220
Yeats, William Butler 10–13, 21, 22, 25, 26, 31, 36, 37–47, 48, 49, 52, 53, 55, 60, 62, 63, 65–67, 69, 71, 73, 78–86, 88–91, 95–101, 104, 107–109, 111, 119, 135, 137, 142–144, 147, 153, 158, 166–168, 172, 176, 177, 188, 194, 202, 203, 205, 207, 219–221, 235, 240, 241, 247